RELIGIOUS FREEDOM IN SPAIN

RELIGIOUS FREEDOM IN SPAIN

ITS EBB AND FLOW

BY

JOHN DAVID HUGHEY

97170

BOOKS FOR LIBRARIES PRESS
FREEPORT, NEW YORK

LIBRARY ST. MARY'S COLLEGE

First Published 1955

Reprinted 1970 by arrangement with John David Hughey

STANDARD BOOK NUMBER:
8369-5378-9

LIBRARY OF CONGRESS CATALOG CARD NUMBER:
77-119935

PRINTED IN THE UNITED STATES OF AMERICA

PREFACE TO 1970 REPRINT EDITION

Since my book was published in 1955 significant changes have taken place in the Roman Catholic Church and in Spain. A brief summary of these changes is in order.

Pope John XXIII opened windows to "let fresh air" into the Catholic Church, A remarkable up-dating and a challenge to medieval attitudes and policies began. Vatican Council II brought the process to a climax. Among many other forward-looking achievements, it put the Roman Catholic Church on the side of religious liberty. Emphasis was placed on the rights of persons in contrast to the older emphasis on the rights of truth for protection against error. Fortunately the older position, though supported by high authority, was never proclaimed as infallible dogma.

The Vatican Council's Declaration on Religious Liberty states that because of peculiar circumstances special civil recognition may be given to a certain religious community. This sanctions the establishment of a particular religion, with inevitable inequalities. It is good that this statement is coupled with the affirmation that "it is at the same time imperative that the right of all citizens and religious communities to religious freedom should be recognized and made effective in practice".

Most of the Spanish prelates in Rome opposed the declaration in the form in which it was adopted. However, since then several members of the Spanish hierarchy have given their support to religious liberty. I stated in 1955 that no change of attitude on the part of the Spanish hierarchy could be expected unless the change should be encouraged by the highest authority of the Roman Catholic Church. That encouragement has at last been given.

There have been other influences on the side of religious liberty in Spain. Of particular importance has been the pressure of foreign public opinion. It is significant that the Minister of Foreign Affairs (who was especially sensitive to foreign opinion) played a leading role in the move towards broader toleration for non-Catholics. Worthy of mention also are the presence of many foreign tourists in Spain, economic and cultural progress, growing secularism and religious indifference, and wariness on the part of many church leaders about being too closely allied with the Franco regime.

Religious liberty is guaranteed by the new Spanish constitution that was adopted in 1966. What was said in the Charter of the Spanish People about the establishment and protection of the Catholic religion is repeated, but the following sentence takes the place of the earlier statement about non-Catholic private worship: "The State will assume the protection of religious liberty, which will be guaranteed by an effective legal guardianship which at the same time will safeguard morality and public order."

Such a general guarantee must, of course, be implemented in legislation. Only after much maneuvering behind the scenes was the Law on Religious Liberty issued in 1967. It is more restrictive than an earlier draft. The following year the Ministry of Justice issued official instructions concerning implementation of the law.

In the spirit of Vatican Council II, the new law recognizes the right of religious liberty as being based on the dignity of the human person and guarantees its protection and the private and public profession and practice of any religion. Less reassuring are statements that religious liberty will be interpreted according to Catholic doctrine, that it must be compatible with the Catholic character of the state, and that it will be subject to limitations imposed by demands of community life and public order.

Various elements of religious liberty are covered by the law: belief, worship, instruction of children, theological education, publications, marriage and burial according to the rites of one's religion, equality of civil rights, church organization, and the right of churches to own property. Much individual freedom is guaranteed, but controls are specified with regard to groups.

The main objection of Protestants to the law is governmental supervision of churches. Guaranteed rights are for officially recognized churches. The law sets forth terms on which "non-Catholic religious associations" may gain recognition. Protestants wonder

vi

why their churches cannot be called churches, and they do not want the state to pass on whether or not a group is entitled to recognition.

The law specifies that religious associations must keep membership records and financial books and that these will be inspected and stamped each year by the authorities. Each "religious association" is required to report to the government donations received, income, and expenses. Ministers are to be registered by the government and given official identification papers. No one who has received Catholic ordination to the priesthood may be registered as a non-Catholic minister unless he obtains clearance from Roman Catholic church authorities. It is further specified that no one ordained to the Catholic priesthood may ever be married unless he is given a canonical dispensation.

The Spanish Baptist Union, the Spanish Evangelical Church, and the Reformed Church declared registration under the new law unacceptable. Other groups accepted registration. By mid-1968 Spanish Protestants were divided about half and half on the matter of registration. Baptists became seriously divided over the issue, and the 1969 Spanish Baptist Convention left local churches free to decide what to do. The Spanish Protestant Defense Committee lost the support of some groups because it advocated registration.

All Spanish Protestants want the law to be changed. They disagree only on what to do in the meantime. Some think that churches should register and thereby obtain permission to hold property and expand their work; as registered "associations" they will have a better chance to work for changing the law. Others are convinced that recognition will bring government interference in church life and is an unacceptable compromise; they demand that the law be changed before their churches are registered.

Even without registration churches face little danger of being closed. They continue to function as in the past—unrecognized and yet known, without freedom to own property and with uncertainty as to what they can do, but actually with a large measure of freedom so long as they do not attract much public attention. The time of closing churches, imprisoning Protestants, denying couples the right to marry, and interfering with burials is past. Annoyances and limitations may continue.

In 1969 Jose Cardona, secretary of the Spanish Protestant Defense Committee, said:

> Spain's future is uncertain in many ways. We do not know how the law will be applied in the future. One thing is certain—the country will continue to have a Catholic government. At present, however, the application of the law is better than the law itself. There are no problems now for registered churches.

J. D. HUGHEY

PREFACE

WHILE living in Spain from 1947 to 1950 as a representative of Southern Baptists, I frequently had occasion to see how religious freedom is denied to Spanish Protestants. My files were soon filled with data on the contemporary situation. Then I became aware of the deep roots which both freedom and intolerance have in Spain, and I began to collect material from other years. Now, with all modesty, for I realize my limitations, I offer to others the results of my observation and research.

I have attempted to describe and analyse the official Spanish attitudes and policies towards Protestantism through the years. Members of minority religions in Spain have at different times experienced persecution, toleration, and freedom. We shall see how the ideal of Catholic unity has led to intolerance and how liberals have struggled for religious liberty. We shall also observe the influence of radicals who have opposed the Catholic Church without really being interested in freedom for all.

Since a book of this kind is worthless unless it is fully documented, I have carefully recorded sources. Constant interruptions from footnotes, however, can interfere with reading for enjoyment, and I have put all notes in the back of the book, where they can easily be found by those who want them, or left unnoticed by those who wish to read more hurriedly.

Much of the material in this book appeared first in a dissertation which I wrote at Columbia University in 1951 on *Spanish Governments and Protestantism (1868–1931)*. The chapters included in that treatise have been thoroughly revised for publication, and several new chapters have been added.

I wish to express my deep appreciation of friends in America and Spain who have helped me obtain source materials and have wisely counselled me in my writing. Their names are too numerous to record here, but they are gratefully and indelibly recorded in my memory.

RÜSCHLIKON-ZÜRICH, *May 1955.*   J. D. HUGHEY, JR.

ix

CONTENTS

THE ORIGIN OF CATHOLIC UNITY

'WE had rather have ten million Communists in Spain than one million Protestants. The worst thing that could happen to our country would be a religious division.'[1] This statement in a Barcelona newspaper in 1949 reflects the centuries-old determination of influential elements in Spain to prevent the growth of Protestantism and to preserve the Catholic unity of the nation.

Non-Catholic religions enjoy only a very limited toleration in Spain today. Protestant worship has been authorized in certain chapels, but they can have no signs on them, and there can be no preaching or religious services in streets or other public places. With only three or four exceptions, permits to open new chapels have not been given since the latter part of 1947. Proselytism and evangelism are officially forbidden, though not fully suppressed. The Bible and other religious literature cannot be published legally by Protestants, and such literature sent from abroad often does not pass the censor.

Spanish Protestants are not permitted to have their own schools, and their children are generally subject to Catholic instruction in the State and parochial schools. Members of the armed services are required to participate in public religious functions unless excused by their officers, and Protestants are denied the right to serve as army officers.[2] Burial with Protestant rites is sometimes forbidden, and marriage outside the Roman Catholic Church is often impossible for those baptized in that Church even though they have become members of another.

After years of broad religious toleration and even brief periods of full religious freedom, Spain has turned back towards Catholic unity, which became a characteristic feature of Spanish national life in the fifteenth and sixteenth centuries. It is the basis of much Spanish legislation and of the 1953 concordat between Spain and the Holy See. The bloody persecution which characterized earlier centuries is not present today, but the adherence to the principle of Catholic unity by Spain's religious and political leaders results in many restrictions upon the activities of religious minorities. This principle is rooted in religion and patriotism.

Many Spaniards are loyal Catholics, deeply interested in the welfare and progress of their Church. They regard their country as eminently Catholic and as obligated, therefore, to further the cause of the Catholic Church and to follow its teachings in all of their implications. A defender of the present régime says, 'The Spain of Franco . . . is Catholic Spain, the only country in the world that at the present time has known how to crystallize in its laws and in its life the full ideal of State Christianity, without the slightest concession to the religious errors of recent centuries; the only country in the world that practises officially and openly the only true religion with all of its agreeable and disagreeable, convenient and inconvenient, consequences'.[3] No other Spanish government since 1868 has sensed so keenly as the present one the obligation to make the country thoroughly Catholic, but there have always been Spaniards who wanted to follow 'the full ideal of State Christianity'.

This ideal points back to the religious unity which prevailed in the later Roman Empire and in medieval times, when the States of Christendom were what would be called today Catholic States. A Catholic State has been defined in recent years as 'a community which is composed exclusively of Catholic subjects and which recognizes Catholicism as the only true religion',[4] and as 'a political community that is exclusively, or almost exclusively, made up of Catholics'.[5] In such a State, as Pope Leo XIII pointed out, the Catholic Church considers it 'unlawful to place the various forms of worship on the same footing as the true religion' or to tolerate other religions except 'for the sake of securing some great good or hindering some great evil'.[6] Advocates of an official policy of Catholic unity in Spain have believed that their country was or could be a truly Catholic State.

Closely tied up with the religious opposition to non-Catholic religions in Spain is opposition inspired by a certain type of nationalism or patriotism. National unity has been regarded by many Spaniards as founded upon and dependent upon religious unity. Well known in Spain is the argument that the Catholic religion in early times overcame the geographical and racial barriers that separated the inhabitants of Spanish soil, later on inspired the struggle for freedom from the Moors, and then guided Ferdinand and Isabella in the unification of Spain and the creation of a great nation.[7] When the Emperor Charles V made Spain the centre of a great empire and King Philip II ruled over a mighty and prosperous nation, Catholicism was an all-important factor in Spanish life. Spain's era of national greatness coincided with a period of intolerance and religious zeal, and intolerance and greatness have been equated by many Spaniards. Towards the latter part of the nineteenth century a distinguished Spanish scholar wrote: 'Spain, evangelizer of half the planet; Spain, hammer of heretics, light of Trent, sword of Rome, cradle of Saint Ignatius—this is our greatness and our glory: we have no other'.[8]

There can be no doubt that the occupation of Spain by Mohammedan Moors and the slow and painful reconquest of the country by Spaniards who professed Christianity gave rise to a fusion of religion and patriotism. It is worthy of note, however, that the period of the Moorish occupation was, on the whole, one of at least limited religious toleration. Christians and Jews lived with a large degree of freedom and tranquillity under Mohammedan rule. During the centuries of the Reconquest, Christian and Moorish kings sometimes forgot their enmities and formed friendships and alliances. In the Christian kingdoms, Christians, Moors, and Jews lived on better terms than would have been possible in most of the rest of Europe. From the thirteenth century on, however, intolerance on the part of people and governments grew in the Spanish kingdoms, and by the latter part of the fifteenth century it had become an integral part of national policy.[9] At that time such a policy was not peculiar to Spain. The singularity of the Spanish nation in this respect rests upon the deep root which the policy took and its continued vigour long after most of the world had forsaken it.

Spain became a great defender of the Catholic faith. That did not necessarily mean subservience to the hierarchy or even to the Vatican, for there was a sharp distinction between the religious and temporal interests of the Church, and the Spanish rulers insisted upon their sovereignty over things temporal. Some of them were even willing to wage war on the Pope when his political pretensions conflicted with their own.[10]

The new national policy of intolerance received clear expression in the establishment of the Inquisition by Ferdinand and Isabella. To this institution, says one writer, the modern Spaniard owes as much, 'whether by attraction or by repulsion, as Britain does to her parliamentary constitution'.[11] The Spanish rulers did not, of course, invent the Inquisition; they only revived it for Spain and gave it a somewhat different form. They began it as a means of dealing with Jews who had falsely professed conversion to Christianity. In 1478 they requested and received a papal Bull authorizing them to set up the Inquisition in their kingdoms, and within a few years the Holy Office was fully organized, with Torquemada as inquisitor general for Aragon and Castile.[12]

The secret procedure of the Inquisition, its use of torture to obtain confessions and incriminations, and its severe penalties made it a dreaded institution. The worst penalty was death by burning (which was executed by civil officials after trial by the Inquisition), but the penances, the floggings, the loss of property, and the long imprisonments were also greatly feared. The Spanish Inquisition presented an impressive combination of the authority of the Church and the power of the Crown, since it represented both Pope and King. In later reigns it was sometimes an instrument of the king's will and sometimes an almost sovereign and all-powerful organization.[13]

In establishing the Inquisition, Ferdinand and Isabella were doubtless moved by both religious and political considerations. Many Jews had professed conversion to the Catholic faith in order to obtain security and privilege, and others had been swept into the Church by persuasive evangelists. Many of these converted Jews and their descendants became prominent in government and even in the Church; but there lingered strong suspicions of their sincerity, and without doubt there were many who made false professions of conversion or of loyalty to the Catholic faith. These false Christians were considered a reproach to the Church and an impediment to the national unity which was being achieved. It was believed that it would help the Church and the State to bring them into conformity, or to eliminate them.[14]

The Holy Office dealt effectively with the Jews who had accepted baptism, but it had no jurisdiction over the others, unless they had committed some offence against the faith such as proselytism. The peninsula was being unified, and it was regarded as necessary to find some means of removing the Jewish hindrance to national uniformity. Other nations—France and England, for example—had expelled the Jews centuries earlier, and this was the solution decided upon by the rulers of Spain. In 1492, following the conquest of Granada and therefore the completion of the Reconquest, the Jews were given the alternative of accepting baptism or leaving the country. This meant, of course, that the way for them to become Spaniards was to be converted to the Catholic religion. Some accepted baptism and remained in Spain, but thousands emigrated, amid scenes of terror and misery. When the Pope granted to Ferdinand and Isabella the title of 'Catholic sovereigns' (which was passed on to their successors), the expulsion of the Jews was listed among the services to the faith entitling them to this honour. Without doubt, however, their reasons were political as well as religious —probably more political than religious.[15]

There remained one great barrier to Catholic unity—and to national unity, so it was believed—the presence of the Moors in Spain. Early in the sixteenth century they began to be faced with the alternative which had faced the Jews: baptism or emigration. Some left the country, but others accepted baptism and remained, though in many cases they continued to hold more or less secretly to their old religion. Eventually all people of Moorish descent, including many who were genuine Catholics, were expelled from the country. To such extremes was the Spanish nation willing to go for the sake of unity.[16]

A new threat to Catholic unity arose in the sixteenth century, when a Protestant Reformation started in Spain. One author states that in 1559 there were probably one thousand Protestants in Seville, one thousand in Valladolid, and one thousand in other parts of Spain[17]; but the number might well be smaller, since the Inquisition in the great *autos de fe* for sentencing and punishing heretics in 1559–62, about which we shall speak presently, condemned only about two hundred Spanish Protestants,[18] and it is not likely that thousands would escape its vigilance. The significance of the Spanish Reformation does not lie in the number of people involved but rather in their strategic position in Spanish society and the influence which in time they might have exerted upon the Spanish State and the life and culture of the nation. Balmes declared, 'Distinguished ecclesiastics, members of the clergy, nuns, important laymen, in a word, individuals of the most influential classes, were found infected by the new errors'.[19] It should be added that there were also people of humble station who became Protestants.

The learned secretary of Emperor Charles V, Alfonso de Valdés, was a convinced Erasmian, severely critical of the clergy and of the low moral and spiritual state of the Roman Catholic Church and desirous of a reformation within the Church. He should probably not be classified as a Protestant, but he, like Erasmus, aroused opposition against the abuses in the Church and was a forerunner of the reformers. He brought upon himself the ire of the clergy by writing (probably in collaboration with his brother Juan) *The Dialogue of Lactancio and the Archdeacon*, which was a defence of the capture and sacking of Rome by the Emperor's forces. The fate of 'the eternal city' was declared to be divine punishment for the vices, ambition, and hypocrisy of high officials of the Church. Alfonso de Valdés was denounced to the Inquisition, but his high standing with the Emperor and the Erasmian tendencies of the grand inquisitor and others who examined his book saved him from persecution. He died in 1532, before Church and State had become fully aroused against heresy.[20]

Juan de Valdés, considered by some to be the greatest of the Spanish reformers, criticized the ignorance, superstition, and corrupt living which were so prevalent in the Roman Catholic Church of his day; but, like his brother Alfonso, he did not break openly with that Church. In his *Dialogue of Christian Doctrine*, which was discovered just a few years ago in Portugal, he voiced the Erasmian hope that godly and enlightened prelates might produce 'a different kind of Christianity' through the reformation and education of the clergy.[21] His writings on theology and his commentaries on different books of the Bible reveal him as an original thinker, unhampered by Church traditions and clearly convinced of the doctrine of justification by faith and of the necessity of personal religious experience. 'I do not understand', he wrote, 'that justification and faith are synonymous, but that they who believe enjoy justification, through the grace of God already executed upon Christ. And I understand that for a man to be justified by this justice is as worthy a cause of pride or of self-esteem and vainglory, as for the thief who is rescued from the gallows in holy week to make his liberation a subject of self-esteem and vainglory.'[22] He valued the Bible highly but gave even greater importance to illumination and guidance by the Spirit of God. The mature Christian, he said, 'attends to the inward inspirations, retaining God's own Spirit as his master, availing himself of the Sacred Scriptures as a kind of holy conversation that refreshes him'.[23]

Juan de Valdés was of aristocratic birth and was wealthy and scholarly. He wrote so well that the severe critic of Protestantism, Menéndez Pelayo, felt constrained to say that as a writer of Spanish, Juan de Valdés must bow only to Cervantes.[24] In Naples, where for some reason he took up residence (perhaps to find security), he gathered a large group of disciples, including noblemen and high ecclesiastics, who met with him to study the Bible and talk about religion. He and his disciples were not molested by the authorities during his lifetime. A few years before his death, however, Emperor Charles V published a severe edict in Naples against persons suspected of heresy, and after Valdés' death in 1541, his followers were scattered or silenced by the threat of persecution. The Italian nobleman Carnesecchi, who had held high positions in the papal court, was beheaded and burned in Rome for his adherence to the teachings of Juan de Valdés.[25]

Among the sixteenth-century Spanish Protestants who lived beyond the borders of their own country, Francisco de Enzinas occupies a position of distinction as the first person to publish a Spanish translation of the New Testament from Greek. He studied in Louvain and Wittenberg and was a personal friend of Melanchthon, in whose home he was often a welcome guest. When his New Testament was ready for publication he had not yet publicly taken his stand with the Protestants, and he hoped to obtain royal protection for his book. In an audience with Charles V he asked the Emperor to be patron and defender of the New Testament, and the Emperor agreed, provided there was nothing suspicious in the book, and charged his confessor with the examination of it. Suspicions of heresy were aroused, however, and Enzinas was imprisoned; but he escaped from prison and was able to make a valuable contribution to the Reformation through his writing and his teaching in the seven years or so remaining to him until his death in 1552. His ability received recognition in his appointment as professor of Greek in Cambridge University.[26]

Michael Servetus, one of the Spaniards persecuted for religious reasons, was regarded as a heretic by both Roman Catholics and Protestants. That he was a man of unusual gifts is demonstrated by his theological writings, his editing of the geography of Ptolemy, his study and practice of medicine, and his discovery of the pulmonary circulation of the blood. Imprisoned by Roman Catholic authorities in France for his unorthodox theology, he escaped and fled, but only to be arrested again when he reached

Protestant Geneva. After a trial in which he was denied the use of a lawyer but spoke himself with great boldness and even impudence, he was condemned by the town council of Geneva, with the approval of Calvin, and was burned at the stake. The specific charges on which he was condemned were that he denied the Trinity (as generally interpreted) and rejected infant baptism. The Code of Justinian was revived to serve as the legal basis for this and other cases of Protestant persecution.[27]

The case of Servetus has lain heavily upon the consciences of Protestants and has served as a reminder that tolerance has not always been a characteristic of their religion. In the beginning most of the reformers accepted the principle of union of Church and State, which logically called for religious unity and the persecution of heretics; but they also believed in free inquiry, which logically called for religious freedom. There are some dark chapters of persecution on the part of Protestants, but Protestantism eventually adopted the principle of religious toleration or, better still, freedom. At the beginning of the twentieth century a group of Protestants erected a monument to Servetus in Geneva, on which the following eloquent words were inscribed: 'We, respectful and grateful sons of Calvin, yet condemning an error which was that of his century, and firmly devoted to liberty of conscience according to the true principles of the Reformation and the Gospel, have erected this expiatory monument.'

The first Protestant who was put to death in Spain for his faith was Francisco de San Roman, a merchant who was converted during his travels in Flanders and Germany and was burned, along with several Jews, in an *auto de fe* in Valladolid, the capital of Spain at that time. At about the same time (in the 1540's) Rodrigo de Valer, a wealthy man of aristocratic birth who had become enamoured of the Bible and boldly denounced the corruptions of the clergy and the Church, was condemned by the Inquisition in Seville to imprisonment for life and the confiscation of his property. His most important influence was seen in the life of Dr. Juan Gil (or Egidius, as he is often called), who was the preaching canon of the Cathedral of Seville. Dr. Gil's preaching took on new power after Rodrigo de Valer had talked with him about religion. He was nominated by the Emperor Charles V as Bishop of Tortosa, but before this appointment could become effective he was accused by the Inquisition of heresy and was condemned to a year of imprisonment and was forbidden to teach or preach for ten years. He died four years after his sentence, and in 1560 his bones were dug up and burned.[28]

In the late 1550's significant Protestant communities were discovered in Valladolid and Seville. By that time the Roman Catholic Church was in full action against the Reformation in Europe, and the liberty of thought which within limits had been allowed a few years earlier was no longer permitted. Dogma was being rigidly defined in the Council of Trent, and debatable ground was being reduced. The Society of Jesus had been organized by the Spaniard, Ignatius Loyola, and had begun its work in support of the papacy. It was an aroused Church which faced the little Protestant movement of Spain.

The powers of the State were also aroused. Charles V had had much trouble with Protestantism in Germany, and he was determined that it should not create divisions in Spain. He and others of his realm had earlier followed a policy of conciliation and had evidently hoped for unity within Christendom. For this reason he had insisted on a Church Council which would reform the Church and thus remove some of the grounds of rebellion. Then he lost hope of a reconciliation between Catholics and Protestants and gave himself wholly to the cause of the Counter Reformation. From his retirement in a monastery, shortly before his death, he urged that heresy be stamped out in Spain as a service to God and country.[29] Philip II accepted as one of the chief responsibilities of his reign the combating of Protestantism at home and abroad. Arms, diplomacy, and the Inquisition were the instruments he used. The Holy Office, which had become quiescent, took on new life.

The group of Protestants in Valladolid included the Italian

gentleman, Carlos de Seso; Dr. Agustín de Cazalla, a highly
gifted clergyman who had been Charles V's chaplain and had
accompanied him for nine years in his travels through Germany
and Flanders; other members of the wealthy and aristocratic
Cazalla family; the Dominican friar Domingo de Rojas; nuns
from local convents; and other people of prominence and influence. It was the practice of these men and women to meet in
the home of Cazalla's mother, Leonor de Vibero, for worship
and Bible study. Arrests were made until, as one writer has said,
the prisons 'boiled with prisoners'. The Inquisition decided to
celebrate an *auto de fe* which would be more solemn and impressive than any Spain had ever witnessed. On 21st May 1559, the
Regent Juana, members of the nobility and clergy, and a great
host of people assembled in the main square of Valladolid to
witness the all-day ceremony for the sentencing of the heretics.
There was a one-hour sermon on the text, 'Beware of false
prophets, who come to you in sheep's clothing, but inwardly
are ravening wolves' (Matthew 7:15). This was followed by an
oath on the part of the princes and then all of the people to
defend the faith of the Church and give all possible aid to the
Inquisition in the discovery and punishment of heretics. Then
came the reading of the sentences, the unfrocking of clergymen,
and the absolving of the penitents who were not condemned to
death. Sixteen people were admitted to reconciliation with
punishments of different degrees. Fourteen were turned over to
secular authorities for execution and were led to a point outside
the city to be put to death. Fear led most of them to profess
orthodoxy, and these were strangled before their bodies were
burned, but one would give no signs of repentance and
was burned alive. The bones of Leonor de Vibero, who had
died several years earlier, were dug up and burned, and her
houses were torn down, the ground sown with salt, and a stone
set up to recall to posterity the shame of what took place
there. A second *auto de fe*, more impressive even than the first
and presided over by Philip II, took place in Valladolid a few
months later. Among the victims were ten Protestants who

were strangled and then burned and two who were burned alive.[30]

The Protestant community of Seville, which owed its origin to Rodrigo de Valer and Dr. Gil, was of even greater significance than that of Valladolid. One of its leading members was Dr. Constantino Ponce de la Fuente, who, like Dr. Cazalla, had served as chaplain and preacher of Charles V and had accompanied him (and also Philip II) on foreign journeys. At the time of his arrest he was preaching canon of the Cathedral of Seville. So eloquent was he that it is said that people went to church at three or four o'clock in the morning in order to get places in the church where they could hear him preach. He was a good writer, and Menéndez Pelayo asserts that his catechism is 'the best-written, though unfortunately not the purest, of Castilian catechisms'.[31] When Charles V heard of his arrest on the charge of heresy, he said, 'If Constantino is a heretic, he is a great one'. There was no doubt of his apostasy from the Roman Church after some of his writings which had been hidden were discovered, for in them he called the Pope Antichrist and referred to purgatory as an invention of the monks to fill their bellies. After two years in prison he died in 1560, and a few months later his bones were dug up and burned.

There were two centres of Protestantism in Seville: the home of Isabel de Baena and the monastery of San Isidro del Campo, whose prior, García-Arias, and the majority of whose inmates accepted the new faith. Many of the Protestants were noble and wealthy, but a man of humble station in life, Julián Hernández (known by the diminutive, Julianillo, because of his small stature), did as much as anybody to further the cause of the Reformation in Spain. He was a muleteer, and he smuggled into the country copies of the New Testament and writings of the Spanish reformers living abroad. His work was brought to an end when a woman denounced him for distributing Protestant books. For three years he resisted all persuasions and tortures and went to his death undaunted in his faith.

There were *autos de fe* in Seville in 1559 and 1560 for eradicating

Protestantism from the city. In the first, twenty-one men and women were burned, some having been strangled and others being burned alive, and in the second fourteen were executed. The majority of these were Protestants; a few were executed for immorality, Judaism, or Mohammedanism. There were many penitents who suffered varying degrees of punishment, and the effigies of several persons who had escaped from Spain were burned.[32]

The Primate of Spain, Bartolomé Carranza, Archbishop of Toledo, was accused of Lutheran heresy and spent seventeen years in prison while he was being tried in Spain and in Rome. His name was frequently mentioned by those who were seized by the Inquisition in Valladolid, and it seems that he was a friend of Juan de Valdés. It is amazing that this distinguished prelate, who had rendered outstanding service to his country, had served as a delegate to the Council of Trent, and had aided in the restoration of Catholicism in England under Queen Mary, should have beliefs suspiciously similar to those of Protestants; and it is fully as surprising that the Inquisition should have had the power to lay hands on him. His arrest was made possible by a special papal decree. For seven years his trial went on in Spain; and then, against the will of Philip II and the Spanish Inquisition, it was referred to Rome. In his sentence in 1576 the Pope declared that 'the Archbishop had imbibed perverse doctrine from many condemned heretics, such as Martin Luther, Œcolampadius, and Philip Melanchthon . . . and had taken from them many errors, phrases, and ways of speaking used by them in their teaching'. The distinguished prisoner was required to abjure sixteen propositions, including the following: 'Christ our Saviour gave satisfaction so effectively and completely for our sins that there is exacted from us no other satisfaction', and 'Only faith without works is sufficient for salvation'. The Archbishop complied with this demand and was absolved but was required to do certain penances and was suspended from his diocese for five years. He died shortly after sentence was passed. Throughout his trial and just before his death he insisted that he had never taught anything contrary to the true teachings of the Church and that his statements had been falsely interpreted. The jealousy and ill-will of certain influential people towards him is a partial explanation of his arrest and trial; but the evidence seems to indicate that he did hold doctrines considered by the Roman Catholic Church to be heresy, though he did not wish to rebel against that Church and the authority of the Pope.[33]

A word must be added about two or three of the Spanish Protestants who in the security of other lands sought to carry on the work of reformation. Juan Pérez continued the task of Bible translation begun by Valdés and Enzinas and also produced several theological works, one of which was an 'Epístola consolatoria' for the consolation of those suffering persecution for their faith. To Casiodoro de Reina belongs the distinction of bringing out a translation of the entire Bible in 1569. This Bible, revised a short time later by Cipriano de Valera, is, with slight alterations, the translation still most widely used among Spanish-speaking Protestants. These men and others wrote copiously with the hope of planting the seed of religious reformation in their fellow-countrymen. They were not granted the joy of seeing the seed take deep root within Spain.[34]

The power of Church and State made the existence of Protestantism in Spain impossible. After the great *autos de fe* in Valladolid and Seville which we have noted, there were several others in which Spanish Protestants were put to death. In later years Protestants occasionally appeared in the lists of those tried and condemned by the Inquisition; but it is correct to say that after the 1560's there was no Protestant movement in the country. As one writer has put it, the Protestants 'were all burnt, or driven by the fear of being burnt into professing themselves Catholics'.[35] The official policy of Catholic unity prevented a religious division.

The ideal of Catholic unity, which thus gained such clear and forceful expression at the beginning of the modern era, has continued through the years and has profoundly affected the policies of Spanish governments. It was unchallenged during the long period of decadence following Philip II; since then it has been challenged but never destroyed. Some Spaniards have regarded themselves as inheritors of the spirit and mission of the Inquisition.[36] Others have wished to avoid the violence of the Inquisiiton but still have found in the fifteenth and sixteenth centuries their ideal for the Spanish nation. The following words spoken by the present head of the Spanish State to a group of Catholic pilgrims from South America in 1950 indicate that he has not forgotten the ideal:

You have wished to come to the place from which your ancestors went to carry the gospel to America, and you find the same Spain . . . of the fifteenth and sixteenth centuries, the same noble and intransigent Spain—intransigent, yes, for in the things of the spirit and of the true faith there must be a noble and holy intransigence. . . . When nations have received the divine blessing of a single faith and are living under the true religion, concessions cannot be made to error. . . . We do not want in our country Masons who come to destroy our spiritual unity and our eternal destiny.[37]

II

THE RISE OF LIBERALISM

CATHOLIC unity as developed in the fifteenth and sixteenth centuries was challenged by the rise of modern liberalism, which brought with it the idea of religious toleration or freedom. In some countries the presence and conflict of different religions has led to a policy of freedom for all; but in Spain, since all other religions besides Catholicism were eliminated at the beginning of the modern era, the achievement of religious liberty has depended almost entirely upon political liberals. In a long and often bitter struggle, they have set themselves against the traditional official policy of Catholic unity and have revived the older Spanish tradition of respect for the rights of religious minorities. By no means is the battle over.

The modern struggle for religious freedom in Spain did not begin in earnest until the nineteenth century, but even before that the domination of life and thought by the Church was questioned and defied. Freedom of thought and reliance upon reason were encouraged by the circulation (on a limited scale) of the *Encyclopedia* and the writings of Voltaire, Rousseau, and other independent thinkers.[1]

The Spanish kings went to great lengths in asserting their authority over the Church. At the beginning of the eighteenth century a papal nuncio was expelled from Madrid, all relationship with Rome was forbidden for a while, and the inquisitor general was exiled. The power of the Inquisition was reduced, and the number of *autos de fe* became fewer and fewer, until in the time of Charles III only four persons were burned at the stake. This energetic ruler also forbade the publication without government consent of any document coming from Rome, and he expelled the Jesuits, surprising them in their homes at night and sending them forthwith out of the country.[2]

In the nineteenth century liberalism took definite form in Spain. The ideas of liberty, equality, and fraternity gained increasing acceptance there as the influence of the French Revolution reached Spain and Spanish people tried to apply in their own country the ideals of that revolution. British and American democracy and liberal thought, and a little later German philosophy (especially that of the now almost unknown Krause) became known and appreciated. Freemasonry gained wide acceptance and contributed to the growth of liberalism and the opposition to clericalism.[3]

Fundamental in nineteenth-century liberalism was its emphasis on human rights and liberties. Freedom of conscience and of worship, freedom of speech and of the press, freedom from ecclesiastical and governmental oppression—these were generally elements of a liberal programme. They became a part of the goal of Spanish liberalism, though, as we shall see, the political parties have been guided at times more by expediency than by devotion to an ideal or programme. Many Spanish liberals have been anti-clerical, in the sense of opposing the power and influence of the clergy, but this has not necessarily meant opposition to Catholicism as a religion, nor has it often implied interest in Protestantism.[4]

It was after the occupation of Spain by Napoleon that Spanish liberals had their first opportunity to put into effect their ideas concerning government. The Spanish people did not submit to French rule, and even while foreigners were in control of most of the country a Spanish Cortes (Parliament), assembled in Cadiz, set about establishing a government for the nation. The fruit of their labours was the Constitution of 1812, which in most respects was extremely liberal for the times. It proclaimed freedom of the press and other civil liberties, but, strangely enough, it did not guarantee freedom of religion.[5] Article 12 reads as follows:

> The religion of the Spanish nation is, and shall be perpetually, Apostolic Roman Catholic, the only true religion. The nation protects

it by wise and just laws and prohibits the exercise of any other, whatsoever.[6]

Some of the lawmakers of Cadiz were free-thinkers and some were liberal Catholics, but none were adherents of any other religion, and they considered the country to be still overwhelmingly Catholic. Their recognition of Catholicism as the only religion of the country, however, did not mean submission to clericalism, and they passed a number of laws which were labelled as measures of oppression by upholders of the rights of the Church. Monasteries and convents with fewer than twelve inmates were dissolved; some church properties were seized; the Inquisition was discontinued; several bishops were imprisoned and exiled; and the nuncio was expelled.[7]

There was strong opposition, especially by the Spanish bishops, to the abolition of the Inquisition, but the majority of the Cortes decided that it was incompatible with the sovereignty of the nation, with the free exercise of civil authority, and with individual liberty and security. After all, the Constitution stated that the protection of the Catholic religion was to be by 'wise and just laws'! In the debate on the question, several delegates declared that the Inquisition could not be abolished without first obtaining the consent of the Pope, but others argued that this was a purely temporal matter, to be decided by the State. One speaker praised the Holy Office as a defender of 'the Christian freedom which has been won for mankind by Jesus Christ, the freedom of the Catholic religion, the true freedom'. Another argued that the object of religion is to give eternal blessedness and that this has nothing to do with civil laws but only with persuasion and preaching. Several of the liberal priests who were members of the Cortes joined in condemning the Inquisition, and they did not hesitate to denounce the temporal ambitions of the popes and to assert the independence of the State as over against the claims of the papacy. In a manifesto to the nation announcing the abolition of the Holy Office, the Cortes declared that 'the ignorance of religion, the backwardness of the sciences, the decadence of the arts, commerce, and agriculture, and the depopulation and poverty of Spain proceeded in great part from the system of the Inquisition'.[8]

When the French were driven out of Spain, Ferdinand VII returned to occupy the throne. His reign was marked by alternate triumphs of reactionary and liberal tendencies. When reaction triumphed, the Jesuits were readmitted to Spain and the Church was favoured in many ways; and when the liberals succeeded in having their way the Jesuits were expelled and many convents and monasteries were closed. The Inquisition was restored for a while but then abolished definitively, though for some time local Committees of the Faith took its place.[9]

The last person to be excuted for heresy in Spain was Cayetano Ripoll, a school teacher, who was condemned by the Valencia Committee of the Faith and was put to death in 1826. He taught his pupils the existence of God and instructed them in the Ten Commandments but ignored the rest of the catechism. The Committee of the Faith found him guilty of heresy and, after fruitless attempts to convert him, handed him over to secular authorities for execution. Death came by hanging, but the old tradition of burning heretics was recalled by flames painted on containers below the gallows. The central government (to its credit let this be said) condemned the execution of Ripoll and ordered the Committee of the Faith to cease its operations.[10]

When Ferdinand VII died in 1833 he was succeeded by his infant daughter, Isabella, whose mother, Maria Christina, became regent. Ferdinand's brother, Carlos, or Charles, claimed the throne, on the basis of a law (annulled by Ferdinand) which denied to females the right of succession to the throne. Since he was supported by extreme conservatives and by many of the clergy, Maria Christina was forced to depend upon more liberal elements. It was out of this sort of situation that the Carlist wars, begun in this period and from time to time resumed later on, arose to scourge the land. The defenders of the cause of Isabella were divided into two main groups: the Progressives, who were thoroughly liberal and at times showed marked anti-clerical tendencies, and the Moderates, who tended towards absolutism and enforced Catholic unity but did not go so far in that direction as the Carlists, who have ever been (even to the present time) the arch-enemies of democracy and religious freedom.[11]

Religious passions rose high in the 1830's. The Carlist War, which lasted for about six years and was renewed later, aroused fanatical devotion to the Church on the part of some and bitter anti-clericalism on the part of others. During a cholera epidemic, rumours spread that monks were poisoning drinking water, and there was an orgy of burning monasteries and killing their inmates. Such was the distrust and hatred of the clergy on the part of some—a minority, to be sure—of the Spanish people.[12]

The Government did not, of course, approve such popular expressions of anti-clericalism, but it, too, was anti-clerical. Monasteries and convents were suppressed, many ecclesiastics were exiled, and ordinations of priests were forbidden. Since there were no relations between the papacy and the Spanish Government, vacancies in the bishoprics could not be filled, and the number of bishops fell to six. The most far-reaching expression of the new policy towards the Church was the nationalization and sale of Church property. This was naturally bitterly opposed by the clergy and applauded by those who resented the great wealth of the Church. It led to the acceptance by the State of the obligation to support the Church and the clergy and has served as the basis of all subsequent claims of the Church to financial support from the government. Mendizabal, the minister responsible for the expropriation of Church property and much of the rest of the anti-clerical legislation, appeared as a demon to some Spaniards and a hero to others.[13]

The Cortes convoked in 1836 to draw up a new Constitution reflected the progress which the idea of religious toleration had made. The article on religion proposed by the committee on the Constitution and eventually adopted recognized the Catholic religion as that professed by the Spanish people but did not declare it to be the only true religion nor specifically refer to it as the religion of the State. It is probably worthy of note that the word 'Roman' was not used, for some liberals who considered themselves Catholics resented the subjection to Rome which the use of the word implied. The article stated only that:

The nation is obliged to maintain the cult and the ministers of the Catholic religion which Spaniards profess.[14]

This article did not satisfy those who wanted an affirmation of Catholic unity, nor those who wanted a clear declaration of religious toleration. Some of the liberals proposed that to it be added the words: 'No Spaniard may be persecuted or disturbed for religious reasons so long as he respects Catholic ideas and does not offend public morality.' One defender of the article as originally proposed denied the necessity of mentioning toleration or freedom of religion, and declared that laws which are intended to produce toleration sometimes provoke disputes and produce the opposite effect. 'The time will come,' he said, 'when civil and canonical legislation will be freed of all intolerance, but at the present time the Cortes can do no more than recognize the indisputable fact that the Spanish people now profess the Catholic religion: what they will do in the future nobody knows.' Another speaker said, 'If there were among us people of different religions I would favour religious freedom, but if religious unity reigns among us, why establish such principles?'[15]

We shall not follow here the struggle between the Progressives, who were responsible for most of the legislation on religion we have been considering, and the Moderates, who followed a much more conciliatory policy towards the Church. Both parties had several opportunities to put into effect their programmes in the 1830's and the 1840's. Mention should be made of the regency of Espartero, during which priests and bishops were removed from office, bishops were appointed without the approval of Rome, and the nunciature was closed. When the Pope protested energetically against the policies of the Spanish Government, an official manifesto referred to the Pope's words as a declaration of war against Queen Isabella and a scandalous provocation to schism, disorder, and rebellion. It added that the time had passed when at a blast from the Vatican thrones trembled and nations were thrown into a panic. The Pope addressed an encyclical to the whole Church on the sad state of the Spanish Church and called upon all Catholics to pray for a change.[16]

In 1843, Isabella, who was then thirteen years old, was declared of age. The Moderates soon gained control of the Government and began to undo much of what previous governments had done, especially with regard to the Church.[17] The Constitution which was adopted in 1845 under their sponsorship declared the Catholic religion to be that of the nation, but it did not go so far as the Constitution of 1812 and guarantee that it would be maintained to the exclusion of all other religions, though perhaps that might be implied:

> The religion of the Spanish nation is the Apostolic Roman Catholic religion. The State binds itself to maintain the cult and its ministers.[18]

The Penal Code of 1848 recognized the Catholic character of the nation as set forth in the Constitution and established penalties for offences against the Catholic religion. It is to be noted, though, that the absolute intolerance characteristic of the days of the Inquisition was absent from this Code—as, indeed, it had been absent from a Code adopted in 1822. There was an implicit recognition of a certain freedom of conscience, for there was no penalty for failing to practise the Catholic religion or for rejecting Catholic dogma in one's mind. Public acts were regarded differently, however, and by the terms of the Code the State would permit no insult or injury to the Catholic religion, nor would it permit public manifestations of other religions. Anyone who might attempt to abolish or change the Roman Catholic religion was liable to imprisonment for twelve to twenty years and perpetual exile if he was in a position of public authority and used his position to achieve that aim. The ordinary citizen guilty of such an offence was liable to imprisonment for six to twelve years and in case of recurrence to perpetual exile. Anyone who might celebrate public acts of worship of a non-Catholic religion was liable to exile for twelve to twenty years. Anyone guilty of publicly inculcating the non-observance of the religious precepts, or making mock of the sacraments of the Church, or persisting in publishing doctrines condemned by the ecclesiastical authorities was subject to imprisonment for a term of six months to three years. Recurrence in such offences was punishable by exile for twelve to twenty years. Any Spaniard who might apostatize publicly from the Roman Catholic religion would be punished with perpetual exile.[19]

The Spanish Government and the Vatican were moving towards a full understanding, and, in 1851, a Concordat based on Catholic unity was signed. This Concordat is of great significance, since it has been used ever since in defence of the principle of Catholic unity. Its first four articles were regarded as valid by the present Spanish Government[20] until a new Concordat was agreed upon in 1953. The first article recognized Catholicism as the only religion existing in Spain and guaranteed it perpetual protection:

The Apostolic Roman Catholic religion, which with the exclusion of all other cults continues to be the only one of the Spanish nation, will be conserved always in the domains of His Catholic Majesty, with all the rights and prerogatives which it should enjoy according to the law of God and the prescriptions of the sacred Canons.[21]

Articles two and three provided that all instruction in universities, seminaries, and private and public schools should be in accordance with Catholic doctrine and under the guardianship of the hierarchy; and that the public authorities should grant their patronage and support to the clergy in the fulfilment of their duties, especially in the control of undesirable propaganda. In other articles the Pope recognized the sale of Church properties and, in turn, received a guarantee of certain rights and privileges of the Church, including financial support by the State and the right of the Church to acquire property. Church and State were prepared to put up a solid front against any advances by Protestantism.

A revolution in 1854 was followed by a two-year period of liberalism, and the antagonism between Church and State was

openly renewed. The Jesuits were again expelled, church properties were again put up for sale, the nuncio and several bishops
were banished from the country, and religious processions in the
streets were forbidden. When the dogma of the Immaculate
Conception was proclaimed, a Madrid newspaper which published it without permission of the government was seized.
Permission was finally given for the publication in Spain of the
papal Bull announcing the dogma, but the authority of the
government to control such things was reaffirmed.[22] Recognition
was given to the rights of those who were not members of the
official Church in an order permitting the construction of
cemeteries for non-Catholics and requiring decorous burial for
them where there was no special cemetery.[23]

In the Cortes called to draw up a Constitution, the question
of freedom of religion was frankly discussed. A proposal of
religious liberty and the separation of Church and State obtained
more than forty votes; and a proposal to tolerate non-Catholic
worship was approved by a standing vote, but when a vote by
names was demanded the motion was lost by four votes. One
of the speakers on the religious question lauded religious freedom
as the greatest of the freedoms and as a necessity for the welfare
of Spain and of the Catholic Church itself. The Minister of
Grace and Justice said that he did not consider it necessary to
authorize full freedom of religion since no one in the Cortes or
out of it asked for such freedom for himself on the basis of not
being a Catholic. Petitions poured into the Cortes from bishops
and others asking for a clear declaration of Catholic unity, and
members of the Cortes made the same plea.[24] The article on
religion in the Constitution went far in the direction of true
religious toleration, though it did not explicitly authorize non-
Catholic worship. It repeated the promise of the Constitution of
1837 to support the Catholic religion 'which Spaniards profess'
but added a guarantee of freedom of belief:

The nation is obliged to maintain and protect the cult and ministers
of the Catholic religion which Spaniards profess.
But no Spaniard or foreigner may be persecuted for his religious

opinions or beliefs, provided that he does not manifest them by public acts contrary to religion.[25]

This Constitution never went into effect, for there was a reaction and change of government, and the Constitution of 1845 was restored. The lines became clearly drawn between the more conservative elements and those who favoured a greater degree of democracy and religious freedom. On one side were the Moderates and on the other the Progressives. The latter were planning for revolution and were moving towards an ever closer collaboration with the Democrats, who were constantly gaining prominence. In various places Republicans and Socialists were trying to take the law into their own hands, and Carlists were also causing trouble. One of the most important parties was the new Liberal Union, made up of former Moderates and Progressives who wished to avoid extremes. They alternated in power with the Moderates during the last years of the reign of Isabella II.[26]

During this period it was definitely established that a meeting is to be regarded as public and therefore subject to regulation by law if it consists of more than twenty persons.[27] This had no immediate significance for Protestants, but later on their meetings would be regarded as private and free from governmental supervision if they fell below that number. Only under the Franco régime has there been any deviation from that practice.

When Pope Pius IX issued the *Syllabus of Errors* in 1864 there was raised again in Spain the question of the right of the government to control publication of documents coming from Rome. Among 'the principal errors of our time' denounced by the Pope were this particular practice and other matters regarding the authority of the State over the Church. The Spanish bishops began to publish the *Syllabus* without awaiting the authorization of the government, whereupon the liberal press loudly protested. The government sought to avoid conflict by officially publishing the document and at the same time reaffirming the right of the State to control such things and promising to harmonize this right with freedom of the press and the rights of the Holy See.[28]

2

The Pope made perfectly clear in the *Syllabus of Errors* that though times had changed the Roman Catholic Church was still opposed to freedom for non-Catholic religions and insisted on its right of absolute control over marriage and education. His pronouncements reinforced the arguments of those Spaniards who were opposed to changing the traditional policy of Catholic unity and alienated some liberals from the Church. The following are some of the 'errors' which the Pope condemned:

15. Every man is free to embrace and profess the religion he shall believe true, guided by the light of reason.

48. This system of instructing youth, which consists in separating it from the Catholic faith and from the power of the Church, and in teaching exclusively, or at least primarily, the knowledge of natural things and the earthly ends of social life alone, may be approved by Catholics.

55. The Church ought to be separated from the State, and the State from the Church.

73. A merely civil contract may, among Christians, constitute a true marriage. . . .

77. In the present day it is no longer expedient that the Catholic religion shall be held as the only religion of the State, to the exclusion of all other modes of worship.

79. The Roman pontiff can and ought to reconcile himself to, and agree with, progress, liberalism, and civilization as lately introduced.[29]

The differences between liberals and conservatives or reactionaries were further sharpened by the question of recognizing the Kingdom of Italy, which was bringing papal temporal power to an end. In the debate on the matter in the Cortes, a deputy deplored the rise of rationalism in Europe and in Spain and declared that modern civilization was imperilled by the modern acceptance of the principle of free inquiry. On another occasion the same man attempted to refute the argument that the interests of Spain demanded the recognition of Italy by saying that the interests of the nation demanded that Spain should be the constant champion of Catholicism and of the Holy See. In spite of such strong opposition, the Cortes voted for recognition of Italy.[30]

The country moved rapidly towards revolution. The gulf

between liberals and conservatives was too broad to bridge. The Queen allied herself with the conservative forces and thereby led to her repudiation by the liberals. Her last ministry of Moderates attempted to strengthen Throne and Church by establishing an iron rule, discharging liberal professors, and consolidating clerical control of education.[31] Nothing, however, could keep the new wine of liberalism from breaking the old wine skins of absolutism and clericalism.

During the years of turmoil leading up to the Revolution of 1868 Protestants were several times heard from; and the roots of 'the second Protestant Reformation', which developed after the Revolution, are found in this period. One of the pioneers was the Methodist, William H. Rule, who attempted to take advantage of the liberalism of the 1830's to establish a Protestant mission in Spain. After visiting various cities, he established a school in Cadiz, where an anti-Catholic political leader lent him support. This school, the first Protestant establishment in Spain, he was soon ordered to close by the military governor. Rule appealed to the authorities in Madrid through the mediation of the British Ambassador, and the mission was re-established, with a school for boys and one for girls, and with services of worship on Sunday. Shortly thereafter orders were given for the work to cease, but Rule refused to discontinue the services of worship on the grounds that they were private meetings in his own home. The Moderate government then in power supported the local authorities and forbade Rule to have schools or to hold meetings with the purpose of spreading doctrines opposed to religious unity. This time British officials did not intervene, and Rule had to give up his work in Cadiz and withdraw to Gibraltar. Other Protestants who by that time had begun to work in Spain were forced to cease their activities. An agent of the Methodist Bible Society was expelled from Cadiz, and another was imprisoned in Algeciras and conducted to Gibraltar. Rule appealed to the Cortes for religious freedom but was ignored.[32]

During this same period George Borrow went to Spain as an emissary of the British and Foreign Bible Society. Through the mediation of the British Ambassador, he obtained an interview with the Spanish Prime Minister, Mendizabal, whom he asked for permission to print the Bible in Spain. The Prime Minister adroitly escaped the issue by telling Borrow to come back when the country was in a more tranquil state. He said that what Spain needed from England was guns and money to carry on the war against the Carlists, and not Bibles. When the Government changed, Borrow repeated his request to the new Ministry of Moderates, and, though he did not receive the permit he wanted, he was given to understand that he could carry out his plans without fear of interference from the authorities. A new Progressive Government was in power when five thousand copies of the Scriptures were printed, including the Gospel of Luke in Gypsy and the same Gospel in Basque. Bibles were also imported from England. Bible sellers were sent out over the country, deposits of Bibles were made in bookshops and other stores in important cities, a Bible shop was opened in Madrid, and Borrow himself travelled from place to place to sell the Scriptures. Valuable assistance was rendered by the British Ambassador and consular officials.

At first Borrow faced little or no interference from the authorities, and there was much interest on the part of the people; but opposition grew on the part of the clergy and the Government, and the work was restricted more and more until it had to cease. Bibles were seized, and Borrow found himself imprisoned several times. He vividly describes his imprisonment of 1838. The Governor of Madrid forbade the sale of the Spanish New Testaments which had been printed there, but since nothing was said about closing the shop, Borrow decided to keep it open and sell the Gospels of Luke in Gypsy and Basque when they were ready. When the Gospels were offered for sale, the shop was raided by the police, the Gospels seized, and Borrow arrested and placed in prison. The British Ambassador immediately intervened, and Borrow was admonished and offered his freedom. He refused to leave, maintaining that he had been illegally imprisoned, and he remained in prison for three weeks. The Governor, by way of apology, wrote to the British Ambassador that Borrow had been imprisoned on insufficient evidence and that no stigma was attached to him.[33]

At the same time that George Borrow was in Spain, the British and Foreign Bible Society had further representation there in the person of Lieutenant Graydon, who served without pay. With the help of the Bible Society, Graydon published in Barcelona Bibles and Testaments in Spanish and in the Catalonian dialect, and he distributed these along the coast as far as Malaga. Entering the field of politico-religious controversy, he gave out pamphlets which were critical of the Government, the Spanish clergy, and the doctrines of the Catholic Church. Inasmuch as he declared his connection with the Bible Society and his association with Borrow, his activities incriminated Borrow, who thereupon protested to his sponsors against Graydon's activities and published in the Spanish press a statement that he was the only authorized agent of the Bible Society in the country. Graydon was upheld by the Bible Society but was withdrawn from Spain for his own personal safety.[34] Borrow's biographer says, 'The work was killed and the Bible Society disavowed the responsibility of the assassination'.[35]

In later years the Bible Society took note as follows of the work of Borrow and Graydon:

The labour of past years has not been labour lost. The seed sown by Mr. George Borrow and Lieutenant Graydon did not all perish. . . . And now when some are met with, who have an acquaintance with the Word of God, and the question is asked how did they obtain it, the answer is that their fathers possessed the Book, and that from their lips they first heard its precious contents. So that there is reason to believe that many who never separated from Rome, because they feared the terrors of her unscrupulous vengeance, yet lived and died in the faith of the Gospel which the Bible revealed to them, but which the tyranny of a cruel despotism prevented them from acknowledging.[36]

When the Revolution of 1854 inaugurated another era of liberalism in Spain, Francisco de Paula Ruet, a Spaniard who had been converted to Protestantism by the Waldensians in Italy, went to Barcelona to share his new faith with his fellow country-men. He attracted considerable attention by his preaching and his writing in a local paper. The Bishop of Barcelona ordered him to appear for questioning, but he refused, declaring that a church to which he did not belong had no jurisdiction over him. He was imprisoned four times, and finally (after the clerical and conservative reaction) he was sentenced to perpetual exile for having apostatized publicly from Catholicism. When he heard the sentence he smiled, and one of the judges said, 'Does it seem funny to you to have to leave your country and friends forever?' Ruet replied, 'You have sentenced me to perpetual exile from my country, but you do not know which will last longer, my life or the present situation'. He was sent to Gibraltar, where he established a church and carried on correspondence with Protestant groups that were springing up in Spain. Many Spaniards who on his instructions signed protests against the Catholic Church and sent them to him were advised that they had been received into the Spanish Evangelical Church.[37]

Ruet was not the only one who in the 1850's tried to introduce Protestantism into Spain. The Spanish Evangelization Society of Edinburgh reported at the end of 1856 that during the two years of its existence it had circulated 100,000 Bibles, Testaments, and Scripture portions in Spain.[38] The British and Foreign Bible Society had ten thousand copies of the Bible printed in Spain, but their sale was not permitted, and they were removed from the country several years later.[39]

A highly significant development for Protestantism was the discovery and publication of many of the writings of the sixteenth-century Spanish reformers. Some of these were excellent in style and content, but when Protestantism was extinguished in Spain the works of the reformers were for the most part lost. Their recovery became the life-work of Luis Usoz y Rio, a learned and wealthy Spaniard who accepted the Evangelical faith. In collaboration with the English Quaker, Benjamin Wiffen, he collected and published at his own expense twenty volumes of the works of the Spanish reformers of the sixteenth century. Since he had his printing done secretly and judiciously and did not offer the books to the public, he never had any trouble with the authorities.[40]

In 1860, Protestants were discovered in several different parts of Spain, and the government took action against them which announced to all the world its determination to maintain Catholic unity. Manuel Matamoros was arrested in Barcelona, and a search of his lodgings revealed letters and documents incriminating him and others as leaders of Protestantism in Spain. Arrests were made in Malaga, Granada, and other places, and a number of people threatened with arrest fled from Spain. It was revealed that in spite of restrictions Protestantism had gained a foothold in Spain, with a rather thorough organization in several centres. During his years of imprisonment, Matamoros carried on an extensive correspondence with people in other countries and aroused interest in himself and his fellow-prisoners. After trials in different courts the final sentence was nine years of imprisonment for Matamoros and three of his companions, and seven years for two others. They had been suspected of connections with political extremists who had caused riots and other disturbances, but these could not be proved, and the crime of which they were convicted was purely religious: they were declared guilty of having attempted to abolish or change the Roman Catholic religion in Spain. It will be recalled that the Penal Code set the penalty for this offence at imprisonment for a term of six to twelve years.

In the meantime, the Protestants of other countries, led by the Evangelical Alliance, had taken the matter up. Petitions were sent to the Spanish Queen or Cortes from groups in Great Britain, Holland, Russia, Sweden, Norway, Switzerland, Austria and other countries. An international committee of prominent people, including noblemen, statesmen, and religious leaders, went to Madrid to ask personally for the pardon of Matamoros and the other prisoners, and the King of Prussia sent a personal ambassador to interview the Queen about the matter. While the committee was seeking to obtain an audience with the Queen (in 1863), she commuted the punishment of the prisoners to exile. Only to that extent would she respond to foreign pressure in favour of the Protestants.[41]

The fate of Matamoros and his companions almost ended the activities of Protestants within Spain for a while. There are, however, little glimpses of Protestant 'cells' in the country. On the eve of the Revolution of 1868, one of the Protestant exiles declared, 'In different parts of Spain there are small societies, mostly from the middle and labouring classes, who hold regular meetings, but, through fear of persecution, this is done altogether in secret'.[42] In other countries some preparations were being made for future Protestant work in Spain, notably the training of young Spaniards for the careers of pastor and teacher.[43] A few months before the Revolution five Spaniards and one Englishman met at Gibraltar in what they called the First General Assembly of the Reformed Church in Spain to get ready for an extension of Protestant effort in the Iberian peninsula.[44] It is obvious that on the part of some Spaniards and foreigners there was hope and a strong confidence that the era of absolute intolerance in Spain would soon come to an end.

III

THE ESTABLISHMENT OF
RELIGIOUS FREEDOM

THE Revolution of 1868, which in many ways heralds a new era in Spanish history, marks the beginning of the legal right of Protestantism to exist in Spain. The policy of enforced Catholic unity gave way to religious freedom—or at least a toleration so generous that no one who was not a member of the official religion could complain of any serious violation of his freedom. The practice of religious liberty was destined to last for only a few years, and those very troubled ones, but after the events of this period it would be impossible to return completely to the old system of absolute intolerance.

The Revolution was a triumph of liberalism, which, as we have seen, had been developing since the beginning of the century and even before. It was brought about by a coalition of Progressives, Democrats, and some Unionists. The Republicans were not accepted by the coalition, but they formed a part of local revolutionary committees and played a prominent part in the evolution of the ideals of the Revolution and helped to carry it forward among the people. There were extremes among the masses, however, which were repudiated by the Republican leaders.[1]

When the Revolution began in September of 1868, with a revolt of the fleet in Cadiz, Generals Topete, Prim, and Serrano, the leaders of the movement, issued a manifesto calling upon the people to rise up against the government and aid in the struggle for legality, decency, honour, and liberty. Among those upon whose sympathetic aid they said they were relying were the members of the clergy. Nothing was said specifically about

33

religious freedom, though freedom in general was exalted.[2] That the principle of religious liberty was not forgotten, however, is indicated by the fact that General Prim told some Protestant pastors who had been living in exile that they were free to enter Spain with the Bible under their arms, to preach its doctrines.[3] City after city and garrison after garrison joined the Revolution, and before the end of the month the Queen had left the country and the entire nation was in the hands of the revolutionists.[4]

The religious question quickly assumed great importance as revolutionary committees were organized in different cities. Among the acts of some local committees in the early days of the Revolution were the expulsion of the Jesuits, the confiscation of many churches and other religious buildings, the closing of monasteries and convents, the establishment of civil marriage, and the expulsion of certain bishops and priests.[5] A large number of Catholic women of Seville sent a petition to General Serrano protesting the policy followed by the revolutionary committee of that city, and stating that fifty-seven churches had been condemned to demolition and that many nuns had been thrown into the street.[6]

The revolutionary committee of Seville had the distinction of being the first to set forth the principle of religious liberty. In a manifesto to the province and the nation, it called for the establishment of human freedom, including religious freedom.[7] A short time later the committee of Madrid issued a declaration of rights which included universal male suffrage, freedom of worship, freedom of instruction, freedom of assembly, freedom of the press, and other rights of free people.[8]

Among the first acts of the Provisional Government were the suppression of the Jesuits, the closing of certain monasteries and convents, and the granting of freedom to establish and operate schools.[9] In a manifesto to the nation the Provisional Government stated that it would attempt to put into effect the various manifestations of public opinion made during the Revolution, and it declared that freedom of religion was the most important of these.[10] In reply to an inquiry, General Serrano wrote to a group of Sephardic Jews that the edict of 1492 expelling the Jews had been made void by the proclamation of religious liberty and that the Jews were free to enter Spain and practise their worship along with the adherents of all other religions.[11]

As we shall see later, this was a period of great activity for Protestants. Only with regard to the importation of Bibles was any difficulty placed in their way, and that was not for religious reasons. Soon after the Revolution the British and Foreign Bible Society attempted to send Bibles into the country, and some passed in the confusion of the times; but then former laws forbidding the importation of Spanish books printed abroad were declared to be still in force. The President of the Bible Society wrote to General Prim about the matter, and he replied that he felt personally sympathetic but could not himself decide the question. In the meantime, some Bibles that had previously been printed in Spain and then removed from the country were permitted to pass the frontier, and Bible depots were opened in Madrid and elsewhere. Plans were made for printing the Bible in Spain. Several months later, through the mediation of the United States Ambassador, the importation of all books, including Bibles, was regularized.[12]

Meanwhile, Catholics were organizing to bring pressure to bear upon the Government to return to the policy of religious unity, or at least to stop strictures on the Catholic Church. Petitions poured in from all parts of the country protesting the suppression of religious orders, the closing of monasteries and convents, the confiscation of churches, and the granting of religious liberty. Articles in the press condemned Protestant literature and called upon landlords to refuse to rent their property for use as Protestant chapels. An Association of Catholics was organized to work against 'the evils brought by the Revolution' through propaganda, aid to schools and churches, the election of Catholic deputies to the Cortes, and every other possible way.[13] This Association denounced the attempt to introduce into Spain 'freedom of worship, freedom of instruction, freedom of the press—in a word, free inquiry, the father and sanctioner of all errors, all absurdities, all vices and crimes'.[14]

The Provisional Government ordered the confiscation of all archives, libraries, museums, and other collections of literature and art held by cathedrals, churches, monasteries, and military orders (but not libraries belonging to seminaries), alleging that these had been hidden away and that they should be made available to the people.[15] The Carlists and others used this order to excite the passions of the people, and the Governor of Burgos was assassinated as he was attempting to make an inventory of the things belonging to the cathedral there. Martial law was declared in the city, and many people, including clergymen, were imprisoned.[16] A few days later the Provisional Government issued a manifesto to the nation calling upon the people to be calm and to submit to the policies of the Government. On the subject of religious liberty it stated:

Religious freedom, which is accepted now in all the nations of the world and which, far from deadening the faith of the immense majority of the Spanish people, will help to revive and fortify it, is now truly established: the Government has proclaimed it in solemn documents and has authorized its practice in all the cases in which requests have been made. The only thing it has considered inopportune to decide is the complicated question of the relations which as a consequence of this liberty must exist between the Church and the State. This is a question which it has felt duty-bound to defer to the free decision of the constituent power. . . .[17]

When news of the murder of the Governor of Burgos reached Madrid, crowds of people circulated through the streets hailing religious freedom and separation of Church and State. The Church of the Italians was invaded, the papal seal was dragged through the streets, and the personal safety of the nuncio was put in danger. The foreign diplomatic corps protested against the threat to the safety of the representative of the Holy See, and the Minister of State expressed the regret of the Government for what had happened but stated that it was understandable, though not justifiable, in view of the fact that the Catholic religion had been used by some as a force of reaction against the Revolution. Relations between the Vatican and the Provisional Government, already rather strained, were not helped by these occurrences, but there was no complete break.[18]

During these troubled days a Protestant chapel was opened in Madrid. A great deal of attention was attracted by the event, and there was danger of violence to the Protestants. The mayor showed his determination to guarantee freedom of worship by sending nine armed guards to protect the chapel and those attending services in it.[19]

Early in 1869 a constituent Cortes was elected. There were not lacking charges of abuses, illegalities, and violence in the elections, but the fact that seventy Republicans and even some Carlists were elected indicates a degree of fairness. The Progressives had the largest number of representatives in the Cortes, followed by the Unionists and the Republicans, with a sizable number of Monarchical Democrats. There were three Unionists in favour of the Bourbon dynasty, led by Cánovas del Castillo.[20]

The Cortes appointed a committee of fifteen, including Progressives, Unionists, and Democrats, to draw up a draft of a Constitution. The committee had trouble reaching an agreement on the religious question, some insisting on the supremacy of Catholicism and the limitation of freedom of worship to foreigners, and others advocating separation of Church and State.[21] The foreword to the constitutional draft indicates that the article on religion represented a compromise:

Only the religious question, the most serious, . . . the most transcendental of all the questions that can be presented to the Spanish nation, that which in itself envelops and enlivens all the rest, has had the legitimate and natural privilege of synthesizing in the last moments and in gigantic proportions all the difficulties which encompass this situation, this assembly, and the revolution. All the individuals of the committee have discussed for a long time, all have doubted, even as the parties and the country have doubted and hesitated. But before the spectacle of the country disturbed, liberty menaced, the revolution threatened, all have dominated their personal sentiments, have hushed their deep-rooted affections, have forgotten old conflicts.[22]

The articles on religion in the draft of the Constitution were as follows:

Art. 20. The nation binds itself to maintain the cult and the ministers of the Catholic religion.
Art. 21. The public or private observance of any other cult is guaranteed to all the foreigners resident in Spain, without further limitations than the universal rules of morality and right.
If some Spaniards profess another religion than the Catholic, all that is provided in the former paragraph is applicable to them.[23]

The Catholic forces of the country, led by the bishops, flooded the Cortes with petitions for a continuance of Catholic unity. The Bishop of Jaen presented a petition sponsored by the Association of Catholics and signed by 2,874,261 people; and he announced that signatures were still being obtained.[24] In an earlier session the Minister of Grace and Justice had declared that Catholic petitions were being signed in obedience to higher orders and that some of the signatures were evidently forgeries, it being clear that on the petitions he had seen four thousand signatures were in the handwriting of four people.[25] As the same Minister pointed out on another occasion, there were also petitions in favour of religious freedom from individuals and groups within Spain and from the Jews of Lisbon, London, Amsterdam, and other places.[26]

The religious issue produced numerous and brilliant discourses in the Cortes. When the constitutional draft as a whole was being considered, many deputies expressed their ideas on the religious question. When the time came to consider the articles on religion, much time was devoted to a debate on the many amendments which had been proposed. Some of the amendments provided for separation of Church and State; some proposed absolute intolerance of non-Catholic worship; and others proposed more or less minor modifications of the draft. After the amendments had been examined and rejected one by one, there were six speeches in favour of the draft and six against it, with interpolations by many other deputies.[27] No attempt will be made to report on all of the speeches but only to indicate through an examination of typical speeches the principal points of view.

One of the positions supported in the Cortes, though by a small minority, was that of enforced Catholic unity, at least so far as worship is concerned. When the plan as a whole was being discussed, Canon Manterola, of Vitoria, declared: 'This plan is not sufficiently Catholic, and the Spanish people—oh, the Spanish people are the most Catholic people of the world.' He added that the Government and the Cortes were saying, in effect, to the Spanish people, 'Up to now we have believed that the Catholic religion was the true one. Now we are not sure, and we open our doors to all other religions.' The Catholic Church, he said, believes in liberty, equality, and fraternity rightly understood, but it teaches that there are no absolute liberties, since individual liberty has to be limited for the common good. The Church has never been intolerant with people, not even with the Jews, but it is intolerant of error. This intolerance is understandable, because Catholicism is authority; but intolerance in Protestantism is inexcusable, since Protestantism believes in free inquiry. The Catholic Church can approve of tolerance of other religions only when this is necessary in order to prevent a greater evil, and no such greater evil faces Spain. The Spanish people, continued the Canon, ought to maintain Catholic unity for patriotic as well as religious reasons, since the maintenance of the Spanish spirit and the national unity depend upon the preservation of religious unity. If Spain should reject religious unity for religious freedom, the great Spain of the past would die, and on the tomb should be written these words: 'Here lies an apostate people who renounced their eternal treasures in order to obtain temporal ones and then were left without the latter after having lost the former.'[28]

Canon Manterola submitted an amendment which stated: 'The Apostolic Roman Catholic religion, the only true one, continues to be and will be perpetually the religion of the State.' In his defence of this amendment he said that the truth has the right to be received by man but that man has duties and not rights with respect to truth. The State also has duties with respect to truth. When the true religion, which is Catholicism, has been preached to a people and accepted by a minority, the civil power has the obligation to protect that religion; and when it has become the religion of the majority, the civil power has the obligation to establish it as the religion of the State. In Spain the people have been and are fervently Catholic. The greatness of the nation in the past was due to her Catholic zeal and her Catholic unity, and her future greatness depends upon the maintenance of the same zeal and the same unity. It is to be feared that those who now betray God are also betraying their country. Catholicism is the foundation of Spanish nationality, and, furthermore, it is the only thing in the nation which guarantees peace, order, obedience to law, and respect for property. It should not be argued that toleration should be granted to others so that they will grant it to Catholics. The Catholic knows that he has the truth and that truth has rights which error does not have. Spaniards do not need to worry about the possible loss of freedom for Catholics in other parts of the world, for when man does his duty God does the rest. When the revealed truth is deprived of certain of its rights, as in England and France, and cannot regain them, it concentrates on rights which it can obtain but never renounces any of its rights. It does not follow that since religious freedom is defended by prelates of France and England it should be established in Spain, for conditions are different. 'In England, I would be in favour of religious freedom, but in Spain, I am in favour of Catholic unity.' The Church has always insisted on the exclusive rights of truth and has always claimed the support of earthly powers to defend the truth when such support could logically be expected.[29]

   Cardinal Cuesta, the Archbishop of Santiago, submitted an amendment which, though milder than that of Canon Manterola, left no room for dissident religions: 'The religion of the Spanish nation being the Apostolic Roman Catholic, the State binds itself to protect it and support, by way of indemnification, its cult and its ministers.' The Cardinal declared in his defence of this amendment that the Church has from the beginning proclaimed religious freedom, which is the freedom to worship the true God, and at the same time has taught that those who have been born and reared in another religion have the freedom not to be forced to change their religion. Mohammedans, and in certain cases Protestants, have used violence to get people to change their religion, but the Catholic Church does not approve of using violence for such a purpose. The charge that the Church used violence in the Inquisition is false, for the Church did not make the legislation calling for the burning of heretics, nor did she execute such sentences. She imposed spiritual penalties on her rebellious sons and left to the Catholic kings the defence of the State, and indirectly the Church, against turbulent and seditious heresies. Catholics do not now want the kind of protection which Philip II gave to the Church, but rather protection against the aggression and propaganda of their enemies. Religious unity is a necessity from the philosophical, the Catholic, and the political points of view—from the philosophical point of view, since God and truth are one, and there can consequently be only one true religion and one manifestation of it; from the Catholic point of view, since the Catholic religion is the only true one, and only a weighty cause such as a struggle between nearly equal forces should lead to the establishment of religious freedom; and from the political point of view, since unity is an element of strength within a nation, and the Catholic religion serves as a bond of unity. There is no reason why freedom of worship and freedom of propaganda should be granted to heretics, and certainly there is no reason for granting special privileges to foreigners, for they have won no victory over Spain.[30]

The other speakers in favour of Catholic unity emphasized many of the same things brought out by Canon Manterola and Cardinal Cuesta, with some additional ideas. There was insistence that religious liberty could not be established in Spain since that would mean breaking an international agreement, the Concordat with the Holy See.[31] One speaker declared that establishing religious freedom would mean imposing on the majority, almost the totality, of the Spanish people the will of a small minority, and he hinted that this might cause a civil war.[32] Another asserted that there were no Spaniards who were not Catholics, though there might be some non-Catholics who claimed to be Spaniards. Protestantism is the beginning of all ills and errors, he said, since it destroys the principle of authority and substitutes for it the principle of individual reason and judgment; and he warned that after Luther came Voltaire with his irreligion, Rousseau with his equalitarianism, and Proudhon with his socialism.[33]

The idea of separation of Church and State was staunchly defended by the Republican members of the Cortes. Some of these attacked religion as an evil in itself and the Catholic Church as the most dangerous form of this evil, while others recognized the value of religion but insisted that the good of the nation and even of the Catholic Church demanded separation of Church and State. A free Church in a free State was their ideal.

The most outspokenly irreligious of the deputies was Francisco Suñer y Capdevila, who proposed the following amendment: 'Every Spaniard and every foreigner resident in Spanish territory has the right and is free to profess any religion, or not to profess any.' In his defence of this amendment and of the idea of separation of Church and State, he declared that his personal wish for the Spanish people was that they should profess no religion, since science, the earth, and man should take the place of faith, heaven, and God. When he attempted to read the Gospels to prove that Mary had other children besides Jesus, there was tumult among the deputies, and the President declared that the Cortes was not competent to discuss religion but only the political form which should be given to religion in Spain. The Republican deputies abandoned the hall when Suñer gave up his attempt to speak.[34] He returned to his theme in a later speech. With many interruptions, he insisted that Jesus had brothers and that he was not miraculously conceived, and that all religions, and especially the Catholic religion, are enemies of progress and civilization. General Topete protested that the speaker did not have the right to ridicule the beliefs and sentiments of the Spanish people. The Minister of Grace and Justice declared that the Republicans lost 90 per cent of their popular support through Suñer's declarations, and he warned that the reactionary forces made use of such things for their purposes.[35]

Francisco Pi y Margall, one of the leaders of the Republicans, made a lengthy and well-reasoned defence of separation of Church and State. He declared that freedom of religion is a necessary condition for freedom of thought, since a religion which claims to be the only true one and is supported in its claims by the civil power dominates thought in all realms, including science, philosophy, and politics. There must be freedom for what is considered error, since what is regarded as error at one time may later prove to be the truth. It is not true that no one wants freedom of worship in Spain. Catholicism has died in the conscience of humanity and in the conscience of the Spanish people. For fifty years the people of Spain have struggled for the liberty denied them by the Church and the State. The moment there was religious freedom, Protestant churches appeared in Seville, Valladolid, and other places. Even if there were no non-Catholics in Spain, however, there should be religious freedom, for this is one of the inherent rights of man. The argument that non-Catholics should be given legal rights in a country only after there is evidence of their existence there would lead to the conclusion that an individual right cannot be granted until there has been a violation of former laws. The draft of the Constitution is unacceptable since it does not go far enough and since it grants religious freedom in a manner that is insulting to Spanish people who are not Catholics. The members of the committee have fallen into the error of the lawmakers of 1854: they have thought that through a show of mildness they could avoid alarming the Catholic Church and arousing its hostility.[36]

Emilio Castelar, also a Republican leader, was without doubt the most eloquent, though by no means the most consistent, of the advocates of separation of Church and State. In the first speech in which he advocated separation of the civil and religious powers there was an anti-religious tone. He declared that the Synagogue was born under the curse of the priests of Assyria and Egypt, the Church under the curse of the Synagogue, Protestantism under the curse of the Catholic Church, and modern philosophy and democracy under the curse of all religions. He attributed Spain's poverty, misery, and ignorance to religious intolerance and showed how the spirit of intolerance had blighted Spain through the Inquisition and the expulsion of the Jews and Moors. He asserted that appeasement of the Church is useless, as the liberal framers of other Spanish constitutions learned, to their sorrow.[37]

In a great speech which is sometimes referred to as the greatest flight of oratory in Spanish history, Castelar recognized the value of religion, provided it is accepted voluntarily, but protested against the abuse of power by the Church and insisted that separation of Church and State is the only way to end this abuse. A State religion is an absurdity, he said, since religion is a personal matter: a State does not confess, nor take communion, nor die. For the good of religion itself religious freedom should be granted:

Great is God on Sinai; the thunder heralds Him, the lightning accompanies Him, the earth trembles, the mountains are rent asunder. But there is a God still greater than He, not the majestic God of Sinai, but the humble God of Calvary, nailed to the Cross, wounded, crowned with thorns, with the gall upon His lips, saying, 'Father, forgive them, forgive my persecutors, for they know not what they do!' Great is the religion of power, but still greater is the religion of love; great is the religion of implacable justice but still greater is the religion of merciful forgiveness; and I, in the name of this religion, in the name of the Gospel, come here to ask you to write upon the face of your fundamental code religious liberty, which means liberty, fraternity, equality among all men.[38]

In a later speech Castelar, while refusing to Catholicism the right of special protection by the State, denied personal sympathy for Protestantism and paid a tribute to the Catholic Church:

I . . . do not belong to the world of theology and faith; I belong, or think I belong, to the world of philosophy and reason. But if some day I should return to the world I have left, I would certainly not embrace the Protestant religion, whose coldness dries up my soul, dries up my heart, dries up my conscience—the Protestant religion, eternal enemy of my country, of my race, and of my history. I would return to the beautiful altar that inspired the greatest sentiments of my life: I would return to bow on bended knee before the holy Virgin who calmed with her smile my first passions; I would return to saturate my spirit in the aroma of incense, in the note of the organ, in the light filtered by the stained glass windows and reflected in the gilded wings of the angels, eternal companions of my soul in its infancy; and upon dying . . . I would ask a haven in the Cross, under whose sacred arms lies the place which I love and venerate most on all the face of the earth: the tomb of my mother.[39]

Other speakers in favour of separation of Church and State followed more or less the same line of reasoning as the ones that have been considered. One declared that he defended religious freedom because intolerance had debased Spain and dishonoured her and separated her from the rest of the world, and because religious freedom is in harmony with the Gospel, the primitive Church, and Spanish history until the time of Torquemada. He charged that Catholics want liberty for themselves and despotism for others and that they talk of fraternity but that their type of fraternity is similar to that of Cain and Abel.[40] Another speaker referred to the Roman Catholic Church as 'that terrible organization which like a spider with a thousand legs holds the Catholic world in domination, with one foot in every country and the stomach and head in Rome'.[41] The Republican leader, Figueras, called the articles on religion vague and hypocritical and said, 'Instead of beginning by legislating for Spaniards in this extremely important article, you commit the error of beginning to legislate for foreigners, and then afterwards saying, "If there is any Spaniard . . . so lost as not to want to be Catholic" '.[42]

The third important point of view on the religious question was that of religious toleration or freedom for all religions but a favoured position for Catholicism. This was what was provided in the constitutional draft, and most of the people who favoured this idea defended the draft, but there were some who objected to the way in which it granted freedom to Spaniards. The speakers were liberals, but they occupied a more conservative position than did those just considered. Most of them emphasized that they were Catholics.

When the draft as a whole was being debated, Segismundo Moret y Prendergast explained that the articles on religion represented a necessary compromise. He himself, he said, was in favour of separation of Church and State, but he realized that it would not be prudent to insist upon the incorporation of this idea into the Constitution, since the majority of the members of the Cortes and the majority of the people opposed it. All that can legitimately be done in such a case is to explain the idea and prepare the way for future implementation of it by the will of the majority.[43] In a later speech Moret said that the committee reached an agreement that there would be no change so far as relations between the Church and the State were concerned but that there would be a change in the matter of rights of non-Catholics.[44] On another occasion he said that religious liberty was not being established in order to protest against the Catholic Church or to weaken it, for religion is a vital factor in human life and in the Spanish nation. Freedom was given to religion, he said, with the belief that in the atmosphere of freedom faith would be revived. The rights of other religions were recognized, since freedom means respect for the rights of all.[45]

Eugenio Montero Ríos declared himself to be a loyal Catholic and at the same time a defender of religious freedom. The early Church Fathers, he declared, asked for religious freedom in the name of human personality and not in the name of revealed truth. There is a great inconsistency in asking for enforced Catholic unity in Spain and at the same time asking for religious freedom elsewhere. People should be guided by what is right and just rather than by what is expedient. If Catholics demand protection of their religion on the claim that it is the true one, they cannot complain when people in other nations, convinced that their religion is the true one, persecute Catholicism. As Lacordaire said, if Catholics want liberty for themselves they must want it for all men; 'Grant it where you are masters, that it may be granted you where you are slaves.' The kind of Catholic unity which some desire is impossible without absolute and unlimited protection to the Church by the civil power, and where there is such a close relationship of the two powers one or the other is apt to lose its rights. Furthermore, State protection for the Church corrupts and corrodes it and destroys its vitality. The Concordat does not bind the State to maintain Catholic unity, for the powers of 1851 had no right to obligate the nation forever to profess and maintain a certain religion.[46]

Another defender of the constitutional draft, Salustiano Olózaga, said that the committee charged with drafting a Constitution recognized the fact that there were foreigners who were not Catholics living in Spain and therefore put into the draft of the Constitution a guarantee of their freedom. There was no evidence of Spaniards who were not Catholics, he said, but just in case there might be or should ever be there was included also a guarantee of their freedom. Spain should conserve her traditions and at the same time make them compatible with the spirit of freedom. Protestantism, he concluded, is not likely to prosper in Spain, for the Spanish people are devoted to the Virgin (who seems more human and closer to man than Christ) and to the religious festivals, and they will not give these up for the reading of the Bible and the cold considerations of Protestantism.[47]

One of the most spirited addresses made in defence of religious freedom and the draft of the Constitution was that of José Echegaray, who declared that the old order had ended and that a new era of individual rights had begun. The Revolution proclaimed individual rights as superior to the law, coming from the nature of man and from God himself. One of these rights is religious freedom. It does not depend upon numbers, and if there were only one Spaniard who was not a Catholic he would have the right to worship God as he saw fit. True freedom is impossible, he continued, without religious freedom, and true religion is impossible without the same freedom, since man is truly religious only when he unites himself freely with the Infinite. Religion is good, but when it is converted into a theocracy dominating society it is bad. All liberals in Spain should unite against the reactionaries to establish and maintain religious freedom. The recently uncovered scene of the *autos de fe* of the Inquisition, he declared, should cause a repudiation of the spirit of intolerance:

The Quemadero de la Cruz is . . . a great book . . . which contains a useful but sad lesson: With her alternate layers, the Quemadero de la Cruz is a bed which I would not call geological but which could in truth be called theological.

In the alternate strata of the Quemadero de la Cruz you will see layers of coal impregnated with human fat, then remains of calcined bones, and then a layer of sand which was thrown over it all; and then another layer of coal, another of bones, and another of sand, and so continues the horrible mass. Not many days ago . . . some children, thrusting with a stick, found in those layers of ashes three objects of great eloquence, which are three discourses in defence of religious liberty. They found a piece of rusted iron, a human rib almost entirely calcined, and a lock of hair burned at the end.

These three arguments are very eloquent. I should like for the gentlemen who defend religious unity to submit them to a severe scrutiny. I should like for them to ask that lock of hair about the cold sweat which its roots absorbed when the flame of the stake burst forth, and about how it stood on end on the head of the victim. I should like for them to ask that poor rib how the heart of the poor Jew palpitated against it. I should like for them to ask that piece of iron, which was perchance a gag, how many woeful groans, how many shrieks of anguish it stifled, and how it began to rust on receiving the blood-laden breath of the victim, for whom that hard iron had more pity, had more compassion, was more human and more merciful than the infamous executioners of that infamous theocracy.[48]

The arguments already noted were repeated again and again by the defenders of the draft of the Constitution, each one adding the originality of his arrangement and perhaps a new thought or two. The Minister of Grace and Justice pointed out that the Church and the State have different objects and methods and that the Church is contradicting one of the fundamental maxims of its Founder when it asks for force to support the truth. He maintained, however, that Spain should not at that time end financial support of the Church, certainly not without paying for the properties which the State seized.[49] Another speaker argued that agreement between the Church and the State, as provided in the Constitution, gives a certain desirable protection to the State and at the same time affords benefits to the Church.[50] Someone else insisted that he and others who favoured religious liberty were not advocating error and did not come under the condemnation of the Church; they were only doing what other good Catholics did elsewhere when religious liberty became necessary.[51] Another legislator declared that only those whose faith in Catholicism is weak and who fear competition and discussion are in favour of enforced Catholic unity.[52]

Antonio Cánovas del Castillo, who was to become the leader in the restoration of the Bourbon monarchy, declared himself to be opposed to both religious persecution and religious freedom, but he did not explain how intolerance could be avoided while the State was maintaining Catholic unity. His conclusion was that 'since there is no other religion in Spain than the Catholic, the State ought to protect, and protect effectively, though by legitimate and liberal means, the Catholic cult'.[53]

The two articles on religion in the constitutional draft were reduced to one, Article 21, but there was no change in the wording. When the time came to vote, Castelar announced that the Republican members would vote against the first part, providing for the maintenance by the State of the Catholic Church, and would abstain from voting (by withdrawing from the assembly hall) on the second part, which provided, but in an unworthy manner, for the establishment of religious freedom. He hailed, however, the disappearance of religious intolerance, which he declared had been the scourge of Spain for so many centuries. The article was approved by a majority vote.[54]

The Constitution was formally promulgated on June 6, 1869. In addition to Article 21, it included other guarantees of rights which would be useful to Protestants. Spaniards were guaranteed freedom of speech and of the press; freedom of assembly; freedom to form associations; freedom to petition the King, the Cortes, and the authorities; and freedom to establish and maintain schools, with inspection only for reasons of hygiene and morality. They were also guaranteed the right to hold public office, with employment determined by capacity and merit, without reference to religion. Foreigners were guaranteed the right to live in Spain and to follow their industry or profession, but they were subject to the laws exacting certificates of aptitude granted by Spanish authorities for certain professions. Some of the rights could be temporarily suspended for reasons of national security.[55]

A new epoch had begun. Religious freedom had taken the place of centuries of religious intolerance. The State was no longer pledged to maintain Catholic unity, and non-Catholics were free to worship God according to the dictates of their consciences and to propagate their faith among the Spanish people.

Now a look may be taken back over the first nine months of religious freedom to see what progress Protestantism had made. The small number of trained Spanish pastors and the unpreparedness of foreign Protestants to take advantage of the new opportunities served as handicaps, but significant gains were made. Spanish Protestants who had been exiled from their native land or who had gone voluntarily to other countries seeking freedom to worship God in the way they believed right returned to Spain; Protestants living in the land exerted themselves to make their religion known to the Spanish people; and missionaries came from various countries to aid in the work of evangelization. They met with an amazing response. In the new atmosphere of freedom, everywhere people were eager to become acquainted with the hitherto unknown Protestant religion. Some of them doubtless connected it in their thinking with the new order introduced by the Revolution.

Upon the outbreak of the Revolution, Juan Cabrera, a former Escolapian friar, entered Spain and made his way to Seville, where he spoke to interested groups of people in cafés, courtyards, and private homes. The nucleus of a Protestant Church was soon formed under his influence, and a former convent was rented and opened as a chapel (the first of this period on the mainland of Spain).[56] Other Protestant groups were formed by other leaders in Seville, and the response was so favourable that by April of 1869, someone estimated that there were 3,500 to 4,000 Protestants in the city.[57]

Another centre of Protestant activity in the first months of religious freedom was Madrid. The Protestant leaders there, Spaniards and foreigners, formed a provisional committee to plan and direct evangelical operations, and this committee drew up an appeal to the Protestants of Europe and America for aid in the evangelization of Spain. For some time services in Madrid were held in inadequate places, and attendance was poor, but when better quarters were found attendance proved excellent.[58]

Protestant work was also begun in Barcelona. An evangelist who went there soon after the Revolution found a ready response. In the first four or five services he held, he called for the signatures of those who wanted to join the Protestant Association and attend the meetings, and more than seven hundred people signed. The room which was rented for a chapel was lost because the owner objected to the sign 'Protestant Association' placed over it, but another chapel was rented.[59]

Other parts of Spain were also reached by Protestants during the first nine months of religious freedom. It was reported, for example, that a Protestant pastor had given three lectures in Valladolid on religious liberty and that the first night he had an audience of about two thousand and the second night four thousand, while on the third night people came in such great numbers that they had to be turned away from the auditorium.[60] Another report (which, like others of the time, might have been coloured by enthusiasm) referred to a congregation of eight hundred to one thousand in Cordova.[61]

In May of 1869 a General Assembly of the Churches in the south of Spain which were sponsored by the Spanish Evangelization Society was held in Seville, with eighteen members present. A provisional Confession of Faith and Code of Church Discipline were adopted, to be considered further in the next General Assembly, and a central Consistory was appointed to supervise the operations of the Church in the meantime. Thus was organized the Reformed Church in Spain (not to be confused with the Spanish Reformed Church, which was established later). In doctrine and polity it was Presbyterian, though different in some respects from Presbyterian churches in other countries. The Consistory was acknowledged by the Spanish Cortes and thereby given a more or less official standing.[62]

Enough has been said to indicate that by the time religious liberty had been definitely established as the law of the land, Protestants had made their message known in various parts of Spain and had laid foundations for future work. They faced no opposition from the government and found the people eager to hear them. It was too early to tell whether or not their religion would gain a firm hold on the Spanish people, but the first indications were encouraging. All were determined to make the most of their new freedom.

IV

THE PRACTICE OF RELIGIOUS FREEDOM

THE years following the adoption of the Constitution of 1869 were years of uncertainty and of changing régimes in Spain. In a very real sense the revolution was continuing, and its outcome was as yet uncertain. Protestants enjoyed the freedom granted them by the Constitution, and laws were passed which guaranteed their rights in specific ways, but they shared in the uncertainty of the times.

For about a year and a half Spain was a regency, with General Serrano as regent, while search was being made for a king. During this period disagreements between the parties of the revolutionary coalition showed that it is sometimes easier to unite against one government than to form another to take its place. Furthermore, Republicans and Carlists were loud in their opposition to the government, and rumblings of civil war could be heard. With calmness and astuteness, however, General Prim, who was President of the Council of Ministers, directed the course of the nation and averted disaster.[1]

A circular letter from the Minister of State to Spanish diplomats abroad—intended to be passed on to foreign governments—listed among the achievements of the Revolution the establishment for the first time in Spanish history of religious freedom. It referred to the unfortunate identification of love of country and pride of race with intolerance at the time of Spain's rise to national greatness, but it stated that through the providence of God, involving suffering, intolerance had been removed from the hearts of many Spaniards. Certain occurrences during the past régime, continued the circular, have led people in other countries to believe that the Spanish people think and feel now as they did at the middle of the sixteenth century, but this is not true, and 'though the religious sentiment and the Catholic faith subsist in their entirety in the immense majority of the people, the nation condemns all idea of violence, all intention of intolerance'.[2]

The introduction of religious freedom in the nation naturally raised the question of attendance upon religious ceremonies of those in military service. In a meeting of the Cortes a member asked if it was not a violation of the Constitution to require soldiers to go to mass and attend other Catholic ceremonies, and General Prim replied that Spanish soldiers were Catholics and did not find going to mass repugnant. He added, however, that he had instructed military commanders to excuse from attendance at mass any soldier who was not a Catholic or who professed some other religion.[3] A circular letter from General Prim, published a few days later, declared that all members of the army were required to attend public ceremonies at which attendance was in line of duty, such as processions and funerals, but that attendance upon mass and the performance of other purely religious acts would not be required of non-Catholics.[4]

The new Penal Code, promulgated in 1870 and destined, with some changes, to last until 1928, offered protection to the adherents and practices of all religions. It provided penalties for forcing people to practise religious acts and for hindering them in the practice of such acts, for disturbing religious services, and for publicly ridiculing the dogmas and ceremonies of any religion having adherents in Spain. In granting protection to religion the Penal Code recognized no distinction between Protestantism and Catholicism.[5]

Logical corollaries of religious freedom are the civil register and civil marriage, both of which were instituted in Spain in 1870.[6] No legal recognition was given to religious marriage ceremonies, but there was, of course, no prohibition of religious ceremonies in addition to the civil service. As would be expected, there was much feeling in the nation over the institution of civil marriage and the removal from the clergy of the registry of births, marriages, and deaths.[7]

Another freedom without which freedom of religion is far from complete is freedom of instruction. The Provisional Government, as we have seen, provided for educational freedom and removed the schools from the control of the clergy, but the question of religious instruction as a part of the curriculum remained to be settled. A discussion took place in the Cortes on this extremely important and inflammatory issue when someone asked the Minister of Public Works, José Echegaray, if the reports were true that he was planning a decree to prohibit the teaching of all dogmatic religion in the public schools. After some evasion, Echegaray replied that ever since he had begun to think of politics he had believed that the teaching of Religion should be suppressed in the schools but that he had not yet done anything to that end. Another deputy declared that the suppression of religion in the public schools would be contrary to the Constitution, which provided that the Catholic religion should be that of the nation, and he threatened the end of conservative support for the government. Another member of the Cortes argued that the secularization of the schools was a natural outgrowth of the Constitution and insisted that religious instruction should be left to the priests in the churches, the Protestants in their chapels, and the Jews in their synagogues.[8] A few months later the government ordered those in charge of schools to grant the requests of Evangelical parents to excuse their children from religious instruction.[9]

The government met with strong opposition from members of the clergy. Some of the priests had abandoned their charges to fight with the Carlists, and the government ordered the bishops and archbishops to take measures against them.[10] There were protests from the hierarchy against this order, and there was great resentment because of the arrest of certain prelates. Resentment increased when a decree ordered members of the clergy, like all other public servants, to take an oath of allegiance to the Constitution. Even though the Pope indicated that there was no obstacle to taking the oath, many of the clergy refused to take it, so aroused had they become by national policies.[11]

The question naturally arises as to the attitude of the Spanish government towards the papacy. Some light is thrown on this subject by a statement made by General Prim in the Cortes not long before the meeting of the Vatican Council. Someone asked what would be the attitude of the government towards this Council if it should attack the principles of the Spanish Constitution, and General Prim replied that if the Council 'should take resolutions that were contrary to the spirit of progress and liberty as established by the Constituent Cortes, it would be for the Spanish nation as if such resolutions . . . had not been made'.[12] There was a spirit of independence shown by the Spanish authorities, and this was matched by a certain intransigence on the part of the papacy. It was probably only the troubles in which the Pope found himself involved in Italy, with the loss of his temporal power, that prevented his giving more attention to Spain.

This was a time of liberty for Protestantism. The British and Foreign Bible Society reported that 'for the present, at least, the Scriptures can be sold as freely in Madrid as in our own metropolis, and the heart that apprehends Christ in the fullness of His grace and love need not hesitate to confess Him before men'. The government sought to avoid giving the appearance of favouritism towards Protestantism, however, and it refused the offer of the British and Foreign Bible Society to furnish copies of the New Testament to the public schools; but many municipal libraries accepted Bibles, and the National Library of Madrid accepted a collection of the various versions of the Bible.[13]

Amadeo of Savoy, son of King Victor Emmanuel II of Italy, was elected King of Spain, and in January of 1871 he entered Madrid, a few days after General Prim, the man who would have been his ablest minister, had been assassinated. The reign of Amadeo was destined to be a time of rivalry between political parties, intrigue, uprisings of Carlists and Republicans, and even full-scale civil war. After about two years, convinced that his efforts to bring peace and unity to the nation were all in vain, he renounced the throne and left Spain.[14]

One of the problems facing the government during the reign

of Amadeo was its relationship with the Spanish clergy and the Vatican. Peace with the Church was sincerely desired, but not at the cost of surrendering such things as freedom of religion, civil marriage, and the civil register; and agreement with the Holy See proved impossible. The problem was doubtless complicated by the fact that Amadeo was the son of the man who had made the Pope 'the prisoner of the Vatican'.[15]

All of the measures looking towards freedom were maintained during the reign of Amadeo, and in at least one respect there was an extension of the rights of non-Catholics. Orders were given that a place be designated within cemeteries for the burial of non-Catholics[16] and that when necessary the cemeteries be enlarged for this purpose. The communication to the provincial governors about this matter emphasized the importance of guarding religious liberty and at the same time avoiding conflicts between civil and ecclesiastical authorities.[17]

Some local officials were not altogether faithful in following the letter and spirit of the guarantees of religious liberty, as can be seen in the case of two citizens of Malaga who wrote to local authorities asking that members of the Evangelical church of that city should not be required to kneel for the Corpus Christi procession. Their request was denied, and they were warned that any demonstration offensive to Catholic Malaga would be punished.[18]

Protestants complained during this time that Catholic prejudice against them continued unabated. An important Spanish Protestant body issued a statement declaring that Protestant teachings were deliberately misrepresented by Roman Catholics, and preachers were insulted in the press and in public speeches; that religious services were disturbed by those opposed to freedom of worship; and that Bibles were often torn up and burned, and sellers of religious books were mistreated and even wounded.[19] Even the best disposed government sometimes cannot control popular expressions of intolerance.

When Amadeo abdicated, the Cortes, under the influence of left-wing liberals, declared Spain to be a Republic. A Carlist war

3

and local Republican uprisings threatened the life of the nation. In many places there was violence to life and property and great hostility to religion. Conditions were such that the Republic was never firmly established, and it came to an end without even having adopted a Republican constitution. Its life was really limited to the eleven months beginning with February of 1873, though it continued to exist in name for a while longer.[20]

The question of the relationship of Church and State was one of the most important which faced the leaders of the Republic. With perhaps different reasons, they agreed on the advisability of the separation of Church and State. One of the clearest statements on the subject was that given in the Constituent Cortes of the Republic by Pi y Margall. He declared that the logical and necessary consequence of religious liberty was separation of Church and State, with all churches regarded as associations subject to the general laws of the nation. Such an arrangement would benefit the Church as well as the State, since the Church would become free to establish its teachings, appoint its bishops, and regulate all of its affairs without governmental interference. But if it should abuse its independence, 'since it would have lost the character which it now has and would be only an association like any other, we would have the right to seize the highest of the powers and place it on the bench as the greatest of the guilty'.[21]

Two drafts of constitutions were drawn up for the Republic (one by the minority of the committee appointed for the purpose[22] and the other by the majority), and both provided for separation of Church and State. The introduction to the majority draft refers to the Constitution of 1869, and says, 'Liberty of cults, there timidly and even apologetically provided, is here a clear and concrete principle'. The articles dealing with religion are as follows:

Art. 34. The practice of all cults is free in Spain.
Art. 35. The Church is separate from the State.
Art. 36. The nation or federal state, the regional states, and

the municipalities are forbidden to subsidize any cult directly or indirectly.

Art. 37. The records of birth, marriage, and death will always be registered by civil authorities.[23]

The *Diario de sesiones* reveals that from time to time there was some debate on the constitutional draft, but a serious consideration of it was prevented by other matters which claimed the attention of the lawmakers. The principle of separation of Church and State was, therefore, never established.

There was serious disagreement among the Republicans as to the treatment of the Catholic Church, some wishing to treat it as an enemy of the Spanish nation, and others being inclined to follow a more moderate and conciliatory policy. On the whole, relations between the Vatican and the Republic were better than those of the time of Amadeo, though the Holy See, like most other governments, did not give official recognition to the Republic.[24] Local Republican groups in many places were violently anti-Catholic, and they seized, destroyed, or profaned churches, tore down monasteries, and assassinated priests.[25]

Protestants suffered local interferences with their activities during the Republic, but on the part of most representatives of the government there was a willingness to protect them and guarantee their rights. This is illustrated by happenings in Granada. In that city a colporteur who began selling Bible portions and giving out tracts at the door of the cathedral was notified by the governor that he could not do this but that he could carry on his work elsewhere. Later on, the same man was the centre of a disturbance when people began burning and tearing up his books, and a policeman carried him off to prison. Not many days afterwards, a group of young men, probably aroused by the incident of the colporteur, entered the Protestant chapel and created a disturbance for which they were arrested by the police. Feeling ran high, and there was danger of a serious conflict in the city. The governor wrote to the pastor of the Protestant church that he had taken energetic measures to protect him and his church and guarantee the liberty of all: 'You may celebrate with the members of your congregation private or public worship and as many religious ceremonies as your beliefs demand, and the authorities will tirelessly defend the rights of all'.[26]

The excesses committed by Republican groups in different parts of the country and also policies advocated or followed by some of the Republican leaders in Madrid alarmed conservatives of all shades of politics. Early in 1874, opponents of leftist rule dissolved the Cortes through a show of military might and obtained control of the government. General Serrano was placed in charge of state affairs. Before the year was out a military pronouncement restored the Bourbon monarchy.[27]

The chief task facing the government of General Serrano was the termination of the Carlist War. This was so serious that other matters had to wait for it. There were Carlist victories everywhere for a while, but it soon became clear that the Carlist star was declining.[28]

The government was recognized by most of the powers of Europe and sought full recognition by the Holy See, but the Vatican chose to keep her relations with Spain on a more or less informal basis. The Spanish Minister of State was encouraged, however, to continue his good desires towards the Church and to demonstrate them by deeds, and he was assured that the Pope never creates obstacles for any government which manifests due respect for the religion of its people and for the rights of the Church.[29] Spanish Protestants were disturbed by the growing rapport between their country and the Vatican, fearing that it implied a return to the old policy of intolerance.[30]

During the rule of General Serrano, Protestants complained of a violation of the principle of religious freedom in various quarters. The Baptist Church in Linares was closed and the pastor banished;[31] a pastor in Cadiz wrote that old chapels were permitted to remain open but that there was evidently a determination in high quarters not to permit the opening of new ones;[32] and in Seville, the mayor, without giving any reasons, forbade the opening of a chapel which had been newly purchased and altered, and it was only after the intervention of the British vice-consul that it was permitted to open.[33] In San Fernando, Protestants were forbidden to open a chapel on the pretext that it did not satisfy requisite conditions of health and safety. After the British Ambassador had talked with the Spanish Minister of State about the matter, an order was sent to the mayor of the town ordering the removal of the obstacles to the opening of the chapel, but the clerk responsible for making a copy of the order 'accidentally' tore it up, and there was a long delay while waiting for a duplicate order to be sent from Madrid. Finally, upon stern new orders from the central government, the mayor permitted the opening of the chapel.[34]

The position of Protestantism in the Spanish nation was still uncertain. Was it to be a permanent part of Spanish life? Had it gained acceptance among the Spanish people? Was there a significant Protestant minority in Spain? Let us look now at the progress made by Protestantism during the five and a half years between the adoption of the Constitution of 1869, and the restoration of the Bourbon monarchy.

The high hopes of the Protestants which arose during the first months of religious freedom continued into this period. Reinforcements were received from abroad, and flourishing Protestant communities were established in many different towns and cities. During the time of the Republic a Spanish Protestant stated that in the first months of religious freedom Spanish and foreign Protestants used all of the means at their disposal for announcing the Gospel, but that it was impossible for them to take full advantage of the opportunities:

The chapels were always filled with multitudes anxious to hear the new doctrines. Bibles were sold by thousands; the tracts printed were all too few to satisfy the universal curiosity. It is much to be lamented that in those days there were not labourers and funds enough to have opened a chapel in every city and town of importance throughout Spain, for, had this been done, there would this day exist as many congregations as there were chapels opened to the public.[35]

The intense interest of the people in the Protestant religion was not destined to last after their initial curiosity had been satisfied, and conditions in the country became so unsettled that Protestant work, like everything else, was greatly interfered with. After a period of spectacular progress, there were serious losses by the churches, due to both external and internal causes, and then a process of consolidation got under way. The varying fortunes of Protestantism in Spain can be seen from a consideration of some of the principal churches and Protestant agencies within the country.

In its annual report for 1871, the British and Foreign Bible Society stated that during the preceding year Bibles had been printed in Madrid and that thousands of copies had been sold.[36] The following year the Society reported that 'eager purchasers do not throng the book stalls with the same enthusiasm as once they did, when the bow of bigotry was first broken and the chains of a cruel despotism fell from their necks, and the conviction first flashed upon them that they were indeed free.'[37] After the advent of the Republic the Society declared that operations had been altogether suspended in some sections because of the civil disturbances, and in other sections continued with interruptions and much discouragement but that the decrease in Bible sales had not been as great as would have been expected under the circumstances.[38]

In the year 1870 several churches and groups formed an Evangelical Union. In their appeal to foreign Protestants for aid they said there were two congregations in Madrid, each with close upon one thousand adherents, affiliated with the Union, and that work had been begun in two other places:

In all of these the interest continues not only unabated but ever increasing. Especially to be mentioned is the mission in Camuñas, a village near Toledo. Here the progress of Protestantism has been such that the cura, or parish priest, has abandoned the place in despair, and left his flock to the tender mercies of the heretic (i.e., Protestant) missionary.[39]

The following year, in a General Assembly of representatives of the Andalusian and Castilian Churches, it was agreed to form a union, to be known as the Spanish Christian Church, which would take the place of the Evangelical Union and the Reformed Church.[40] The Consistory of the Church (which was essentially Presbyterian in all but name) issued a report indicating good attendance and a large membership in the churches. There were schools for boys and girls in connection with most of the churches.[41]

In 1872 another Assembly, consisting of representatives from four congregations in Madrid and twelve in other cities, adopted a confession of faith and completed the union of the churches.[42] The report of an Assembly held the following year indicates internal problems, for it is stated that several cases of discipline were dealt with and some unworthy evangelists dismissed.[43]

Several miscellaneous news items may be cited to show the state of the work of the Spanish Christian Church during this period. In 1870 it was reported that Cabrera had enrolled two thousand people in his church in Seville,[44] and several months later a magnificent old Jesuit church building was inaugurated as the place of worship of this church,[45] but by 1873 it had settled down to a regular membership of 258.[46] The church of Madera Baja Street in Madrid had 464 members and 1300 'adherents' in 1871,[47] but three years later it reported only 367 old members, 72 new ones, and 283 friends who attended and contributed but had not united with the Church.[48] A periodical serving members of the Spanish Christian Church stated in 1873 that some people had stopped attending Evangelical services for fear the Carlists would win the war and wreak vengeance on the Evangelicals,[49] and a few months later the same magazine declared that in Spain there was nothing to prevent the preaching of the Gospel but that there was great indifference and little progress.[50]

A number of foreign missionaries were associated with the work of the Spanish Christian Church. One of the most prominent of these was the German, Fritz Fliedner, who was sent out by a committee of Berlin with instructions not to try to set up a new denomination but rather to aid in the work where aid was needed.[51] We shall catch glimpses later of the extensive activity of this capable missionary.

The Spanish Christian Church was the leading branch of Protestantism in Spain, but not the only one. This period marks the beginning of denominationalism in the country. As a Spaniard of the times expressed it, in the first months following the Revolution there was no thought of differences of denomination, but soon 'the different religious tendencies of each of the directors became apparent. Some declared their adoption of the Presbyterian form, others manifested their Baptist proclivities, while others declared their adherence to the Plymouthites.'[52] Congregationalists, Methodists, and Episcopalians also entered the field.

Among the pioneers of Protestantism in Spain were Plymouth Brethren. One of their leaders was George Lawrence, of England, who, with Barcelona as his main centre of operations, carried on an extensive work with churches and schools and travelled widely selling Bibles and distributing tracts and other religious literature. The American Tract Society reported in 1870 that in the preceding year he sold at a nominal price 300,000 copies of the Bible, in whole or in part, and that in two and a half days he and his six helpers sold 60,000 copies from their tent in front of the city hall in Barcelona.[53] The life of this missionary was full of adventure. Once when King Amadeo went to Barcelona, Lawrence and a companion, with their Bible coach, sold Bibles to the people waiting to see the royal procession. The police ordered them on, claiming that they were blocking the street. They protested but eventually obeyed orders. By that time the King had passed, and the Bible sellers dropped into the royal procession only a few carriages behind the King. The people cried, 'Look, look! There is the Protestant coach!' As Lawrence and his friend went down the street behind the King they sold and gave away many Bibles and Scripture portions.[54]

An important work was begun in Madrid and several other places by an American Baptist, William Knapp, who went to

Spain originally as an independent missionary. In April of 1870 he wrote that during the seven months he had laboured in Spain 1325 professed converts had been enrolled in his books, largely through the efforts of Spanish people working with him. During these first months he had no church organization, but then he formed a relationship with two Presbyterian missionaries, who aided in the formation of a Presbyterian Church, with forty-five charter members. Under his direction were church services in two places, a day school for boys and another for girls, and a theological class.[55]

A short time later Knapp changed his mind about the expediency of following Presbyterian polity in his work, and he organized the First Baptist Church of Madrid, with an initial membership of thirty-three. The American Baptist Missionary Union adopted the mission and appointed Knapp as its missionary. The work was expanded in Madrid; a Baptist Church was organized in Alicante; and work was also begun at other points.[56] The 1874 report of the American Baptist Missionary Union showed four churches in Spain, four native pastors and evangelists, three schools, sixty-two baptisms during the preceding year, and a total membership of 244.[57]

Like other denominations, the Baptists suffered disappointments after the first period of progress. Some of their pastors proved unworthy and created scandals, and the disturbed conditions in the country also hindered their work. The report of the American Baptist Missionary Union for 1873 includes the following statement:

Our operations in Spain have been hindered by various causes, both external and internal. The work, like that of all denominations in the country, remains in statu quo. All expect that the separation of Church and State will redound to our benefit, but State decrees do not change hearts or excite interest in evangelical religion. . . .

The unsettled state of the country renders it very difficult to work there effectively. The ways in many instances are blocked or obstructed ; and everywhere the attention of the people is held to political subjects and excitements, so that there is little chance for the gospel.[58]

The Methodists did not long delay in beginning work in Spain. By April of 1871 the Wesleyan Methodists had 163 boys and 151 girls in schools in Barcelona, and religious services were being held five times a week. There was one church member, and eight persons were being considered for membership.[59] Three years later, work was being carried on in Barcelona and Port Mahon, and there were 102 church members, thirteen prospective members, and 503 day pupils.[60]

The American Board of Commissioners for Foreign Missions (Congregational) turned its attention to Barcelona and Santander. The work in Barcelona proved very discouraging and was abandoned after a short time, but there was more success in Santander, where William H. Gulick was in charge. Services were begun in a small way, but the congregation grew until it reached three or four hundred on one Sunday.[61] By July of 1874 the attendance had shrunk to an average of about thirty, and Gulick stated that the day of large, and fluctuating, congregations had passed, but that a steady work could be done. He was planning then to organize a church.[62]

The above account of Protestantism in this period is only partial, but the limits of this book do not permit a fuller treatment, and we shall turn now to a summary of Evangelical activities in 1874. William H. Gulick reported in that year that Evangelical work was being carried on in nineteen cities and towns. There were twenty-seven foreign Protestant men and thirty-two women, including three single women, and eighteen native pastors, and fourteen evangelists working in the churches and mission points. Help was extended through missionaries, or financial aid or both by the United Presbyterian Church of Scotland, the Presbyterian Church of Ireland, American Baptists, American Congregationalists, English Wesleyans, English Brethren, Anglicans, the Spanish Evangelization Society of Edinburgh, a German committee, committees of Switzerland and Holland, and other groups. In some cities there were several churches, and the total number of preaching places was thirty-six. The average total attendance at Sunday services was 1840, and the average total daily attendance at forty-three Protestant schools was 1783, The British and Foreign Bible Society had fifteen colporteurs, not included in the above number of workers, and the National Bible Society of Scotland had seven. There were four Evangelical periodicals, one of which, *El cristiano*, had a circulation of 1400.[63]

Protestantism had still not touched the wealthy and aristocratic classes of Spanish society, and it had not gained wide acceptance among the poor and uneducated. The masses of the people still had their children baptized in the Roman Catholic Church and looked to that Church for marriage and burial. Catholicism was regarded as the religion of Spaniards and Protestantism as a religion of foreigners. The foreign character of Protestantism was enhanced by the fact that its propagation in Spain depended so largely upon money and people from abroad.

At first Protestants profited from the political and social ferment of the times, and many of them tended to look with sympathy upon the cause of Republicans and other left-wing liberals, but they seem soon to have been disillusioned. The British and Foreign Bible Society stated in its report for 1872: 'At the commencement of the Revolution, far more importance was attached to the opinions and countenance of liberal men who sided with the Protestant movement, without, perhaps, realizing its value, or imbibing its spirit. It is now felt that an arm of the flesh is of little value'.[64] The following year a Spanish Protestant said, 'Few Liberals, and hardly any Republicans, in certain provinces, will hearken to a word of religion'.[65] It was evident that Protestants could expect little response to their religious message from the political leftists.

A Spanish pastor wrote in 1874 that field after field was being relinquished by the Evangelicals and that this endangered the future enjoyment of religious freedom'.[66] He was right. The best guarantee of freedom would have been the growth of a large and influential Protestant minority in Spain. There were many Spaniards who believed with Balmes that 'every government which professes a religion is more or less intolerant with other religions, and this intolerance diminishes or ceases only when those who profess the hated religion make themselves feared by being very strong or scorned by being very weak'.[67] Spanish Protestants were not insignificant enough to be ignored nor strong enough to be greatly feared.

V

THE ESTABLISHMENT OF RELIGIOUS
TOLERATION

INTENSE struggle between two opposing tendencies often ends in a compromise. Such was the case in Spain. After the uncertain triumph of liberalism over extreme conservatism in 1868 and the years immediately following, there was a settlement designed to satisfy both moderate liberals and moderate conservatives. The settlement came with the restoration of the Bourbon monarchy in the person of Alfonso XII, who is known as 'the peacemaker'. On the religious question, the compromise meant exchanging religious freedom for religious toleration. Protestants continued to have the right to exist in Spain, but their activities were circumscribed in deference to the Catholic religion.

The Restoration was brought about by a military pronounce-ment in favour of Alfonso by General Martinez Campos on December 29, 1874. Antonio Cánovas del Castillo was, however, the real father of the Restoration. For several years he had been working for the enthronement of Alfonso by peaceful and legal means, and after the military pronouncement (with which, incidentally, he was displeased), he took charge of the govern-ment. Opposition to the new movement quickly disappeared, and when the King reached Spain early in January he was enthusiastically received by the people.[1]

Cánovas del Castillo was a conservative, but a conservative with somewhat liberal ideas. He took no part in the Revolution of 1868, and he never renounced his loyalty to the Bourbon rulers of Spain. His liberal background is indicated, however, by the fact that he wrote the revolutionary manifesto which played a prominent part in the liberal upsurge of 1854, and by the fact that during the latter part of the reign of Isabella II, he opposed the reactionary policies of her government. As the moulder of the monarchy in the new epoch, he sought to avoid extremes both of reaction and of liberalism.[2]

The leaders of the nation in the time of the Restoration sought the participation in public affairs of all who would accept the constitutional monarchy or limit themselves to peaceful means in opposing it. The policy of conciliation won over the greater part of the friends of the Revolution. Some joined the party of Cánovas, to be known in time as the Conservative Liberal (or Conservative) Party, and others allied themselves with the supporters of the Constitution of 1869, known as Constitutionalists (later as the Liberal Party) and led by Práxedes Mateo Sagasta. At a mass meeting in Madrid in 1875, Sagasta laid down the platform of the Constitutionalists. Among other things, he affirmed allegiance to Alfonso XII; said that there was no need of a new constitution, since the country already had that of 1869; and declared that he and his associates would defend all kinds of freedom, including religious freedom.[3]

The Carlist War continued into this period, but a number of Carlists joined Alfonso, who appealed to them to follow him as a Catholic king and a repairer of the injustices which had been done to the Church. A determined military effort was made against the Carlist armies, and early in 1876 the war was brought to a close. There being then no serious threat to the security of the nation, the government could direct its full attention to the work of consolidation.[4]

When we turn to an examination of the religious question, our attention is attracted, first of all, to a manifesto issued by Alfonso from Sandhurst, England, shortly before the Restoration. This manifesto set forth the programme of the monarchy, if it should be restored, and appealed for the support of all Spaniards. Both the Constitution of 1845 and that of 1869 were declared null and void, and all political questions were said to be reserved for future decision by Cortes and King. Alfonso referred to himself as both Catholic and Liberal:

For my part it is a debt I owe to misfortune that I am in contact with the men and conditions of modern Europe; and if Spain does not attain in Europe a position of independence and sympathy as well as a position worthy of her history, it will not be my fault, either now or ever. Whatever my lot may be, I shall not cease to be a good Spaniard, or, like my ancestors, a good Catholic, or truly liberal, as becomes a man of our generation.[5]

In the first days of the monarchy, the clergy and members of the Roman Catholic Church were assured of the Catholic character of the State. In fact, promises were given which later proved embarrassing to the government. Even before the arrival of the King, the Minister of Grace and Justice wrote as follows to the Spanish hierarchy:

A Ministry-Regency has been formed, and I consider it my duty to give official notification to you . . . of the happy occurrences to which it owes its origin. . . . The Church has suffered with the Spanish nation countless evils from the past sterile political disturbances, but with the coming to the throne of an illustrious Catholic prince determined to repair the damages done, it can expect brighter and better days. The proclamation of Alfonso XII as our king brings those disturbances to an end and begins a new era, in which our good relations with the common Father of the faithful, unfortunately interrupted by the injustices and excesses of these latter times, will be re-established; in which we shall proceed in everything which might affect these reciprocal relationships in accord with the advice of our wise prelates and in agreement with the Holy See; and in which the Church and its ministers will be given all the protection that is due them in a nation which like ours is truly Catholic. In the performance of its task, the government counts on the efficacious co-operation of you . . . and your worthy companions of the Episcopate . . . and the aid of good Catholics. . . .[6]

A decree on the press included as one of its articles the provision that any publication which contained insults to religious persons or things would be suspended for a period not to exceed eight days.[7] La luz commented that much would depend upon the interpretation of this article and expressed the hope that setting forth Evangelical doctrines would not be considered an insult to Catholics.[8] There is no evidence that it was.

A circular letter from the Minister of the Interior to the

provincial governors forbade public meetings without special authorization. Any meeting attended by more than twenty persons and held in the open air or in a building where all the persons present did not have their regular residence was construed as a public meeting. Religious processions and religious meetings held in church buildings (and also attendance upon performances in theatres and other such establishments) were not included in the prohibition.[9] The circular letter was an emergency measure and was intended primarily to control political meetings, but it meant that Protestants also would have less freedom for holding meetings.

Civil marriage was abolished for members of the Catholic Church. Canonical marriage was re-established for them as the only legal form of marriage, and civil marriage was retained only for those not qualified for marriage by the Catholic Church. The civil register was kept, but for persons married canonically only a simple inscription by the priest in the register was necessary. Those who had been married by the Catholic Church without civil sanction since 1870 were declared legally married. Persons ordained by the Catholic Church or bound by vows of chastity were declared ineligible for marriage even though they had renounced their faith, and if they had married under the former law their marriage was declared of no effect but their children were given the legal rights of legitimate children.[10] A Protestant pastor wrote from Spain at this time that the withdrawal of the right of marriage for those who had taken religious vows was a serious blow for Protestant ministers, many of whom were former priests.[11]

One of the governmental orders of this period forbade university professors to teach anything contrary to the Catholic religion or the monarchy.[12] Other measures taken by the government included the return of certain properties to the Church, the increase of the financial grants to the clergy, and the restoration to the Church of confiscated archives, libraries, and other such possessions.[13] The policy of the government was definitely one of favour towards the established religion.

The first measures of Alfonso's government won the approval of the Catholic Church. A new Spanish ambassador was sent to the Holy See, and a nuncio went to Madrid.[14] Upon the arrival of the nuncio in Spain, Protestants and Liberals were alarmed by a statement from him that the Vatican hoped for a restoration of religious unity in Spain. Their fears were allayed somewhat by statements in the newspapers regarded as mouthpieces of the government that Spain would not surrender liberty of conscience. Such statements showed that Cánovas and his associates intended to guard their liberty and that of the nation. The editor of La luz was disturbed, however, because the term 'liberty of conscience' rather than 'liberty of worship' was used.[15]

Protestants feared that their chapels were going to be closed by the government, but their fears proved in large part unfounded. It is true that some churches were closed, but, on the whole, there was no interference with Protestant worship unless it could be shown, on the basis of true or false evidence, that the churches were involved in politics.[16] There were cases of interference with the work of colporteurs, and priests taunted them that their days in Spain were limited, but the sale of Bibles continued.[17]

Light is thrown on the attitude of the authorities towards the rights of Protestantism by the reply which the governor of Cadiz made to a request by the bishop of that region that Protestant schools and churches be closed. Reporting that a Protestant centre of propaganda had been opened in San Fernando and that another was to be opened in Algeciras, the bishop stated that it was understandable that religious error should be propagated during the period of revolutionary disturbances through which the country had passed, but that it was unthinkable that this should be permitted to continue in the shadow of the throne of King Alfonso. The governor replied that he was seeking information on the case of Algeciras and that he had given orders that the Protestants in San Fernando should not engage in any propaganda outside their chapel or do anything which might disturb public order. He added, however, that he did not have the right to close the chapel in San Fernando.[18]

When the drawing up of a Constitution began to be considered, the religious question assumed gigantic proportions. A committee of prominent men charged with preparing the draft of a Constitution to be submitted to the Cortes when that body assembled experienced great difficulty in agreeing on the status the various religions were to have in Spain, and, in fact, the agreement of all members was never obtained.[19] The majority proposed an article on religion which represented a compromise:

Art. 11. The Apostolic Roman Catholic religion is that of the State. The nation binds itself to maintain the cult and its ministers.

No one will be molested in Spanish territory for his religious opinions nor for the observance of his respective cult, provided that he shows due respect to Christian morality.

Public ceremonies and manifestations other than those of the religion of the State, however, will not be permitted.[20]

As soon as the work of the committee on the Constitution was known in Rome, the papal Secretary of State informed the Spanish Ambassador that Article 11 was contrary to the Concordat and that approval of it might disturb the relations between Spain and the Holy See. The Spanish government protested that because of political conditions and relations with other countries a return to the legal situation which existed before 1868 was impossible. While affirming respect for the Concordat and a desire to observe it wherever its provisions did not interfere with internal rights, the Spanish authorities made it clear that they did not regard Catholic unity as an invariable and eternal principle.[21] There is some question as to just what was the reply of the Vatican. The Spanish Ambassador telegraphed to Madrid that the papal Secretary of State had told him that it was impossible for the Holy See to approve liberty of cults as a principle, but that under the circumstances such liberty could be permitted in Spain and that if there were Protestant chapels in the country the Vatican would close its eyes to them. The Nuncio insisted, however, that the Ambassador had not understood well what was said to him.[22]

A little later there was published in Madrid a pastoral letter of the Archbishop of Toledo, Cardinal Moreno, in which there was inserted a communication from the Pope condemning Article 11 of the constitutional draft and upholding the principle of religious unity. The Pope declared that the article violated the Concordat, cleared the way for error, and did violence to the Catholic religion. The papal communication was published without governmental authorization, and the Spanish government saw one of its ancient prerogatives flouted, since official permission had long been required for the publication of such documents in Spain. The newspaper which published the letter was confiscated, but the declaration of the Pope was already known, and it served as ammunition for the defenders of Catholic unity.[23]

The Spanish clergy sought through pastoral letters, sermons, and other means to arouse the people to a defence of Catholic unity. The faithful were exhorted to use all possible legal means to keep friends of religious liberty from forming a part of the Cortes.[24] The elections, however, were a disappointment to the hierarchy. The majority of the members of both the Senate and the Congress of Deputies were supporters of the policies of Cánovas or of the more liberal policies of the Constitutionalists.[25] As we shall see, however, the forces opposed to the toleration of non-Catholic worship were represented in the Cortes, and Cánovas and his followers had to do battle with them.

A Protestant periodical published an open letter to the Cortes by the editor appealing for religious liberty. The following paragraphs show his unwillingness—and that of other Protestants —to accept religious toleration in lieu of religious freedom:

We do not ask mere liberty of conscience, for conscience remains free in prison, under torture, and even in fire. We ask for religious liberty, with civil rights; that is to say, the freedom to live according to our consciences in our country. We do not want our pure and immaculate faith to be an article of contraband; we do not want the practice of our cult to be a crime according to law; we do not want to live hidden in the shadows, avoiding the vigilance of the agents of authority and fearing the accusations of the prosecuting attorneys and the sentences of the judges; we do not want to live as men without religion, without temple, without worship, and without God. We

ask you, therefore, to consecrate anew and affirm freedom of cults in
our beloved country. Thousands of our fellow-citizens, thousands of
Spaniards, request it. How can their just petition be ignored and their
rights disavowed?

In the name, therefore, of civilization, in the name of humanity, in
the name of the God of the heavens and the earth, we appeal to you.
Maintain the rights of conscience and of human personality; keep the
Spanish people on a level with the citizens of all civilized nations;
consolidate liberty of cults in Spain.[26]

A lengthy discussion took place in both houses of the parliament on the religious question. As in 1869, many amendments
were proposed to the article on religion in the draft of the Constitution, most of them this time providing for a return to the
Constitution of 1869, or for the restoration of Catholic unity.
The arguments in both houses of the Cortes were about the same,
but the intransigents among the Moderates and clericals made a
stronger stand in the Senate than in the Congress. The three chief
points of view were the following: (1) Spain should maintain
Catholic unity; (2) the settlement of 1869 should be continued;
(3) Article 11 of the new Constitution should be accepted. The
eloquent defender of the principle of separation of Church and
State in the Cortes of 1869, Castelar, was heard from again, but
he spoke with greater restraint. The most that liberals could hope
for from the Cortes was acceptance of Article 21 of the Constitution of 1869, and the composition of the body gave little
hope even for that.[27]

It will be worthwhile to summarize or refer briefly to some of
the typical speeches in the Cortes. Much that was said on religious
unity in 1869 was said again at this time. So far as possible, the
arguments already noted as having been used in 1869 will not be
repeated. The Constitution was not considered by the Senate
until it had been approved by the Congress, but we shall consider
together the speeches in the two houses.

It is somewhat surprising to find that the cries of certain
Catholics in the Cortes against Article 11 were fully as loud as
the protests against Article 21 of the Constitution of 1869 had
been. Roman Catholicism had suffered a severe blow in the

Revolution, but by 1876 it had made a recovery, and there were some who thought that it would be possible to restore it to its old position as the only legally authorized religion in Spain. That there were limits to the spirit of intolerance is shown, however, by the fact that no one asked for a return of the Inquisition.

The deputy, Pidal y Mon, declared that he opposed Article 11 as a monarchist, as a Spaniard, and as a Catholic. The article, he said, is a crime against the monarchy, since it breaks with all the traditions and interests of the monarchy on the religious question. The Revolution of 1868, which overthrew the monarchy, brought freedom of religion; the Restoration should bring a renewal of Catholic unity. Article 11 is also a crime against Spanish nationality, since it introduces the germ of disunity and discord in the nation. It is a crime against religion, since, as the Pope has said, it violates all the rights of truth and of the Catholic religion. There is no need of toleration in Spain, since there are no strong forces of non-Catholics to disturb the tranquillity of the nation if they are not tolerated. Protestants have the right to read their Bibles in their homes, but they should not be permitted to have temples. If Protestant propaganda and bribery should be suppressed, in a very short time the few who now call themselves Protestants would return to the Catholic fold. Article 11 represents a compromise with the materialistic, rationalistic, atheistic spirit which has swept over Europe and which found expression in Spain in the Revolution of 1868. The Catholic can make no such compromise.[28]

The Bishop of Salamanca stated in the Senate that the question presented by Article 11 was not just political, as was maintained by some, but also religious, and that he would have to speak as both bishop and senator. He quoted the *Syllabus of Errors* to show that liberty of cults is an error, and he dealt at length with the letter written by the Pope to Cardinal Moreno. He indicated that the pontiff had also written to other prelates, including himself, and he stated that the condemnation of Article 11 by the Pope should settle the matter for all Catholics. He explained, however, that he did not mean that one who voted for Article 11 would be guilty of heresy or should be excluded from the Church. He appealed for observance of the Concordat and the consequent maintenance of Catholic unity. If Article 11 is approved and legal liberty granted to dissident cults, he said, Spanish legislation and the Spanish state will lose their Catholic character. When a state disregards its religious obligations, especially the obligation to impede public apostasy and the propagation of doctrines contrary to Catholicism, it loses its right to be known as Catholic. In a Catholic state there can be toleration when necessary of those born and reared in error, but there can be no toleration of apostates. All of the non-Catholics in Spain are apostates and recent ones. They can claim in their defence only a Constitution which has never been taken seriously by the Spanish nation, and their numbers and influence are too small to be taken into account. Protestants entered Spain with great hopes after the Revolution of 1868, but the Spanish people have laughed at them, and they have lost ground until now it is difficult to find a Protestant chapel. Protestanism will disappear completely if the government takes a firm stand on the religious question.[29]

The Bishop of Orihuela also defended Catholic unity, but he showed a greater spirit of tolerance than did the Bishop of Salamanca. After condemning dogmatic tolerance and also the civil toleration of dissident cults except when conditions within the nation or international obligations demand it, he said that if Spain had incurred certain obligations which required her to permit some Protestant chapels to remain open, that might be done, but that no new obligations should be accepted. If a certain degree of tolerance should be practised for reasons of necessity, he declared, the government should make sure that full respect was maintained for the Catholic religion and that all possible protection and aid were given it.[30]

The Senator, Benavides, referred to the expulsion of the Jews and the Moors, which, he said, was necessary but very costly to the nation. After achieving Catholic unity at such a price, he asked, how can we establish religious tolerance when there is no need of it? Our religious unity is the only unity we have, except for that of the monarchy, and if we lose it, all is lost.[31]

The Constitutionalists insisted that Article 21 of the Constitution of 1869 was the best possible solution of the religious question. Advocates of religious freedom, they opposed the principle of Catholic unity and also the compromise represented by Article 11 of the constitutional draft.

Victor Balaguer was one of those who insisted on the uselessness of compromise on the religious question. He said that the article did not satisfy the liberal parties, because they already had Article 21 of the Constitution of 1869 and some wanted to change even that in a more liberal sense. Certainly it did not satisfy the members of the Moderate Party, the clergy, and certain other conservatives, for petitions in favour of Catholic unity were pouring in to the Cortes, and the clergy and the Pope were denouncing the constitutional draft. The framers of the Constitution were being called heretics, and it would have been no worse for them if they had retained Article 21 of the Constitution of 1869. On the religious question there is no middle ground, said Balaguer: there must be either Catholic unity or liberty of cults.[32]

Cipriano del Mazo denounced in strong terms the ambiguity of Article 11 of the draft, insisting that it could mean either religious liberty or intolerance, depending upon the interpretation given it by the government. Like other speakers, he asked for a definition of 'public manifestation' and a clear explanation of the significance of the article. Even while professing himself a Catholic, he appealed for a maintenance of the independence of the civil power in the face of demands from the Church and denounced ultramontanism and religious intolerance. He sought to show through a comparison of Scotland and Ireland, North America and South America, and northern and southern Europe that religious freedom brings or at least accompanies the progress of civilization. He stated that the establishment of religious freedom does not necessarily exclude state protection to or preference for a certain religion, since the state, though incapable of judging matters of faith, can judge questions of social advantage and might find it advantageous to give official support to a certain religion.[33]

Soon after the opening of the Cortes, before the draft of the Constitution was read, Sagasta, who was later to serve often and long as president of the Council of Ministers, made a defence of religious freedom. Affirming that religion is a matter between man and God and that no one has the right to force a person to seek his salvation by means of rites and symbols that his conscience rejects, he insisted that when once religious freedom has been established in a country it is inhuman to revoke it.[34] During the debate on Article 11 of the constitutional draft he declared that his party would always stand in opposition to any administration that opposed religious liberty and would seek to modify any laws which were contrary to freedom of religion:

Why, instead of granting religious liberty, do you establish a two-edged sword, which will serve on the one hand to cut religious intolerance, and on the other hand to cut religious freedom? Why? Why do you who want religious liberty not establish it? Because you are afraid that those who have never wanted it will abandon you . . . that this majority will break up. . . . I want the country to know and I want Europe and the entire world to know that in Spain there is a party which is liberal—but that believes in law and order—which does not compromise . . . with any power that violates with sacrilegious hand the first, greatest, noblest, and most sacred of all the liberties: religious liberty. . . . .

The Constitutionalist Party . . . will not accept as its own and reserves for itself the right to modify all laws which ought to set forth that liberty and do not, and . . . it will not submit to any power which . . . considers that the party that proclaims . . . [religious freedom] is not . . . capable of directing the destinies of the nation.[35]

Representatives of the government and of the committees on the Constitution in the Congress and Senate, together with other members of the Cortes, spoke in defence of Article 11. They answered some of the questions raised by other lawmakers as to the meaning of the article, and their speeches serve as a more or less official interpretation of it, even though they were not in complete agreement. In spite of being staunch Catholics, they upheld the tradition of Spanish regalism, the sovereignty of the State in the face of demands from the Church.

Cánovas del Castillo sought to show that there was no question of going from Catholic unity to religious toleration but rather of going from religious freedom to religious toleration. He stated that it was impossible to ignore the fact that religious liberty had been practised in Spain for several years, that Protestant churches had been opened, and that treaties of commerce containing guarantees of freedom for Protestantism had been signed. Under such circumstances the nation could not return to the old policy of intolerance. Furthermore, said Cánovas, Spain must be guided at least in part by the practices of other nations if it wishes to live in harmony with them, and religious toleration or freedom of religion has been established almost everywhere. The Concordat does not bind the government to suppress or exclude non-Catholic religions; it merely states in its first article the historical fact of Catholic unity. It is incorrectly argued that the number of Protestants in Spain is insufficient to justify religious freedom. The one thousand or two thousand Spaniards who are Protestants may seem few as Protestants but as prisoners they would seem many.[36]

In a later speech in the Senate Cánovas said that some who opposed Article 11 of the Constitution were trying to get people to believe that its adoption would mean the suppression of Catholicism, whereas in reality the old relationship of Church and State would be fully maintained. As for other religions, he said, Article 11 simply provides that no one will be carried to court or condemned to prison for practising a non-Catholic cult. Such a provision, he continued, is not contrary to Catholic theology. The government accepts fully the *Syllabus of Errors* but insists that it does not condemn Article 11. The *Syllabus* condemns the idea that the existence of dissident cults is a good thing. The question being decided by the Cortes is not whether or not it is good to have other religions but rather what must be done since such religions already exist in Spain. Naturally, the Pope has not been able to approve toleration as a principle. When someone consulted him about the Spanish Constitution, he said, in effect, that the Church represents absolute truth and cannot compromise; but the pontiffs have never condemned civil tolerance or even liberty of cults when they have been established for valid reasons in a nation. When the popes were temporal rulers they practised toleration of the Jews, and more recently they even tolerated an Anglican church in Rome. Furthermore, the Spanish nation alone is qualified to decide the question of the status of the various religions within its borders. The prelates have the right to maintain the ideal of Catholic unity and to seek to give to God what they think is God's, but the government must use the right given it by God to render to Cæsar the things that are Cæsar's. There can be no sacrifice of the sovereignty of the state. Spanish rulers have always insisted on this; regalism forms an intimate part of Spanish history. Philip II and other Catholic rulers of Spain did not give absolute and unquestioning obedience to every letter and every warning from the Pope. If a letter like that of the Pope to Cardinal Moreno had been published without authorization in the time of Ferdinand the Catholic, Philip II, or Charles III, the prelates who published it would have been exiled from the kingdom. If the king of Spain and the legislators are required to obey without question every mandate of Rome in matters that are not of dogma or even morality, then it should be proclaimed openly that there is only one power on earth, that of the Church, and that from now on the Pope and the bishops will govern the Spanish nation.[37]

Francisco Silvela, a member of the committee on the Constitution in the Congress, attempted to explain the meaning of Article 11. He denied that it was ambiguous and stated that it clearly guaranteed respect for the worship of non-Catholics within their temples and for the external manifestations of the religion of the State. According to this article, he said, only the religion of the majority will have the right of publicity and propaganda. Matters of detail will have to be decided by future legislation. It would seem clear, however, that signs will not be permitted on non-Catholic temples, since they are external manifestations. The question of public employment will probably be decided by each branch of service. There is no reason to demand a profession of the Catholic faith from those of certain occupations—mine engineers, for example—but there is reason for such a requirement for the directors of orphanages and people in similar positions. Cemeteries for non-Catholics have long existed in Spain, and will doubtless continue to exist, but the integrity of the Catholic cemetery will surely be respected.[38]

Count de Coello de Portugal declared that intolerance started in Spain in modern times at the same time that it started in other countries, but that it had disappeared everywhere except in Spain. He said that the opposition to Article 11 was difficult to understand, since the article meant no more than respect for dissident cults, and did not give freedom of propagating in the press or on the platform doctrines or principles contrary to the Catholic religion. What really ought to concern Spanish Catholics, he said, is the glacial indifference which exists everywhere. It is strange that months should be spent deciding whether or not to authorize the opening of a Protestant temple when no attention is given to the weightier problem of religious indifference. If religious toleration is voted by the Spanish Cortes, the Pope will accept it even as he accepted the fact of religious toleration in the Catholic nations of Portugal, France, and Austria.[39]

Both the Congress and the Senate approved Article 11 and the entire Constitution by large majorities. The final vote (that of the Senate) was on June 22, 1876.[40] That date marked the legal establishment in the Spanish nation of the principle of religious toleration as distinguished from religious freedom.

The Constitution of 1876 included other guarantees of individual rights. Those which were of especial interest to Protestants were much the same as those in the Constitution of 1869. One noteworthy difference was that the right of holding public office was not said specifically to be independent of religion. Furthermore, the article dealing with education implied a closer governmental control of the schools than was the case under the former Constitution, but the right to establish and maintain private schools was clearly recognized. This would be of great significance for Protestants, who would be able to have their own schools and admit whomever they pleased to them.[41]

What would be the effect of the new Constitution on the Protestant movement? Much would depend upon the official interpretation of it. Clearly, there would be a reduction of religious freedom, but the extent of that reduction was not yet fully apparent.

VI

THE PRACTICE OF RELIGIOUS TOLERATION

THE national policy of religious toleration which was established by the Constitution of 1876 continued until the monarchy came to an end in 1931. Protestants were assured of the right to practise their religion in Spain, but the amount of their freedom depended upon the interpretation given to Article 11 by those in power. During the reign of Alfonzo XII and the regency of Maria Christina, Conservatives alternated with Liberals in directing the affairs of Spain. The principles of the two parties on religion as well as on other things were different in the beginning, but in time the differences almost disappeared.

During this period there were several pronouncements from the Vatican which showed that the Roman Catholic Church was still opposed in principle to the growth of freedom for other religions. In 1885 the encyclical letter, *Immortale Dei*, of Pope Leo XIII, insisted that 'it is not lawful for the State, any more than for the individual, either to disregard all religious duties or to hold in equal favour different kinds of religion', and that 'the unrestrained freedom of thinking and of openly making known one's thoughts is not inherent in the rights of citizens, and is by no means to be reckoned worthy of favour and support'. The same document stated that the Church 'deems it unlawful to place the various forms of divine worship on the same footing as the true religion, but does not, on that account, condemn those rulers who, for the sake of securing some great good or hindering some great evil, allow patiently custom or usage to be a kind of sanction for each kind of religion having its place in the State'.[1] The encyclical letter, *Libertas humana*, a few years later, condemned freedom of thought, of the press, of education, and of worship and declared that any liberty except that which means submission to God and subjection to His will as interpreted by the Church is unintelligible and that generally the state which makes fewest concessions to such evils as liberty of cults, other things being equal, is the best.[2]

The pull towards Catholic unity was strong in Spain, but so also was that towards tolerance and freedom of thought. A landmark in the development of liberal thought was the founding in Madrid of the 'Institución Libre de Enseñanza' by Francisco Giner de los Ríos as a protest against clerical and state control of education. Through the influence of this school, and naturally through other influences as well, the thought of many Spaniards left traditional channels.[3]

Conservative ministries were in power from the time of the Restoration until 1881, and thus the men who led in the adoption of the Constitution were those who first applied its principles. Cánovas del Castillo, as President of the Council of Ministers during most of this time, had ample opportunity to put into effect his ideas on the religious question.[4]

The adoption of Article 11 of the Constitution did not bring a break with the Holy See, as some had feared it would. The papal Secretary of State protested to the Spanish Ambassador against the violation of the Concordat and the rights of the Church; but, mentioning the declarations made in the Cortes by representatives of the government during the debate on the Constitution, he expressed the hope that these statements implied that there would be a recognition in future laws of the prerogatives of the Catholic Church. He indicated that the Holy See expected that instruction in universities and public and private schools should be in keeping with the Catholic religion, that bishops should be guaranteed the right to supervise the religious education of the young, and that the authority of the State should aid the bishops in their attempts to prevent the printing and circulation of books harmful to the faith and to morality.[5] The expectations of the papacy were in large part, though not fully, met by the government.

In the first months following the adoption of the Constitution, efforts were made by the Catholic clergy, zealous laymen, and certain local officials to reduce the liberties of Protestants. There were fines for disturbing other people by singing and for accompanying children to and from Protestant schools. The mayor of one town ordered the Protestant pastor there to remove the design of the Bible from the church building and to conduct services with the doors of the chapel closed, since otherwise people in the street could see and hear what was going on inside.[6] A Protestant religious service was interrupted by a government official. After protests were made, he insisted that it was a school rather than a church which he had entered,[7] and the central government upheld him and affirmed his right to inspect schools.[8]

Of especial significance were developments in Madrid. The pastors of the churches there were ordered to remove from buildings all signs or advertisements relative to worship, schools, and the sale of religious books. The agent of the British and Foreign Bible Society was told to efface the signs over the Bible depot and to remove all books from the window, but he obeyed only in part, since a written order was not given him. He obliterated one sign, and he closed the books in the windows and turned them with their backs inside, so that the titles could not be seen from the street. When Cánovas del Castillo heard about this, he expressed regret for the orders that had been given and encouraged the reopening of the books.[9]

In October of 1876 there was a royal order setting forth the official interpretation of Article 11 of the Constitution. It was of great significance, since this interpretation of the principle of religious toleration lasted for more than thirty years. Among the rules governing dissident religions were the following:

1. From this date all public manifestations of the cults or sects dissident from the Catholic religion are forbidden outside the precincts of their temples or cemeteries.

2. For the effects of the previous rule, by public manifestation will be understood everything in the street or on the exterior walls of the temple or of the cemetery which gives knowledge of the ceremonies,

rites, usages, and customs of the dissident cult, including signs, banners, emblems, advertisements, and posters.[10]

The order went on to state that purely religious meetings within places of worship would enjoy constitutional inviolability. Protestants thus had freedom of worship within their chapels, but they could not put signs on them, nor could they hold services in the streets. The government was to be informed twenty-four hours in advance of the opening of any dissident chapel or cemetery, and meetings celebrated outside the places regularly set apart for them would require special authorization. Schools were to be independent of places of worship, and subject to governmental inspection.

Events of subsequent years showed the policy of religious toleration in practice. In some cases Protestants saw their rights vindicated, and in others they were painfully reminded that full religious freedom did not exist in Spain. We shall look at some of the typical cases and note some of the significant developments.

A Protestant who had resisted the attempt of the local priest and certain other people to persuade him to let his children be baptized in the Catholic Church, agreed to permit the baptism after the mayor had intervened in the matter. Then the father reported to the Ministry of the Interior that he had been caused against his will to submit his children to baptism, and the central government censured the mayor for using the influence of his position for securing the performance of a religious act and affirmed its determination to maintain freedom of conscience and religious profession. The governmental order contained derogatory statements about the Protestant father, but it was a victory for the Protestant cause.[11]

The Bishop of Cadiz instigated the mayor to send policemen to a Protestant chapel to break up a meeting in which about four hundred people were present. The British consul intervened and referred the matter to the Ambassador. The central government thereupon instructed local authorities to refrain from intervening in affairs of the dissident religions without instructions from Madrid.[12]

Colporteurs went all over Spain selling Bibles, but in some places they met with much opposition from priests and other people, including local officials,[13] and the central government also placed limitations on their freedom. It was announced that the preaching of doctrines and the sale of books contrary to Catholic dogma were public manifestations when carried on outside the places set apart for them and that under such circumstances they were forbidden. The sellers of books were not permitted to enter shops or factories for the purpose of selling to the workers and directing exhortations to them.[14] The British and Foreign Bible Society summed up the situation as follows:

The restraints imposed upon the circulation of the Scriptures remain in force. . . . A colporteur, it may be, arrives early one morning in a town where he has good hopes of success. Scarcely has he arranged his books, when a priest steps up, who in insolent tones denounces his work and demands to see his licence. . . . A constable is fetched, who bids him follow to the house of the Justice of the Peace. The latter examines his books and papers, and orders the officer to take possession of the former and convey the man himself to the lock-up. A word of appeal is met by the remark that the Constitution gives him full liberty to define what is a public manifestation, and that he is prepared to accept the responsibility. By nine o'clock the poor colporteur finds himself in confinement, and it is not until the same hour has struck at night that he is released; and then only on condition of his leaving town, while his books are detained, in order, it is said, that they may be forwarded to the governor of the province. This is no extreme case; often the colporteurs are exposed to personal injury besides. In the full sense of the word, they cannot sell publicly, but they do venture as best they may to carry on their honourable calling. In some districts a tacit permission is accorded, and they are practically free; but the time is ardently desired when the decrees which press upon them so closely may once and for ever be removed.[15]

Protestants rather frequently found themselves charged with offences against the Catholic religion. One of the most interesting cases was that of the pastor of Alcoy, who was accused of interrupting a religious service. A local priest went unbidden to the home of a sick member of the Protestant church and began conducting the Catholic rites for the dying. The Protestant pastor

4

was sent for by the members of the family, and he entered the room where the priest and the dying woman were. He was arrested and sentenced to three years and eight months of imprisonment. A higher court annulled the sentence, however, declaring the article of the Penal Code under which he had been sentenced applicable only to disturbances of public religious functions.[16]

A question destined to be referred many times to the courts was whether or not a person should be required to take off his hat for religious acts such as burials, processions, and the passing of the *Viaticum*, or sacrament for the dying. In 1879 there was a decision to the effect that an unmotivated refusal to remove the hat on such occasions or an unjust resistance to doing so was an offence to the Catholic sentiments of the majority of the Spanish people and was punishable under the Penal Code.[17] This was not a final answer to the question, since, as subsequent trials showed, it was difficult to determine what was an unmotivated refusal. Though it will mean anticipating events somewhat, it may be stated here that in the trial of three Protestants in 1886 the Supreme Court ruled that the failure to take off one's hat for the *Viaticum* was not punishable when the meeting was accidental and there was no intention of offending Catholic sentiments.[18] Even this, however, did not prevent new cases from arising.

Another difficult problem was that of burial, since the Catholic clergy claimed the right to bury all children who had been baptized by their Church. In 1880 the government ruled that parents have the right to decide where and how their children shall be buried.[19] The clergy did not accept this ruling, and ten years later a bishop obtained from the government an order declaring that the Catholic Church has the right to decide who dies in communion with it and is, therefore, entitled to Catholic burial.[20] Protestant parents were naturally very resentful of the fact that in certain cases their children could be taken away from them in the moment of death and buried in a place where they themselves could not be buried.

A law of 1880 dealt with the right of peaceable assembly,

which was guaranteed by the Constitution. After defining a public meeting as one attended by more than twenty persons and held in a place not the habitual residence of those convoking it, the law stated that the only condition for holding such a meeting within a building was that authorities should be notified in writing twenty-four hours in advance concerning the object, place, and time of meeting. Meetings held in streets or public squares would require written permission from the authorities. Representatives of the government would have the right to attend all public meetings, and they would have the authority to dissolve them under certain circumstances. Catholic processions and meetings of the Catholic Church or of other tolerated religions held within temples or cemeteries were not subject to the provisions of this law, and meetings of less than twenty persons were regarded as private and therefore free from all governmental control.[21]

When Cánovas del Castillo resigned in 1881, the Liberals took over for a period of about three years, led most of the time by Sagasta.[22] The status of non-Catholic religions did not change greatly during this period, but two or three matters are worthy of mention. The first is that the order of 1875, which had forbidden professors in the universities to teach anything contrary to the monarchy or the Catholic religion, was revoked and the professors who had been discharged for political or religious reasons were reinstated. The Nuncio protested against this, but his protests were of no avail.[23]

A second thing that showed the liberal character of the government was the announcement that Article 11 of the Constitution would be interpreted in a broad and liberal sense and that, as provided in the Penal Code, offences against all religions would be prosecuted.[24] An evangelist who had been imprisoned and fined on the charge of having preached to a crowd gathered in the street was pardoned, and proceedings against several other Protestants were dropped.[25] Those interested in Protestantism were greatly encouraged.

When the Liberal ministry resigned, a Conservative cabinet

presided over by Cánovas del Castillo took its place and continued in office until the death of the King in November of 1885.[26] This was a time of reaction. A Protestant missionary reported that the position of Protestants in Spain (especially outside Madrid) was more difficult than at any other time since the Revolution of 1868.[27]

The desire of the government to gain Catholic favour was shown by its decrees on education. Inspection of municipal and provincial elementary schools by representatives of the Catholic Church was insisted upon.[28] Catholic schools were given a boost by the provision that schools maintained by private funds should be eligible for financial aid from the state. Protestant educators were placed in a precarious position by the requirement that the directors of private secondary schools should be taxpayers or have sponsors who were and that they should obtain certificates of good conduct from the mayors of their home towns. Protestant schools were put at a distinct disadvantage by the provision that school directors should let the authorities and the parents of their pupils know immediately whether or not they intended putting their schools under the spiritual direction of the parish priests.[29]

In this period, as in others, there was a fair degree of freedom of the press. The Supreme Court ruled that criticism of the dogmas of the Catholic religion was not a crime, but that the tenacious scorning of the dogmas of religion with the purpose of offending was an offence punishable under the Penal Code.[30] One is impressed with the freedom with which Protestant and secular magazines dealt with controversial religious questions and criticized the government for its denial of full religious freedom. The liberal principle of freedom of expression had a greater triumph than did the liberal principle of freedom of worship.

Following the death of Alfonso XII, his widow, Maria Christina, became regent. Several months after the death of her husband, Maria Christina gave birth to a son, who became Alfonso XIII. The situation of the throne was precarious, with a foreign woman as regent, and Cánovas del Castillo called upon all monarchists to rally to the defence of the throne. He resigned, and a new ministry, headed by Sagasta, was appointed. The two men alternated as heads of Spanish cabinets until Cánovas del Castillo was killed in 1897. The real political differences between them practically disappeared, and a change of ministry did not mean a fundamental change of policy or procedure.[31]

During this period much publicity was given to the violation of the rights of Protestants in the Caroline Islands, over which, following a dispute between Spain and Germany, Spanish authority had recently been recognized. In spite of Spain's promises to recognize Protestant missions, the governor arrested an aged and influential American missionary there and sent him to Manilla. Higher authorities removed the governor from office and permitted the missionary to return to his post.[32] It was stated at the time of these occurrences that never before in the history of Spain had the public press so freely discussed a subject connected with Protestantism.[33]

One of the achievements of these years was the growth of a better understanding between the Catholic Church and those who called themselves Liberals, in spite of the continuing hostility to liberalism in many Catholic quarters. When the question of a new Civil Code containing articles recognizing both civil and canonical marriage was discussed with the Vatican by representatives of the Liberal government then in power, the Holy See approved what was stated in the draft of the Civil Code with regard to marriage between Catholics and let it be known that the government's decision with reference to the marriage of non-Catholics would be tolerated. The Spanish authorities, fully satisfied, announced that the time of hostility between the liberal parties and the Church had come to an end.[34]

The new Civil Code, which went into effect in 1889, followed the decree of 1875 on the subject of marriage. Article 42 stated: 'The law recognizes two forms of marriage: canonical, which those who profess the Catholic religion must contract; and civil, which will be celebrated in the manner determined by this Code.'

Another article forbade marriage for those who had been ordained or had taken a religious vow of chastity, unless they had received canonical dispensation authorizing them to marry.[35]

An example of local intolerance and of the desire of the central government to control it was afforded by events in the village of Campo de Criptana, of the province of Ciudad Real. The opening of a chapel there by George Lawrence aroused great opposition, and one day during a Catholic religious procession a tumult arose and the crowd threw stones at the Protestant building. The mayor ordered the chapel closed provisionally, and it remained closed for many months. Lawrence and his family were insulted and stoned whenever they left their house, and he was fined for singing in a family devotional service. He was kept in prison twenty-four hours on a charge by priests that he did not take off his hat when the cross passed by. Under pressure from the central government, the local officials permitted the chapel to reopen and offered protection to the Protestants. The Minister of the Interior indicated that he was determined that toleration of cults should be a reality in Spain, and he invited the Protestants who visited him to appeal to him immediately whenever their rights were violated. He counselled prudence, however, in order to avoid conflicts.[36]

Roman Catholic opposition to freedom of worship was brought to light by the construction of an imposing building for the Protestant Church of the Redeemer in Madrid. In spite of the opposition, the building was authorized and completed, but its inauguration was postponed, first by Conservatives and then by Liberals,[37] Permission to open the church was given only after a cross and the inscription, *Christus Redemptor aeternus*, had been removed from the façade. Even then the Minister of Grace and Justice requested that the front door be kept closed and that entrance be through the adjoining building in order to avoid arousing the reactionaries. It was not until twelve years later that permission was finally given to open the door.[38]

There was a discussion in the Cortes about the new Protestant church building. A senator protested that a building which was clearly distinguishable as a church had been built by Protestants in Madrid and that the newspapers had announced the opening of a chapel for public worship. The government, he said, had permitted the opening of the chapel in spite of the requests to the contrary from the Nuncio, the bishops, distinguished ladies, and Catholic groups in various parts of Spain. He claimed that Article 11 of the Constitution had been violated by the construction and use of a building which served as a public manifestation of the Protestant religion.[39]

The Minister of Grace and Justice replied that neither in Madrid nor in any other part of Spain was there a Protestant church open for public worship—that all dissident worship was private, as the Constitution exacted that it should be. He stated that the plans of the building were duly approved by the municipal authorities and that these plans had obviously been followed. He said that it was true that the building could be recognized as a religious structure but that there was nothing about it to indicate Protestant beliefs or practices, and that neither those who approved the plans nor those who permitted the opening of the church were guilty of any infraction of the Constitution.[40]

There were several important developments in the field of education during this period. The Liberal ministry appointed just after the death of Alfonso XII revoked the decrees on education issued by the preceding ministry and restored earlier decrees granting educational freedom.[41] Even before this the liberal character of the government had been shown by an order declaring innocent of any transgression of the law a school teacher who had refused to take his pupils to mass.[42]

A later Liberal ministry attempted to show that it was not hostile to Catholicism by issuing a decree calling for the introduction of a Religion course in the institutes, or secondary schools. Registration for the course would be voluntary, and no one would be required to declare his faith when the matter of registration came up, but attendance for those registered would be obligatory.[43]

The decree did not satisfy certain Catholics. A member of the

Senate complained that Religion was assigned a place of lesser importance in the curriculum than other courses, which were required, and he expressed the fear that few students would take the course. He argued that it would be better to make the study of Religion obligatory for all except those who asked to be excused from it, and he said that the prelates had accepted the plan not because they liked it but because they thought it better to have Religion included in the curriculum as the decree provided than not to have it included at all.[44]

The Minister of Public Works insisted that it was unjust for the Liberal Party to be criticized for not making Religion a required course in the secondary schools. When the Conservatives were in power, he said, they did nothing towards putting Religion in the institutes. The Liberal government had introduced Religion, he continued, but in such a way that no one was compelled to take the course, since Liberals could not consent to compulsion in religion.[45]

In a later speech the same Minister gave a remarkably frank statement of how the Liberals had made concessions on the religious question—in order, he said, to achieve peace and harmony in the nation. One suspects that the chief reason for the concessions was the desire to gain favour with the Catholic forces of the country or at least to avoid arousing their active hostility. The Minister said that the old Progressive Party, which was a liberal party, was characterized by a certain hostility towards the Church, since on the part of the Church there was hostility towards liberalism, but that liberals had sacrificed some of their goals in order to reach an understanding with the Church. They wanted liberty of cults as set forth in the Constitution of 1869, but for the sake of peace they accepted Article 11 of the Constitution of 1876, and also the order of 1876 which interpreted the article in a restrictive sense. On the question of civil marriage, out of deference to the Holy See, they accepted a formula which was not their own, and more recently, in consideration of the requests of the prelates, they introduced Religion into the secondary schools. The Liberals are not hostile to religion, declared the Minister, but there is a limit to what they can concede.[46]

The Spanish Liberal Party had abandoned its earlier advocacy of religious freedom and, for the time being, at least, accepted the policy of religious toleration, with special privileges for the Roman Catholic Church. It still maintained certain rights of non-Catholics in such areas as education and marriage, and thus showed that it was not altogether false to its heritage. The policies of the Liberal Party after it came to power, however, were a far cry from the pronouncements of Sagasta and other Liberals in earlier years.

The construction by Fliedner of a large Protestant school building in Madrid created almost as much furor as had the building of the Church of the Redeemer a few years earlier. Negotiations for approval of the plans began while the Liberals were in power, but the actual construction took place during the last administration of Cánovas del Castillo. The Nuncio, Catholic bishops, ladies of the aristocracy, and other people of influence sought to prevent the building of the school; and the papal Secretary of State wrote to the Queen Regent asking her to intervene. Cánovas del Castillo took a firm stand, however, and the building was authorized and completed. His only concession to Catholic pressure was a request that certain features of the building which gave it an ecclesiastical appearance should be removed from the plans.[41]

When Cánovas del Castillo was killed, the magazine published by the Fliedner mission paid the following tribute to him:

It is not incumbent upon us to point out here his merits in politics, but we do have the duty to note the influence which he has exercised in religious life during the past twenty-five years. One could not expect from a Conservative the maintenance of all the liberties achieved in the Revolution of '68. The reaction of 1875 converted liberty of conscience into religious toleration. The merit of Cánovas on this point consists in having maintained unbroken the limits to which he himself had reduced the liberties, without permitting them to be narrowed further, either by intolerant governors, the reactionary clergy, or fanatical ladies. Cánovas was a person of sound character;

for him to promise was to fulfil; . . . we can proclaim his merits in a simple word: 'He did justice'.[48]

After the death of Cánovas del Castillo, there was a Liberal ministry, then a Conservative, reactionary government, and then again a period of Liberal rule. The differences between Right and Left were accentuated, as was the bitterness on political and religious questions. The defeat of Spain in the Spanish American War brought a wave of pessimism and of dissatisfaction with the national leaders. During these last years of the regency (which ended in 1902), Spain was in transition.[49]

This period witnessed a revival of prejudice against Protestantism in some quarters and a bid for Catholic leadership in the regeneration of Spain. The most notable Catholic triumph came when Conservatives ordered that civil marriage should be permitted only when there was a sworn declaration from those marrying that they did not profess the Catholic religion.[50]

Of even greater significance was the revival of anti-clericalism. The strength of popular feeling against clerical control of life was demonstrated not long before the end of the regency by the reaction to Benito Perez Galdos' play, *Electra*, whose theme is the prevention by clericals of a young girl's marriage to a progressive man of science and her confinement in a convent. The play was enthusiastically received by liberals and radicals, and strikes and attacks on convents were traced to its influence.[51]

A Protestant missionary society commented that the popular outburst over *Electra* was 'a clear indication of the state of public opinion, and . . . another step in the direction of religious liberty'. With real insight, however, it added that the forces of irreligion might become stronger and therefore more dangerous than the old forces of clericalism.[52] A Spanish Protestant leader wrote as follows:

We are passing through a political, social, and religious crisis. Religiously, Spain is breaking away from Rome, and in so doing seems about to throw herself into the arms of incredulity and atheism, just as France did, the natural outcome wherever Romanism has taught and ruled. The change is so rapid that we can see it. We do not have to fight against religious fanaticism, but against social fanaticism. We have not so much to fear persecution and insults from the clergy, though there are instances of such, the last efforts of a dying giant, as we have to fight against the indifference of the people. But we have liberty enough, and the Book.[53]

An inquiry may now be made as to the activities and strength of Protestantism from 1876 to 1902. In general, we can say that though Protestantism continued in Spain its progress was not striking. In some places and on the part of some denominations there was a marked decline in membership and activity.

The American Baptist missionary, William Knapp, left Spain in 1876 greatly discouraged because of disappointments in Spanish pastors and the lack of permanent progress in the work.[54] Spaniards continued the Baptist witness, with some help from America, but the work in Madrid and other points occupied by Knapp and his associates steadily declined and eventually ceased. The Baptist position in Spain would probably have been lost altogether had it not been for Eric Lund, who went there from Sweden and worked under American Baptist auspices,[55] and some other Swedes who worked under the sponsorship of Swedish Baptists. Near the turn of the century there were 76 church members in Valencia[56] and 114 in the region of Catalonia,[57] but there was then no Baptist church in Madrid.

One of the most prosperous missions in Spain during this period was that supported by American Congregationalists. In 1902 the American Board of Commissioners for Foreign Missions reported one ordained missionary and four American women working in Spain, together with twenty-four Spanish workers. There were eight churches and seventeen regular preaching stations, with 354 church members and 1510 'adherents'. There was a boarding school for girls with thirty-four students which enjoyed the respect of Spanish authorities and people of culture, and there were fifteen other schools, with a total enrolment of 772. Most of the growth had taken place since the Restoration.[58]

In 1880 a schism occurred in the Spanish Christian Church. Juan Cabrera, the capable Spanish pastor who had built up a large congregation in Seville and then had gone to Madrid to serve as pastor of the Church of the Redeemer, led several churches in organizing the Spanish Reformed Church, of Episcopal rite and polity, he himself being elected bishop of the Church.[59] Five years later there were eight congregations affiliated with the new organization, and this branch of Spanish Protestantism had become one of the best-known and most influential.[60] The construction of a large and attractive church building in Madrid has already been noted.

Another important development in Protestant work during this period was the establishment by the Presbytery of Andalusia of a seminary for the training of pastors. Spasmodic efforts towards the development of pastoral leadership had been made earlier, but nothing so significant as this.[61]

In 1886, an Assembly in Madrid of representatives of the congregations of the Spanish Christian Church which had not followed Cabrera changed the name of their organization to the Spanish Evangelical Church. It was hoped to avoid denominationalism, and overtures were made for union with the Congregationalists, who in the previous year had formed the Iberian Evangelical Union.[62] Three years later union was achieved. All distinctively denominational terms, formulas, and titles were avoided so far as possible, and a large degree of autonomy was left to the individual churches and missions.[63]

A missionary in Spain wrote in 1886 as follows:

The late history of the Protestant movement in Spain is certainly peculiar. To the enthusiasm and curiosity of the first years has succeeded an almost absolute stagnation over the whole peninsula. The new places which have been begun during the last ten years might almost be counted on the fingers of one hand, certainly on those of both hands.[64]

A few years later the same missionary was more optimistic concerning the growth of Protestantism in Spain, but he mentioned the alarming growth of scepticism.[65] Someone else who was well acquainted with Protestant work in Spain stated in 1891 that the number of congregations was greater than ever before and that, though there were no congregations so large as a few which were formed soon after the Revolution of 1868, the total number of members and the total regular attendance at services were as large if not larger than ever before.[66] Religious statistics from Spain are always open to question, but the report given at about that time probably indicates fairly accurately the strength of Protestantism. According to the report, there were 122 houses or rooms used for chapels or schools; 9000 people who attended Protestant services of worship; 3600 communicant members of the churches; and 5000 pupils in the schools.[67]

Protestantism had made some progress since 1876, but its progress was still slow. Would there be greater growth if full religious freedom were granted? Many believed that there would be, and they hoped that the twentieth century would bring the achievement of that freedom.

VII

THE PRACTICE OF RELIGIOUS
TOLERATION—(*continued*)

DURING the long reign of Alfonso XIII, the policy of religious toleration was continued, but with differences of degree. From 1902 to 1923, when Liberals and Conservatives alternated in forming ministries, liberalism tended to prevail, and the bases of religious toleration were broadened. From 1923 to 1930, while General Primo de Rivera was dictator, reactionary forces triumphed, and the practice of religious toleration became more restricted.

Liberal leadership passed to less cautious men than Sagasta, who died soon after the beginning of this period, and some of them took a strong stand on the religious question. Many regarded religious liberty as the ground on which all liberals, including Republicans and Socialists, could unite. Eventually, however, most political leaders lost interest in religious freedom or became afraid to advocate it.[1]

Spanish Protestants, unwilling merely to be tolerated, hoped that full religious freedom could be achieved, and they conducted campaigns, with mass meetings, in favour of it, and sent petitions to the Cortes and the heads of the Spanish government. Hitherto they had largely depended upon others to contend for their rights, but in this period they spoke up boldly in their own name.

The most spectacular Protestant campaign for religious freedom took place in 1910. In many cities Protestants organized public meetings which were attended by hundreds and even thousands and which received much publicity in the press. The crowning act of the campaign was the presentation to the Cortes of a petition for religious liberty signed by 150,000 people.[2]

Since by no means all who signed the petition were Protestants, the message to the Cortes had to be phrased in general
terms. It included the following paragraphs:

The most interesting pages of our national history are . . . those
which reveal respect and mutual tolerance in the sphere of religious
thought—respect and tolerance demonstrated in the living together
of races of distinct religious confessions. . . .
The undersigned leave to the enlightened and elevated judgment
of the worthy representatives of the nation in the Cortes [an estimate
of] the transcendental effect of a measure which would place our
beloved nation on the same spiritual plane with those nations which
have proclaimed liberty of cults as a fundamental dogma of modern
democracy. . . .
Well deserving of the country would be the liberal Cortes if it
should respond to the noble desire for spiritual liberation represented
in the present petition by establishing in the fundamental laws of the
Kingdom complete liberty of cults, or at least by repealing those laws
now in effect which are opposed to that sacred principle.[3]

The petition, beautifully bound in four volumes, was presented
by a committee of Protestants to the President of the Congress,
who left the president's chair during a meeting to receive the
committee in his office. The spokesman for the group, after
expressing the gratitude of Spanish Protestants for what the
Liberal government had done in their favour, voiced the hope
that religious toleration would give way to full religious freedom
and gave many examples of denials of freedom. The President of
the Congress listened courteously and indicated the timeliness
of making known the need of liberal reforms. Declaring
that the Liberal Party hoped to broaden the bases of religious
toleration and arrive finally at full liberty, he counselled prudence and patience and said that progress would be gradual but
certain.[4]

Progress towards religious liberty was much too gradual to
suit Protestants, and they conducted other campaigns and sent
other petitions to those in authority. The following paragraph
from a petition of the Spanish Evangelical Alliance to the
President of the Council of Ministers several years later expressed

the dissatisfaction of Protestants with their inferior status as citizens:

We have never complained because the Roman Church received a favoured treatment in Spanish legislation. We do not long for favour, nor do we envy those who enjoy it; but we do desire that justice should be done to us, that what is ours by natural law, which is divine law, should be given to us. We call for respect for our human personality in all the moments of life, today clouded by vexatious laws of exception which follow us from the cradle to the grave. We want to enter the public school, military service, matrimony, and our last earthly resting place in enjoyment of the rights of complete citizenship . . .; we do not want to be persons who are tolerated because they cannot be exterminated.[5]

Conservatives and Catholics were by no means dormant while these things were going on, and they did their utmost to prevent an extension of religious freedom or to reduce it further. Pastoral letters from bishops, public meetings, and written protests made known the opposition to religious liberty.[6] A letter from Pope Pius X to the Archbishop of Toledo made clear where his sympathies lay:

It must be maintained as a certain principle that in Spain it is possible to support, as many do in fact most nobly support, the Catholic thesis, and with it the re-establishment of religious unity. It is, furthermore, the duty of every Catholic to combat all the errors condemned by the Holy See, especially those included in the *Syllabus* and the *liberties of perdition* proclaimed by the new law, or liberalism, whose application to the government of Spain is the cause of so many evils. This action of religious reconquest must be carried out within the limits of legality.[7]

The reasons for Protestant petitions for religious liberty, and also the progress of liberal reforms during the period from 1902 to 1923, appear in the matters of burial, marriage, education, military service, and worship. These were the old areas of tension in Spain, as they are in most places where there is a problem of limited religious liberty.

With regard to burial, Protestants resented the fact that in many places there was no civil cemetery or it was inferior to the Catholic cemetery,[8] and they continued to chafe under the ruling that the Catholic Church could decide the question of the burial of minors who had been baptized in that Church.[9] They received some consolation, however, from the fact that a governmental order censured a mayor for forcing a non-Catholic to bury his two children in an open field, and stated that small villages were not exempted from the requirement set forth in previous orders that a decorous place be provided for the burial of religious dissenters.[10]

In the matter of marriage, liberalism made a slight advance, only to be pushed back a short time later. A Liberal government ruled in 1906 that those who wished to contract civil marriage would not be required to make any declaration whatsoever regarding their religion.[11] The Minister of Grace and Justice stated at that time: 'For the State there are no Catholics, nor Protestants, nor Jews; there are only citizens, who can profess the religion they choose, and for them the State must legislate, since all have rights and duties'.[12] When the Conservatives came to power they abolished this order on marriage, and thereby made it necessary for those contracting civil marriage to make a declaration that they were not Catholics.[13] Liberals did not return to their original position, but in 1913 a Liberal government did reprimand and fine a judge who had refused civil marriage to a couple who declared they were not Roman Catholics. The governmental order made it clear that a declaration of non-membership in the Catholic Church by one or both of the persons wishing to contract matrimony was sufficient reason for the authorization of civil marriage.[14]

Public education was not altogether free from the influence of the dominant religion, for the Catholic faith was taught in the schools of the State, but there was a large degree of educational freedom. As we have already seen, students in the secondary schools could be excused from the study of Religion, and in 1913 the government made clear that children in the public primary schools might also be excused from taking Religion if their parents belonged to a faith other than the Roman Catholic.[15] Of perhaps even greater significance was the fact that Protestant schools suffered no interference with their activities on account of religion.

An interesting discussion took place in the Cortes over the invitation extended to the director of the Protestant school in Bilbao to the dedication of a statue in that city. Since the school director was also a Protestant pastor, some saw in his official invitation to a public function a violation of the Constitution. A Carlist deputy declared that the Constitution did not permit public manifestations of dissident religions, and it certainly did not permit public exhibitions of the ecclesiastical authorities of such religions on equality with the Catholic clergy. He referred to a protest which several hundred Catholic women of Bilbao had made against this offence to the religion of the State. Representatives of the government replied that the director of the Protestant school was invited because the directors of all schools were, and that an invitation to a public ceremony which was not a religious act involved no violation of Article 11 of the Constitution.[16]

There were several important developments during this period with regard to the practice of religion by members of the armed services. An order in 1906 declared that the ruling of 1870 on this subject was still in force, and it gave certain specific directions to clear up misunderstandings. All members of the army, the order stated, were required to attend public religious rites and ceremonies and to perform whatever military acts were called for in relation with them when the unit of which they formed a part was ordered to attend; but attendance upon prayers in the barracks and upon confession and communion was not required. All military authorities were instructed to deal with particular cases in such a way as to respect the religion of the State and also the religious convictions of individuals, but without permitting the relaxation of military discipline.[17] In subsequent years members of the armed services were sometimes penalized for failing to meet the requirements, and most Protestant petitions for religious liberty mentioned freedom of conscience for those in uniform. Since so much was left to the discretion of commanding officers, there was no uniformity of practice.

The case of a Protestant sailor who was imprisoned for refusing to kneel when he was required to go to mass attracted wide attention. The liberal press pleaded his case and insisted on new laws which would guarantee the rights of conscience of those in military service, while the conservative and Catholic press took the position that this was merely a case of military insubordination which deserved punishment. A committee of Protestants paid several visits to members of the cabinet, and the Universal Evangelical Alliance intervened in favour of the sailor.[18]

In the Cortes a deputy called for freedom of conscience for members of the armed services and insisted that a matter so vital should not be left to the discretion of those in command of military units. The President of the Council of Ministers replied that the government was seeking a way to guarantee the rights of conscience of soldiers and sailors without sacrificing military discipline.[19] Early in 1913 there was issued an order clarifying the earlier order and setting forth clearly that all who stated in their official documents upon joining the armed services that they did not belong to the Apostolic Roman Catholic Church would be excused from attending mass.[20] About a month later the sailor, who had been sentenced by the highest military court to six months and one day in prison, was pardoned.[21] A few years later the government recognized the right of those in military service to change their religion after their induction.[22]

The case of a Protestant colonel of the naval artillery who refused to attend the compulsory Mass of the Holy Spirit before a court martial at which he was to be one of the judges brought to public attention the question of attendance at such services. The officer was arrested, but the Liberal government set him free provisionally and announced that a bill would be introduced in the Cortes to abolish the compulsory Mass of the Holy Spirit for the judges in a court-martial in the navy, as it had already been abolished in the army. The bill was introduced, but a few days later the ministry fell, and a Conservative cabinet was appointed. The colonel was court-martialled and was sentenced to six months' imprisonment. There was a widespread public demand that he be pardoned, and a pardon was granted by the King. Even while passing sentence in order to comply with the law, the military court had recommended pardon.[23] Some time later (in 1916) a governmental order stated that until a law was passed on the subject attendance upon the Mass of the Holy Spirit would not be obligatory.[24]

The most important measure of this period with regard to religious freedom had to do with Protestant places of worship. It was the work of José Canalejas, an advanced liberal who was opposed to the political power and privilege of the Roman Catholic Church and devoted to the cause of equal rights for all. In 1910 he issued an order which gave a new interpretation of Article 11 of the Constitution with regard to public manifestations of dissident religions. Declaring the second paragraph of the order of 1876 on this subject void, it stated that henceforth there was no prohibition of inscriptions, banners, emblems, announcements, placards, and other signs revealing the buildings, ceremonies, rites, usages, or customs of dissident religions. Public manifestations (which were forbidden by the Constitution) were defined as meetings held in the open air with the purpose of making known the collective sentiments or beliefs of those assembled.[25] The governments which followed that of Canalejas felt it necessary to accept the new interpretation of Article 11.

In an article published a few days after the appearance of this order, a Protestant pastor expressed the gratitude of members of his religion for permission to put signs on their places of worship. He mentioned Evangelical disillusionment with Liberals who had not dared to change the order issued by Cánovas del Castillo, and he expressed the hope that the measures taken by Canalejas augured the early establishment of full religious freedom. After referring to Spanish Catholic and Vatican protests against the new policy towards dissident religions, he expressed the confidence that Canalejas and his programme enjoyed the support of all liberals.[26] A letter to the President of the Council of Ministers assured him of the gratitude of Protestants.[27]

In the Cortes there were Catholics who criticized Canalejas for interpreting Article 11 in a liberal sense, and there were liberals who criticized him for not changing the Constitution. One speaker accused him of doing an absurd and tyrannical thing in taking to himself the right to interpret the meaning of the law and in drawing up a royal order which was clearly opposed to Article 11 of the Constitution. The opposite point of view was presented by a spokesman for the Republican minority who asked for full freedom of religion, civil marriage without religious impediments, the secularization of cemeteries, and the freedom of schools from clerical control and influence. Holding that he did not oppose Catholic dogma but rather Catholic politics, he declared that the religious question was the fundamental one in Spain and that all Spaniards were divided on that question into rightists and leftists, ultramontanes and liberals.[28]

The high point of religious toleration was reached during the Canalejas régime. After his assassination in 1912, some liberals continued to plead the cause of religious minorities, and some advances were made, but, as we have already pointed out, political expediency prevented the determined, long-range advocacy of religious freedom which would have brought its establishment. At one time liberals announced their intention of changing the Constitution to grant full freedom to all religions, but Roman Catholic opposition and the inertia of many liberals led to an abandonment of the plan.[29]

This survey of the practice of religious toleration from 1902 to 1923 would not be complete without mention of some of the trials of persons accused of having committed offences against the Catholic religion. Some of the typical cases which reached the Supreme Court will be cited, but it should not be supposed that they were isolated cases, for there were many such. Some men who removed their hats but did not kneel when the cross was borne past them were declared innocent of any infraction of the law.[30] A man who had courteously refused to take off his hat at the passing of the *Viaticum* and had given as his reason that he belonged to another religion than the Catholic was absolved,[31] but one who, when asked by a priest to take off his hat for the *Viaticum*, said that he would not do so for anybody or anything was declared guilty of an infraction of the Penal Code.[32] There were cases of writers who were condemned for making mock of the Catholic religion,[33] and of others who were absolved on the grounds that in setting forth ideas contrary to the Catholic religion they had no intention of ridiculing that religion.[34]

In September of 1923 General Primo de Rivera issued a proclamation to the Spanish people announcing his intention of taking charge of the nation and saving it from the disaster to which the politicians had brought it. He was supported by a large part of the military forces and was promptly accepted by the King as head of the government. The Constitution was suspended, and opposition was rigorously suppressed, so far as that was possible. The dictator did many things which were applauded by the nation, but opposition to him increased as time went on, and in January of 1930 he resigned. It has been said of him that he gave Spain six years of material peace and public order, but that without knowing it he hatched a revolution.[35]

For Protestants the dictatorship meant a more limited toleration of their religion. In most cases their chapels and schools were permitted to remain open, but it was extremely difficult to begin work in new places. Protestants received many reminders that the Catholic religion enjoyed the favour of the authorities to a greater extent than had been the case for many years.

Not long after General Primo de Rivera took charge of the government, there was an official declaration that the same thing could be said of Spain that Mussolini had said of Italy: that some asked for work and others for justice, but that no one asked for freedom, since everybody had enough to conduct himself as a good citizen.[36] The officers of the Spanish Evangelical Alliance wrote to the dictator that there were thousands of Evangelical Christians who asked for religious freedom.[37] A few weeks later Spanish Protestants were alarmed when General Primo de Rivera said to a reporter from Cuba who asked about liberty of cults in Spain, 'At no time have we thought of that'.[38]

A Protestant missionary organization with work in Spain reported in 1926 that the leading men of the government had not personally interfered with Protestant activities but that little hindrance had been placed in the way of clerical and reactionary elements which were intent upon reducing the influence of Protestantism. Since the constitutional guarantees had been suspended, it was necessary to obtain permission for holding mass meetings and other unusual gatherings, and local officials often showed particular unwillingness to authorize Protestant meetings. One governor who granted permission for holding a meeting in a theatre without understanding clearly it was to be Evangelical in character, after learning the nature of the meeting, ordered the principal speaker not to make any allusion to religion, to the Church of Rome, to Protestantism, or to liberty of worship. The speaker obeyed the order, but his veiled allusions to the religious situation were so well understood that he was frequently interrupted by applause.[39]

There was censorship of the press during the dictatorship, and Spanish Protestant magazines could not publish all they wished concerning the reduction of religious liberty in Spain; but some things were published, including a letter from a committee of the Spanish Evangelical Alliance to the Minister of the Interior in 1927. This letter gave a list of cases in which Protestants had been denied certain rights. Included were the denial of permission to publish an Evangelical paper, refusal to authorize the opening of a chapel, and denial of permission for holding a special meeting. Listed also were the closing of a school, the prosecution of a pastor who spoke at a funeral in an unwalled place, and the exile of a pastor from a village because certain Protestants had allegedly insulted the local priest. The letter appealed to the central government to give instructions to subordinate officials on matters relating to religious toleration.[40]

The situation of Protestants in Spain was dramatized in 1926 by the arrest of a woman named Carmen Padín for saying in public that the Virgin Mary had other children after the birth of Jesus. She was condemned to two years, four months, and one day in prison. After insistent requests from the Spanish Evangelical Alliance and other groups that she be pardoned (and after most of her term of imprisonment had been served), her sentence was commuted to exile from her village for the remainder of her term.[41]

In 1928 a new Penal Code was adopted. The Code of 1870, which had remained in force until that time, was based on the Constitution of 1869, which established religious freedom, and it made no distinction between the Catholic religion and others, though in practice, as we have seen, certain articles of the Code were applied only to offences against the Catholic religion. The articles on religion in the new Penal Code were based clearly on the principle of religious toleration (rather than religious freedom) as established by the Constitution of 1876, and Protestants were given an inferior status. It was made a crime to attempt by force to abolish or change the religion of the State. This reminds one of the Code of 1848, though that Code did not include the words 'by force'. Disturbances of Catholic services were punished more severely than were disturbances of services of the dissident religions. Making mock of the Catholic religion was made a legal offence, while there was no prohibition of the scorning of other religions. A penalty—imprisonment for three to six years—was established for celebrating non-Catholic religious ceremonies or manifestations outside of temples or cemeteries. It will be recalled that the Code of 1848 punished with exile the celebration of acts of worship of a non-Catholic religion.[42]

On the seventh anniversary of the régime, in a manifesto dealing with some proposed changes in the Constitution, General Primo de Rivera said, 'If in a country of twenty million inhabitants nineteen and a half million are well protected in their rights, it is not of great importance that the remaining half million want fuller rights'. He stated that the ideal of Spain was to guarantee to its citizens all of the individual and collective rights which among modern peoples have been found good, well-founded, and useful. A Protestant commented that there was no right more fully proved by experience to be good, well-founded, and useful than complete liberty of cults.[43]

Protestants felt the effects of a mere toleration when a Spanish Evangelical Congress was held in Barcelona in 1929 and the use of a public hall was denied to the delegates.[44] The Congress considered the fact that in the proposed changes of the Spanish Consitution no alteration of Article 11 was contemplated, and it petitioned the government for religious freedom:

> The Spanish Evangelical Congress, in its closing session, agrees by acclamation to direct to the Government of His Majesty the respectful petition that measures be taken for the establishment in Spanish law of full liberty of cults. In the experience of half a century Article 11 of the present Constitution has proved completely inadequate for avoiding real molestations for Spanish Evangelicals, with the consequent blot upon the name of our beloved nation. The Congress earnestly desires legal guarantees for the rights of conscience in all the manifestations of life.
>
> This conclusion reflects the feeling of some 20,000 Spanish Protestants, who love their country intensely and wish to live in it with their heads held up, as citizens equally respected like the rest. No one excels them in the fulfilment of duties towards the nation, and they consider it their moral right that the future Constitution of their country should grant them, not mere religious toleration, but liberty of cults, which is a fundamental right of every human being.
>
> They desire that the impediments to civil marriage, founded on purely ecclesiastical reasons, should disappear; that the present separation of cemeteries, with its sequel of the indecorous state of many of the so-called 'civil' ones, should end; that there should not be imposed upon the dissident military man an obligation to submit to the official cult in 'acts of service'; that the conscience of the non-Catholic teacher and pupil in the national schools should be guaranteed; and that, finally, the other remainders of the intolerance which for several centuries has been the moral scourge of Spain should be erased.[45]

When General Primo de Rivera resigned, a Protestant missionary wrote of the difficulties experienced by Protestantism during his period of rule and added:

> Our Evangelical work has not been destroyed, as would have been

the desire of the 'great friends' of Primo de Rivera. With the Roman Church it is necessary either to be energetic, like Cánovas, or to submit to all of its exigencies. Primo did neither, and he fell, and great was his fall.[46]

After the resignation of General Primo de Rivera, there were two short-lived ministries, during which widespread dissatisfaction and disorder served as signs of the end of an era. Municipal elections held in April of 1931 resulted in many places in the victory of Republicans and Socialists. Seeing in the elections and the demonstrations of the public a repudiation of the monarchy, the King abandoned Spain, and a peaceful transition was made from a monarchy to a republic.[47]

Shortly before the elections of 1931, an article in a Protestant magazine showed that at least some Spanish Protestants shared the widespread disillusionment with the monarchy. The author refused to identify Protestantism with any particular form of government or political party, but he stated that Evangelicals would probably be openly on the side of any political movement which proposed freeing Spain from clericalism and effecting separation of Church and State.[48] Protestants were not active in politics and were very far from revolutionary plotting, but any régime which would grant them freedom and dignity would doubtless receive their gratitude and loyalty.

An examination of Spanish Protestantism during the reign of Alfonso XIII reveals several significant developments. Among these was the organization of the Spanish Evangelical Alliance on a national scale, in co-operation with the World's Evangelical Alliance, which since the time of Matamoros had demonstrated its interest in Spain. Under the auspices of the Spanish Evangelical Alliance a great Evangelical Congress was held in Madrid in 1919; and a second Congress was held in Barcelona ten years later, with 696 registered delegates. On a number of occasions the Alliance appealed to the authorities for greater religious freedom, and it rose to the defence of Protestants who found themselves in difficulties because of their religion. It also fostered the observance of joint prayer services among Evangelicals.[49]

A further move towards unity among Spanish Protestants was the suppression of several separate magazines in order to make possible a co-operative periodical. The new magazine was excellent and was widely read, but some denominational publications were continued.[50] Church union on a limited scale took place when in 1928 the Wesleyan Methodist Churches of Catalonia and the Balearic Islands joined the federation of the Spanish Evangelical Church.[51] The International Spanish Evangelization Committee was set up to co-ordinate the work of several mission committees sponsoring work in Spain.[52]

Schools—some good and some bad—continued to be operated by Protestants. The Fliedner school in Madrid, whose founding has already been noted, and the Model School in Alicante, which was developed with the help of the Methodist Episcopal Church of the United States, were numbered among the best schools in the country.[53] The highly significant educational work of the American Board of Commissioners for Foreign Missions was severely curtailed in this period. Whereas in 1903 this agency had a boarding school for girls, with twenty-six students, and fifteeen other schools, with 886 boys and girls enrolled, in 1931 it reported only four secondary school students and four primary and elementary schools, with four hundred pupils.[54]

There was a difference of opinion as to the value of Protestant schools. Their service to the children of Protestants was obvious, but many people doubted their evangelistic value. On the other hand, friends of the schools, while admitting that few of the pupils from non-Evangelical families became church members, were convinced that the schools helped to break down prejudices against Protestantism and to prepare the way for an evangelistic appeal later on.[55] It is certainly true that on more than one occasion Spanish Protestants have encountered friendliness and helpfulness in government officials and others who received their education or a part of it in Evangelical schools and therefore felt kindly disposed towards Protestants.

During this period some Protestant denominations grew and others declined. Congregationalist work showed much promise for a while, but then there was retrogression, and by 1931 only six organized churches, with 320 members, could be reported.[56] The various little Baptist groups in the country were consolidated under the direction of the Southern Baptist Convention of the United States, following an agreement to that effect by the Baptist World Alliance in 1920; and there followed a period of expansion until the financial depression in America made curtailment necessary. Spanish Baptists increased from about 600 adult members in 1922 to 1005 in 1931.[57] A non-denominational mission under the direction of Percy Buffard, a Baptist of England, carried on a rather flourishing work in the centre of Spain.[58] The various other Protestant groups were apparently holding their own or growing slowly.

On the whole, Protestant work was at a standstill. As we have already seen, the petition to General Primo de Rivera in 1929 referred to 'some 20,000 Spanish Protestants', but many of these were merely members of Protestant families or were 'sympathizers' and not communicant members of churches. A well-informed man wrote in 1923: 'After fifty years of effort by about ten denominations there are at present in Spain scarcely four thousand evangelical Christians'.[59]

On one subject Protestants were all agreed: the winning of Spaniards to their faith and to active participation in their churches was difficult. By no means, however, had they lost their conviction that Spain needed the Gospel which they proclaimed.

SEPARATION OF CHURCH AND STATE

THE Republic was inaugurated on a wave of enthusiasm and optimism in April of 1931. Representing a culmination of liberal and radical tendencies which had long existed in Spain, it was supported by persons of widely different points of view, including Catholics and atheists, middle-class Republicans, Socialists, and radicals of various kinds. Niceto Alcalá Zamora, a moderate liberal who was a devout Catholic and a recent monarchist, was made President of the Provisional Government, but his influence in the government was limited by men of less conservative convictions.[1]

One of the great achievements of the Republic was the separation of Church and State, which had been dreamed of before by Spaniards but never achieved. The glory of the achievement at this time was diminished by the fact that it was accompanied by anti-clericalism and was destined in a few years to be undone by clericalism.

Among the first acts of the Provisional Government was the proclamation of religious liberty.[2] It is not strange, therefore, that Protestants greeted the advent of the Republic with joy. An article in a Protestant magazine hailed the new régime and stated:

Liberty of cults . . . will permit the Gospel of Christ to be preached with full freedom; and those who have the honour of being known as Spanish Evangelicals will be able to work for the cause of the Gospel with the same freedom that those of other religious creeds have.

May God guide the Provisional Government of the Republic.[3]

By no means so hearty was the reception accorded the Republic by leaders of the Catholic Church. Cardinal Segura, Archbishop of Toledo and Primate of Spain, issued a pastoral letter in which he referred to the triumph of 'the enemies of the Kingdom of Jesus Christ' and placed himself in frank opposition to the Republic. The result was that he became an exile from his native land. Some members of the hierarchy, more prudent than Cardinal Segura, expressed their loyalty to the Republic and stated that the Church stands above national politics; but the general impression was that the Catholic Church was not friendly to the new régime.[4]

Hardly had the new government been instituted when violent anti-clericalism, manifested in the burning of churches and monasteries, broke out in various parts of Spain.[5] Though the responsibility for this vandalism has not been determined, we may suppose that it was connected in some way with the reaction to Cardinal Segura's pastoral letter. It was a disquieting augury for the future of the Republic. Spain's great weakness still lay in the strength of the extreme Left and Right.

Among the measures of the Provisional Government which were intended to implement the earlier proclamation of religious liberty were two that made religious freedom a reality in the army and navy. For soldiers and sailors attendance upon mass was made purely voluntary, and orders were given that officers and enlisted men should attend no religious functions in an official capacity and that military bands of music should take no part in religious acts.[6] This was quite an advance over the ruling of the monarchy that those who stated officially upon joining the armed services that they did not belong to the Roman Catholic Church would be excused from attending mass.

The practice of religious freedom was extended to the prisons of Spain through a decree that attendance upon mass by prisoners should be on a purely voluntary basis and that religious acts should be held only on the request of the prisoners. The corps of prison chaplains was to be gradually disbanded, but any prisoner would have the right to request any kind of religious service which might be possible where the prison was located, and expenses for such services would be paid by the State.[7] This meant that Protestant ministers and Catholic priests would have the same rights with regard to ministering in prisons.

One of the great bones of contention during the monarchy had been the question of religious instruction in the schools. The Catholic Church had always claimed the right to control education, and the most the liberals had ever been able to achieve was exemption from religious instruction for those children of the primary schools whose parents requested it and voluntary enrolment in Religion courses in the secondary schools. The Provisional Government of the Republic ruled (in a decree called by a Protestant magazine exactly what the Spanish Evangelical Alliance had been asking for)[8] that religious instruction should not be obligatory in the schools of the State but that it should be provided for those children whose parents requested it. In case the teachers should not wish to give this instruction, it would be given by priests, whose services would be offered free of charge. A paragraph in the preamble of the order indicated the desire of the government to measure up to the standard of religious liberty set by other nations:

One of the postulates of the Republic, and therefore of this Provisional Government, is religious liberty. With the recognition of this right, Spain places herself on the moral and spiritual plane of the democracies of Europe and of those democracies of America which, separated from Spain, inaugurated earlier those measures just taken here. Religious liberty, so far as the school is concerned, means respect for the conscience of the child and the teacher.[9]

The provisions of this order were amplified a little later in a circular letter which stated that teachers were freed from all obligation to engage in religious acts with their students or attend religious services or ceremonies. The symbols of religion could still be used in connection with school life only where the teacher and the parents of all the children wished it. The normal schools would cease to require Religion and would offer it only to those who might desire it.[10]

In a broad and at the same time explicit pronouncement on religious freedom, the Provisional Government declared that all religions were authorized to practise their cults privately or publicly, that no one in the military or civil service of the nation would be required to manifest his religion or be permitted to ask that other people manifest theirs, and that no one would be required to take part in religious ceremonies and practices. The establishment of religious liberty, said the decree, was in harmony with the practice of other nations and had been a goal of those who had worked through the years for the creation of the new, modern state of Spain. Mention was made of the advocacy of religious freedom by the Roman Catholic Church in countries where there are other State churches or where there are obstacles to her own freedom of action.[11]

One more measure taken by the Provisional Government must be mentioned: that concerning the question of burials, which during the monarchy had been a source of so much strife. It will be recalled that there was an official ruling that parents had the right to decide where their children would be buried, but this was reversed later when the government announced that the Catholic Church had the authority to decide who was to be buried with Catholic rites. The Provisional Government of the Republic ordered that municipal authorities should have full charge of the civil cemeteries (taking the place of the priests who had in some places kept the keys), that parents or guardians of children under age should decide where they would be buried, and that the expressed wish of a deceased person or his relatives' interpretation of this wish should decide whether or not he would have Catholic burial.[12]

The decrees of the Provisional Government were merely emergency measures, and the main task of lawmaking was left to the Constituent Cortes, which was elected to draw up a Constitution. The members of this body, when it assembled, agreed that the Church should be separated from the State; but some wished to treat it as an honoured institution with special rights and privileges in Spanish society, while others wished to deal with it as a hostile power and end its influence. An examination of a few of the speeches in the Cortes will throw light on the ideas and feelings with regard to the religious issue at that time.

The Minister of Justice, Fernando de los Ríos, made an eloquent plea for separation of Church and State as a means of ending the domination of the State by the Church and also governmental meddling in religious affairs. Calling himself a son of the Erasmians, he said that those like him had had their consciences strangled for centuries. There had been no respect, he declared, for their persons or their honour. and in the moment of death they had been separated from their parents. They were not Catholics, he said, not because they were not religious, but rather because they wanted to be.[13]

A member of the Cortes who said that he spoke in the name of free thought and liberalism declared that he also spoke as a Christian, since he found in Christianity the essence of democracy and freedom. He denied, however, that he was or ever had been a Catholic.[14] It is significant that he and others who said they were Christians but not Catholics were not Protestants either. There was, unfortunately, no one in the Cortes to speak in the name of Evangelical Christianity.

One of the speakers in favour of separation of Church and State insisted that it is axiomatic that the State should have no official religion, and he added that even if the Constitution were to say that neither the State nor the family nor the individual needed religion he would not object, for neither he nor his family had found religion necessary to live morally and æsthetically. He insisted that all religious orders should be dissolved and that the Church should be watched as the worst of all associations. There is talk about arousing the Catholic majority of the nation, he said, but there ought to be concern lest the anti-clerical minority be aroused. He quoted Anatole France as saying that the Church considers itself persecuted if it cannot persecute others and said that such was the case in Spain at that time. Quoting Bakunin to the effect that man goes to church and to the saloon because in his misery he wants illusions and dreams about a better world, the speaker predicted the disappearance of religion when better

5

conditions of life should be created. His was the point of view of the extreme Left, which should be classified as radical rather than liberal.[15]

Gil Robles lent the weight of his influence and oratory to the cause of the Catholic Church. After declaring that he did not oppose religious freedom, since the Catholic Church recognizes that it is sometimes necessary, he insisted that the Church be recognized as an independent, perfect society in its sphere; and he attacked the plan for dealing with the religious orders as contrary to individual liberty, freedom of association, and religious freedom, all of which were guaranteed in the Constitution itself. The constitutional draft, he declared, is a draft of religious persecution, and Catholics cannot accept it. He warned that if it should be approved he and others would use all possible legal and peaceful means to change it. The struggle might be long, he said, but the outcome of it was certain.[16]

A priest who was a member of the Cortes declared that those who had created the Republic did not know how to preserve it. A wise revolutionary, he said, would not have raised the religious question, certainly not in the exaggerated way it had been raised, but would have given everybody to understand that, though there would be great democratic and social advances, the profoundly religious sentiments of Spain would be respected. Any attempt to create an anti-Catholic Spain, he predicted, would meet with disaster.[17]

A spokesman for the Basque-Navarra minority in the Cortes called for religious freedom for the Catholic Church, which he said was being persecuted, and argued that the Spanish people were Catholic and that the State should be officially Catholic. He said that he and those for whom he spoke were willing to accept whatever concessions the Church felt were called for as a result of the revolution, but they were not willing to agree to conditions imposed upon the Church. He declared that the family was being destroyed and the school secularized, and he attacked especially the proposed laws concerning religious orders. It is anti-Catholic and contrary to human dignity and freedom, he said, that one type of association should be denied rights granted to others. The freedom of all organizations and of all individuals should be respected. If you try to persecute the Catholic Church, he threatened, you will be defeated—you will go to Canossa, just as the German Emperor, the other Spanish Republic, and many other powers have done.[18]

Niceto Alcalá Zamora, the President of the Provisional Government, gave a clear and logical statement of his opposition to the articles on religion in the proposed Constitution. He said that he did not identify himself with the Basque minority, since they ask for religious freedom only at the time of misfortune and defeat for the Catholic Church, whereas he advocated it all of the time and for all people; nor could he join with the majority of the Cortes, since they wanted a solution to the religious question which was not democratic and just. The proposed Constitution, he said, violates the rights of Catholics and contradicts its own basic principles. The assumption of some legislators that the Revolution gave a mandate to the Cortes to destroy the Catholic Church is false, for among the participants in the Revolution were Catholics as well as free thinkers. In keeping with a Spanish and Christian tradition, he continued, the civil power should defend itself against the encroachments of the religious orders, but the regulation of these orders should be left to flexible laws and not be determined in the Constitution. Separation of Church and State is good, he said, but this should be achieved through a Concordat with the Vatican instead of being decided unilaterally. Separation can be effected unilaterally in Protestant countries without great difficulty, since the Church is subordinated to the State; but the Catholic Church has never been completely subject to the power of any state. Its unity and universality demand that if separation is attempted it should be through mutual agreement, for if unilateral separation is achieved the visible head of the Church still remains outside the domination of the State and there may ensue a struggle which will be disastrous for the State. To be sure, the State must always keep the possible weapon of unilateral action but should try not to use it. A good formula, said Alcalá Zamora, is the following: a concordat neither imposed nor impeded, unilateral legislation only if the intransigence of the Church makes it necessary, encouragement to agreement so that if the comprehension of the Church permits there may be no wasteful struggle between Church and State. If the door to negotiation is closed now, he warned, there will be negotiation at another time when Parliament cannot defend the rights of the State. If the Constitution as proposed should be approved, concluded the speaker, he would not abandon the Republic, but for the good of the country and of the Republic he would turn to the Catholic masses of the country and to the unbelievers, free thinkers, heretics, and all others with a sense of justice and seek their aid in bringing about a change in the Constitution.[19]

Manuel Azaña, then Minister of War and soon to be head of the government, made a brilliant but provocative speech in which his major thesis was that Spain had ceased to be Catholic. He began by referring to the three great problems with which the Republic had to deal and whose solution would bring the transformation of the nation: the problem of local autonomies, that of social reform (with reference especially to property), and that of religion. The religious problem, he said, has back of it the premise that Spain has ceased to be Catholic. In the sixteenth century the nation was Catholic, in spite of the fact that there were many and important dissidents then; and Spain has ceased to be Catholic in spite of the fact that there are many millions of Spanish Catholics. What makes a country, a people, or a society religious is not the number of beliefs or believers it has but rather the creative force of its mind and the trend of its culture. For centuries European and Spanish thought were within the framework of Christianity, but that is no longer true. The Spanish State must be organized in keeping with the new spirit, the new Spanish culture. There is, continued the speaker, no altogether good solution to the religious problem of Spain. Freedom of conscience must be respected, but the Republic must also be protected, and that means elimination or strict control of whatever is dangerous to the State. Religious orders which are dangerous to the State must be suppressed, and education must be removed from the control and influence of the religious orders. The sad state of Spanish life is due largely to the influence of these orders on the consciences of the young, and the welfare of the nation demands that this influence be broken. Just as it would not be permitted that a professor in the university should teach the astronomy of Aristotle or the medicine of the sixteenth century, it cannot be permitted that the religious orders continue their antiquated teachings and methods. In the moral and political sciences they have the religious obligation to teach the very opposite of the basic principles of the modern state.[20]

So strong were the objections of Alcalá Zamora to the constitutional provisions on religion and to certain statements made by representatives of the government (especially Azaña) that he resigned as President of the Provisional Government, and another man resigned from the ministry for the same reason. Azaña, whose point of view was more nearly that of the majority of the Parliament, was named head of the government.[21]

The various articles on religion in the Constitution were approved by parliamentary majorities, and on 9th December 1931 the entire Constitution was approved. It provided for separation of Church and State which the first Republic had hoped for but had not achieved; and it established freedom of conscience and of worship and provided for the secularization of cemeteries, freedom to hold public office without reference to religious affiliation, and the secularization of schools. Churches were recognized as having the right to teach their doctrines in their own establishments. The family was declared to be under the protection of the State, and marriage was pronounced subject to dissolution by mutual agreement or by the request of either of the parties concerned when, in the latter case, a just cause was alleged. Norms were set for a future law on religious associations. The very extensiveness with which the religious question was dealt shows its importance in the minds of the legislators. The following articles are of particular interest:

Art. 3. The Spanish State has no official religion.

Art. 26. All religious confessions will be considered as Associations under a special law.

Neither the State, the regions, the provinces, nor the municipalities will maintain, favour, nor help economically the Churches, Associations, or religious Institutions.

A special law will determine the total extinction of the subsidy to the clergy within a maximum period of two years.

Those religious orders which, by their statutes, impose, in addition to the three canonical vows, another special vow of obedience to any authority other than the legitimate authority of the State, are hereby dissolved. Their possessions will be nationalized and devoted to charitable and educational ends.

The remaining religious orders will submit to a special law voted by this Constituent Cortes on the following bases:

(1) Dissolution of those which, by their activities, constitute a danger to the security of the State. . . .

(3) Incapacity to acquire or keep (directly or through intermediate persons) more property than that which can be shown to be used as living quarters or in direct connection with the fulfilment of their particular mission.

(4) Prohibition of activity in industry, commerce, or education. . . .

The property of the religious orders can be nationalized.

Art. 27. Liberty of conscience and the right to profess and practise any religion freely are guaranteed in Spanish territory, except for due respect to the demands of public morality.

Cemeteries will be subject exclusively to civil jurisdiction. There may not be a separation of parts within them for religious reasons.

All religions may practise their cults privately. Public manifestations of the cult must be authorized in each case by the government.

No one may be compelled to declare officially his religious beliefs.

The religious condition will not affect civil or political capacity, except for what is set forth in this Constitution for the naming of the President of the Republic and for serving as President of the Council of Ministers.[22]

Spanish Protestants naturally rejoiced over the adoption of a Constitution which granted them full freedom and placed them on an equality with their fellow citizens. The Constitution of 1869 had granted religious liberty in practice, but it had done so in such a way as to imply inferiority on the part of non-Catholics, and it had left the Roman Catholic Church as the official Church. It can be said, therefore, that religious freedom, in the strictest sense of the term, was implanted in Spain for the first time in 1931. The union of Church and State which had characterized Spain for centuries was ended. The following words express the satisfaction of one Protestant (and probably of many others) over the achievements of the Republic:

The new Spanish Constitution is one of the best of modern constitutions, superior to many that are in existence in countries which were and are considered more advanced than Spain. It does not fall into the radicalisms that some wanted, but it is a Constitution of leftists, and it has solved problems which, like that of the separation of Church and State, have taken thirty years to solve in some countries, such as the French Republic, and have not yet been solved in some countries, such as the Argentine Republic. . . . The Constitution is especially satisfactory for us as Spaniards and Evangelicals because it has solved the religious problem. . . .

We Spanish Protestants owe much to the Constituent Cortes, to the Provisional Government of the Republic, and, especially, to the Minister of Justice, Don Fernando de los Ríos, who with such skill has solved the religious problem, bringing an end to the legend of black Spain, which four centuries of monarchy could not end.[23]

Another Protestant statement is equally striking:

We Spanish Evangelicals, who have been calling for so many years for liberty of cults, secularization of cemeteries, civil marriage, respect for the conscience of soldiers and sailors, and the restoration of civil rights to former clerics—how could we fail to be content with the Republic, which has done these things in so few months?[24]

Cries of persecution went up from Roman Catholics. A Protestant pastor, in a defence of the régime against the Catholic charge of persecution, said that except for the lamentable burning of religious buildings some months earlier (the blame for which had not yet been determined) there had been absolutely no violation of the freedom of Catholics or of the legitimate rights of their Church. The Republic, he declared, had done nothing more than take away some of the special privileges which had been granted by other régimes, and that was not persecution.

He called for one step further, the ending of diplomatic relations with the Vatican.[25]

Following the adoption of the Constitution, Alcalá Zamora was elected President of the Republic, probably in an attempt to appease the more conservative sectors of public opinion. A Protestant leader, hailing his election as a good omen for the future, referred to him as the father of the Republic and as a man of moral integrity, broad vision, unshakable optimism, and patriotic abnegation. The religion of the President, said the writer, was different from his own, but it was gratifying to know that the first official of the nation was a man of religious faith.[26]

For nearly two years there was a period of leftist rule, with Azaña as Prime Minister. The rightists were by no means content, and at one time there was armed conflict. The Government proceeded with legislation which converted from theory into practice the provisions of the Constitution, including, of course, those dealing with religion. The Jesuit order was dissolved, and the budget for the clergy was reduced and then suppressed. In some respects the anti-clericalism of those in authority led them beyond the implications of the Constitution.[27]

A decree on education ended the teaching of Religion in the public schools.[28] This was in harmony with the constitutional requirement that education should be laical, but the Provisional Government had probably been more prudent when it ruled that Religion could be taught in the schools for those children whose parents desired it. Roman Catholic resentment of this measure could be expected, for education was not only taken from the control of the Church—it was completely secularized.

The 'petty, almost vindictive anti-clericalism' of the leaders of the Republic was revealed by their regulations concerning burial.[29] Not only were municipal cemeteries opened to all citizens, as one would expect after the establishment of religious freedom, but the walls between civil and religious cemeteries were torn down wherever the two were contiguous, and municipal authorities were given the right to expropriate parochial cemeteries wherever it might seem advisable to do so. Not content with deciding that the kind of burial to be given to minors and legally incompetent persons should be decided by their families, the Cortes ruled that no one who had reached the age of twenty could be given religious burial unless he had so determined before his death.[30] Some notaries who circulated printed blanks for people to sign indicating their desire for Catholic burial were reprimanded, and such acts were forbidden.[31] Instructions were given that soldiers should be given religious burial only when the wish for such burial had been duly manifested.[32]

Of equal gravity for the Roman Catholic Church were the regulations of the Republic regarding marriage. Catholics naturally objected strongly to the constitutional recognition of the right of divorce, and much of the subsequent legislation on marriage was equally unacceptable to them. First, orders were given that those who applied for civil marriage were not to be asked for any statement regarding their religion,[33] and then the Cortes passed a law that there would be only one legal form of marriage in Spain, civil marriage.[34] Though there was no prohibition of a religious ceremony in addition to the civil service, it had no legal validity. Marriage was thus not only completely removed from the control of the Church; its religious character lost all official recognition. A less anti-clerical régime would probably have seen the wisdom of permitting the Church to continue to preside fully over the marriages of those who wished Catholic marriage.

A new Penal Code, or at least an adaptation of that of 1870, continued the protection offered in the earlier Code to the adherents and practices of all religions. It provided penalties for forcing persons to engage in religious acts or hindering them from engaging in such acts, for disturbing religious acts or ceremonies, for profaning religious objects, hindering the functions of any minister, or ridiculing the beliefs or practices of any religion having adherents in Spain. In keeping with the Republican Constitution, the new Code established penalties for any public official who might obligate a person to declare officially his religious beliefs or to engage in religious acts. Penalties were also stipulated for those public officials who might try to hinder a person in the free exercise of his religion or who might seek to prevent a religious group from practising freely its cult.[35]

During this period Protestants enjoyed full freedom of action and received courtesies and consideration from officials of the government. Such would certainly be the testimony of the National Committee of Evangelical Propaganda which was organized to direct efforts to make the Protestant message known in Spain through public meetings and otherwise. A delegation of Protestants representing this committee called on the Socialist leader, Prieto, who was a member of the cabinet, to ask for his assistance. In spite of being very busy, he received them cordially and had a long conversation with them, after which he gave them a letter to the Ministry of the Interior that obtained for them an interview there. The Minister of the Interior sent telegrams to the governors of the provinces recommending to them that they place no obstacle in the way of the Committee of Evangelical Propaganda but rather see that help was given in case of any attempt at obstruction. The governors forwarded the instructions to the mayors, and the Protestant committee was able to carry on its work without the slightest difficulty.[36]

In 1933 the Cortes passed a Law of Confessions and Congregations which brought Roman Catholic opposition to the Republic to a climax. By the terms of this law, the property of the Catholic Church was nationalized, though all needed for religious functions could still be used by the Church; and the religious orders were forbidden to take part in commerce, industry, agriculture, and general education (as had been set forth in the Constitution). Mention should also be made of some provisions of the law which applied to Protestants. All religious groups had freedom to organize themselves as they might see fit, on the condition that their administrators and office holders were Spaniards. This meant that foreign missionaries would not be able to figure officially as pastors of churches or directors of church organizations. The right of the churches to found and administer schools for the teaching of their doctrines and equipment of their members was recognized. The non-Catholic confessions were required to report to the government the territorial location of their activities and their adherents.[37]

The Pope wrote an encyclical letter condemning the Law of Confessions and Congregations and other measures which he said indicated that the Republic was forsaking the Spanish tradition of good will towards the Catholic Church. He declared it was an error to affirm that separation of Church and State was licit and good in itself, and that the error was especially blameworthy when the nation concerned was almost wholly Catholic, as was the case with Spain. Charging that the new legislation seemed to be aimed at ruining the Church and putting it at the mercy of the civil power, he called upon Catholics to use all legitimate means to bring about a change in the laws.[38] The bishops of Spain condemned the Law of Confessions and forbade Catholics to send their children to State schools.[39] The Catholic Church now appeared in a new rôle as the great protagonist of religious liberty.

New elections held the latter part of 1933 resulted in the defeat of the Left, and a period of rule by the Right and the right Centre. It was immediately apparent that the anti-clerical measures of the Constitution would not be strictly enforced. The plans for suppressing education by the religious orders were held in abeyance, and priests were granted a part of their salaries. During this time a long-brewing leftist revolt broke out. A general strike paralysed most of Spain; there were armed rebellions in various parts of the country; churches, monasteries, and convents were burned; and priests and monks were killed. The government took a firm hold to restore order, and the Right enjoyed full control of Spanish affairs for a while.[40]

The various rightist parties formed an anti-Marxist alliance for the elections of 1936, and the leftists (Republicans, Socialists, Communists, Anarcho-Syndicalists, and others) formed the Popular Front.[41] Leaders of the Catholic Church actively entered the lists in favour of the rightist coalition, but most Protestants, fearing a return of intolerance and despotism should the rightists win, tended to look upon the Popular Front as the less dangerous of the two coalitions. The enemies of Protestantism in later years made much of the fact that one prominent Protestant openly endorsed the leftists.[42]

The Popular Front won a majority in the elections, and Azaña, who may be regarded as belonging to the left Centre, became Prime Minister. A little later President Alcalá Zamora was removed from office by the Cortes, and Azaña was elected in his place. There was only a small Communist minority in the Parliament, but more important was a rather extreme Socialist fraction led by Largo Caballero. Another Socialist group, led by Prieto, was far more moderate and was willing to join others in a gradual and orderly unfolding of leftist policy. A violent and bloody struggle between the two Socialist factions helped to weaken the State.[43]

The country was clearly on the edge of a precipice. The violence and lawlessness of extremists of the Left was matched by that of the Falange and other groups of the Right. Leftists and rightists were assassinated; churches and convents were burned; street fights took place; and strikes crippled industry and commerce. In a speech to the Cortes, Gil Robles indicted the government for leniency towards the doers of violence and stated, among other things, that 160 churches had been destroyed and 251 set on fire and otherwise attacked. Many officers of the army were dissatisfied because their privileges had been reduced, and they were thinking in terms of a military pronouncement such as those which had so often in the past changed the government of Spain. They could count on the support of many monarchists, Carlists, members of the privileged classes, and the higher clergy.[44]

In July of 1936 civil war started with the revolt of the garrison in Morocco. Many military units in Spain went over promptly to the Rebels (or the Nationalists, as they came to be called), for the movement was endorsed by most of the army officers; but a large part of the country, including Madrid and Barcelona, and also the Basque country (which was Catholic but wanted regional autonomy), remained true to the Republic. The Nationalists were unified under the leadership of General Francisco Franco. The civil war, complicated by the assistance of Italy and Germany to the Nationalists and by that of Russia to the Republicans or Loyalists, lasted for nearly three horrible years. The central government of the Republic swung sharply to the left and eventually fell largely under the control of Russian agents and Spanish Communists.[45]

Leftist extremists took things into their own hands in Republican Spain during the first days following the outbreak of civil war; and prominent people were killed, churches and other religious buildings were destroyed, and priests and monks were murdered in large numbers. Order was restored by the Government, but there was never complete domination of extremists by the forces of law and order. The Catholic Church was the object of hatred and violence, since from the beginning of the civil war it was clearly on the side of the enemies of the Republic. The Government itself was not friendly towards the Catholic Church, and no Catholic worship was permitted in most of Republican Spain until near the end of the war. The exact number of persons executed and murdered for religious reasons will probably never be known, but it is certain that there were thousands.[46]

On the whole, Protestants enjoyed as much freedom in Republican territory as could be expected in the abnormal circumstances of civil war. In the early months of the war a Protestant writer expressed gratification that churches were unmolested in Madrid and certain other places, but he expressed concern over the closing of Protestant churches in some parts of Spain, notably in Catalonia.[47] The British and Foreign Bible Society reported that in Barcelona reprisals against the Roman Catholic Church at the beginning of the civil war resulted in the burning of nearly every Catholic church in the city, but that none of the Protestant churches were destroyed. One was set on fire, but when the mob realized it was a Protestant church they helped to put out the fire.[48] In 1938 the Bible Society noted that the religious situation was complicated, and that though theoretically religious liberty existed in both Nationalist and Republican Spain there were wide areas in the former where Protestant work had been stopped and pastors had been killed or imprisoned, and there were places in the latter where Roman Catholic priests could not safely resume their religious functions.[49]

It appears that Protestants, as a general thing, remained loyal citizens of the Republic, though not in sympathy with the radical leftists who became dominant in the civil war. During the war a Spanish pastor expressed confidence that Spain would never be Communist, and he stated that if the Republic should win the war the nation would probably have some kind of Socialist administration.[50] He was probably echoing a widespread hope that more moderate elements would regain control once victory had been achieved.

A backward look may now be taken at the activities and growth of Protestantism during the Republic. In a great Socialist meeting in 1931, Indalecio Prieto lamented that there was no dissident religion in Spain to challenge the Roman Catholic Church. A Protestant pastor and editor wrote in reply that there were 200 Protestant churches and chapels in Spain, 200 schools, 2 hospitals, several magazines, and 20,000 Protestants. There *is*, he said, a dissident religion in Spain, and it is with the Republic in opposing the abuses of power and influence by the Catholic Church.[51] The numbers were obviously only an estimate.

In 1933 a rather thorough survey of Protestantism in Spain by Araujo and Grubb[52] listed 166 organized Protestant churches, 6259 communicant members (almost all Spaniards), and a total Evangelical community, including children of Protestants and people who attended services but were not members, of 21,900. The Protestant schools had an enrolment of 7459. There were 123 foreign workers, including wives of missionaries, and 142 national workers in the various churches.

Spanish Protestants were divided into four main groups: the Spanish Evangelical Church, the Plymouth Brethren, the

Baptists, and the Spanish Reformed Church. The Spanish Evangelical Church, which, as we have already seen, is a federation or union of churches whose main elements are Presbyterian, Congregationalist, and Methodist, contained 30 per cent of the Protestants in the country. Twenty-seven per cent of Spanish Evangelicals were affiliated with churches of the Plymouth Brethren, 17 per cent with Baptist churches, and 8 per cent with the Reformed Church (which is Episcopal). In addition to these four main groups, there were miscellaneous small bodies which comprised 18 per cent of the strength of Spanish Protestantism.

Araujo and Grubb commented—correctly, it would seem—that though the Spanish Evangelical Church and the Brethren were about equal numerically, the former exerted more influence in promoting the general growth of liberal views, since it had more and better educated national workers and was dominated to a lesser degree by foreign missionaries, and since it was spread more generally over the country. They noted, however, the superior evangelistic zeal of the Brethren and Baptists.

After more than sixty years of missionary work in Spain, the churches were still largely dependent upon foreign financial assistance and to a somewhat lesser degree upon the help of missionaries. Among the foreign groups helping the Spanish Evangelical Church or certain units of that Church were German committees, the Presbyterian Church in Ireland, the Wesleyan Methodist Church of England, the American Board of Commissioners for Foreign Missions, a Dutch committee, and a French mission. The Spanish and Portuguese Church Aid Society of the Anglican Church gave financial backing to the Spanish Reformed Church, and there were close ties between that Church and the Anglican Church in Ireland. The churches of the Brethren received financial aid and personal assistance from England, and the Baptists got help from America. The British and Foreign Bible Society and the National Bible Society of Scotland rendered invaluable service to the Protestant cause as a whole. More than half of the foreign Protestants working in Spanish churches were English Brethren, and there were Englishmen working in other branches of Protestantism. Next to the British, the Germans were the largest group of foreign missionaries in Spain, with thirteen workers.

The general situation of Protestantism at the end of the Republic was not greatly different from what it was in 1933. The advantages resulting from the establishment of religious freedom were to a great extent neutralized by the growth of religious indifference and even opposition to all religion. A Spanish pastor was quoted as follows in 1934:

The moral and religious level of the Spanish people has confessedly descended in an accentuated manner. The campaigns against the Roman Catholic Church have been many times confounded with things against the idea of God, and the activity of atheist literature increases the loss of faith, especially among the lower classes. . . .

To sum up, we would say that the republic has lost part of its liberal spirit; that the economic life of the nation is unstable because of the lack of tranquillity and because of the disorder which rules the land; that the moral and religious spirit of the people is on the down-grade; and that every kind of violence is the order of the day.[53]

Protestant expansion was also limited by a lack of funds. The period of religious freedom in Spain coincided with a financial depression in America and other parts of the world, and since Spanish churches were dependent upon foreign financial help for their support, a reduction of financial aid meant in many cases a reduction of the number of pastors and even the closing of some churches. New work could not be begun on any great scale by some denominations. A representative of the Baptists wrote in 1935, 'It is to be greatly regretted that we are unable to take advantage of the new and very great opportunities afforded by the Spanish Republic for the free preaching of the Gospel'.[54]

Still, there was Protestant activity and some progress. A number of new chapels were opened,[55] and mass meetings were held in an effort to make the Evangelical religion known in Spain. There was large attendance at some of the meetings, and much enthusiasm, but few conversions.[56] The numerical increase of the churches was slight. Baptist statistics, showing 1005 members in 1931[57] and only 1054 five years later,[58] may be taken as typical, though there were doubtless some groups which grew more than Baptists did. It was evident that however desirable religious liberty might be it was not the open-sesame of Protestant growth. The civil war naturally halted all progress and brought great losses to the churches.

The 'second Protestant Reformation' in Spain was having a hard time getting under way. At the end of the Republic, Protestantism had still not become a real and significant part of Spanish culture. That is one reason why reactionaries would not find it difficult to reduce religious liberty.

RETURN TO CATHOLIC UNITY

THE civil war, resulting in the dictatorship of General Franco, brought a revival of the ideal of Catholic unity in Spain. Under the present régime there have been no *autos de fe*, as in the sixteenth century, nor has Protestantism been completely suppressed, for times are different; but privileges and favours have been granted the Roman Catholic Church, and Protestants have found their freedom more limited than at any time since 1868. Indeed, 'the Spain of Franco . . . is Catholic Spain'.[1]

We shall look first at the movement towards Catholic unity during the period from 1936 to 1945. Then we shall see how the bases of religious toleration were broadened, and finally we shall take note of a new tendency to restrict the practice of toleration.

The 'crusade for God and country' conducted by General Franco and his Nationalists enjoyed the blessing of most of the leaders of the Catholic Church in Spain. In a joint pastoral letter soon after the outbreak of hostilities, the Spanish bishops referred to 'the continuous outrages' perpetrated by the Republic and affirmed that resort to force had been necessary to save the nation and its fundamental principles.[2] The Church thus joined with the army, Traditionalists (or Carlists), and Falangists to change the Government of Spain.[3]

From the very beginning General Franco manifested his intention of favouring the Roman Catholic Church. In a statement to an American newspaper reporter in 1937, he said, 'Our State must be a Catholic State in the social and spiritual sense, for the true Spain has been, is, and will be Catholic'.[4] At the same time there were assurances that the government of General Franco would practise religious toleration. The Spanish representative in London, the Duke of Alba, wrote as follows:

I think you should know that complete toleration now exists in
National Spain for all Christian communions, and that complete
toleration will continue to be the policy and practice of the National
Spanish Government after the war.
I make this statement on the authority of General Franco himself.[5]

Dr. Rushbrooke, Secretary of the Baptist World Alliance,
asked in a letter to the London *Times* what General Franco meant
by 'complete toleration' and enumerated the essential elements of
religious freedom as stated by the Oxford Conference. Among
these were freedom of public and private worship, freedom of
instruction, freedom of church organization and practice, and
freedom of Christian service and missionary activity at home
and abroad.[6] An authorized person wrote in reply: 'I have full
authority for saying that the complete toleration guaranteed by
General Franco connotes the "religious freedom" which Dr.
Rushbrooke so precisely defines'.[7] Experience was to prove that
it did not. It was not possible to create a Catholic State in Spain
without limiting the rights of religious minorities.

Many of the early measures of the Franco government showed
its Catholic character. The bishops were given the direction of
religion in prisons;[8] the day of Corpus Christi was declared the
national festival of Catholic unity;[9] and the Society of Jesus was
given the right to function in Spain.[10] The religious orders were
restored to the position they occupied before 1931, and the church
properties that had been nationalized were returned.[11] After the
final victory of the Nationalists, the support of the clergy was
introduced into the national budget by a law which referred as
follows to Catholic unity and to the clergy's aid in the war:

The Spanish State, conscious that its unity and greatness rest upon
the pillars of the Catholic Faith, the supreme inspirer of its imperial
undertakings, and desirous of showing once more and in a practical
way its filial attachment to the Church and of repairing at the same
time the iniquitous spoliation that the liberal governments made of
her patrimony . . ., proposes by this law to render due tribute to
the unselfish Spanish clergy, most efficient co-operators in our
victorious crusade.[12]

The lack of religious freedom was felt very soon in the Nationalist army and navy. There was an order requiring members of the armed services to pay military honour to the Holy Sacrament and to members of the hierarchy,[13] and there was a revalidation of the ruling of the monarchy that non-Catholic soldiers and sailors, though excused from personal religious acts such as confession and communion, would have to participate in corporate acts of honour to the Catholic religion.[14] Since the advent of Franco, many Protestants have been penalized for refusing to kneel during Catholic mass or other religious ceremonies which they were required to attend with their military units.[15]

The Catholic character of the new State was manifested clearly in its regulations on education. Protestant schools, which since the Revolution of 1868 had enjoyed full freedom, were closed,[16] and the Catholic religion became a required course of study in all schools.[17] It was a source of great sorrow to Spanish Protestants that their children, unless excused by a tolerant teacher, were required to study a religion which was not their own. The deference to the Catholic Church in education was strikingly stated in an order on intermediate education:

The teaching of religion, as can be inferred from the very nature of the Church and its code of Canon Law, belongs to the Roman Pontiff, as supreme Doctor of all the Church, and to the Bishops of the dioceses, as true teachers.

Spain, which today more than ever takes pride in its glorious seal of Catholic, proclaims the sovereignty of the Church in the matter of Religion and recognizes in all its fullness the bishops' inherent right to teach. Because of their divine mission and their competence, they will direct, watch over, and care for the instruction and Christian life in all centres of education.[18]

The Franco government did not long tarry in repealing the legislation of the Republic on cemeteries. A law stated that 'the sectarian spirit which animated all the legislation of the Republic of 1931 was expressed also in this matter of cemeteries, . . . and it even prohibited the religious burial of every person over twenty years of age who had not expressly manifested his desire [for it] . . . a regulation so sectarian that it probably has no precedent in the law of any civilized state'. Municipal authorities were ordered to rebuild the walls between civil and Catholic cemeteries and to return to the Church the cemeteries that had been expropriated. Ecclesiastical authorities were given the jurisdiction over Catholic cemeteries, and orders were given that all inscriptions or symbols which might be offensive to the Catholic religion should be removed from monuments and walls.[19] From this time on Protestants would sometimes have just cause for complaint over the lack of a decent place to bury their dead. There were also cases in which freedom of burial with Protestant rites was denied, though in most cases such burial was permitted.[20]

It is natural that the new State should seek to bring Spanish law and practice regarding marriage into harmony with Canon Law. The Republic's law of divorce was repealed,[21] and so was the law establishing civil marriage as the only legally recognized form of marriage in the nation.[22] The right of civil marriage for non-Catholics, as provided in the Civil Code of the monarchy, was recognized, but the government indicated a desire to limit the right:

Article 42 of the Civil Code recognizes the requirement of canonical marriage for all who, wishing to contract legal matrimony, profess the Catholic religion. The defective composition of this article, which did not even distinguish between the non-Catholicity of both of the contracting parties and only one, and also the faultiness of various other dispositions in the Code, . . . more marked since the publication of the new Canonical Code, incorporated in Spanish legislation . . . [in] 1919 . . ., calls for a careful revision of those articles. But this does not prevent them from having their due application while they are in force. . . .

Municipal judges will not authorize other civil marriages than those of persons who do not belong to the Catholic religion and who give documentary proof of their non-Catholicity, or, in case this documentary proof should not be possible, who present a sworn declaration of not having been baptized, to the accuracy of which declaration are bound the validity and civil effects of such marriages.[23]

The immediate significance of this order was with regard to

the documentary proof of not being a Catholic. The most the monarchy had ever required was a sworn declaration that those who applied for civil marriage were not professing Catholics, but now a documentary proof of not being Catholics would be expected of those who could not swear that they had never been baptized as Catholics. For several years this posed no particular difficulty for Protestants, since a letter from a Protestant pastor was accepted as proof of the non-Catholicity of those getting married. As we shall see further on, however, in time marriage became much more difficult for Protestants.

The extensive work of Bible colportage, which had been carried on for more than seventy years without interruption, became completely impossible under the Franco régime. The stock of more than 100,000 Bibles and other books and booklets in the offices of the British and Foreign Bible Society in Madrid was confiscated, and orders were given that all Bibles published by the Society should be seized wherever found.[24] Eventually compensation was given for the seized books, and the Bible Society was able, without authorization, to continue its operations on a very limited scale.[25] A few Protestant books have been published since Franco came to power, and a few are sent into Spain from abroad; but official permission has never been given for such publications, and books mailed into Spain often do not pass the censor.

Of perhaps even greater gravity for Protestants than all that has been thus far mentioned was the denial to them of freedom of worship. In some places in Nationalist territory (Seville, for example, and Madrid, after its occupation) Protestant churches were permitted to remain open, but in most areas they were closed. Just after the end of the war the British and Foreign Bible Society stated:

It is true that some Protestant churches are open and crowded with worshippers, but these are the exceptions. A study of Evangelical work in 147 Spanish towns and villages shows that in only thirty-three of them was the church open. In a number of cases the building had been sacked and furniture destroyed.[26]

Many of the Protestants whose chapels were closed met secretly for worship in private homes. The attendance was necessarily limited, and there was always danger of apprehension by the authorities. There were numerous arrests, fines, and imprisonments for holding clandestine religious meetings. A typical case of this kind was that of the small group of Baptists in Villafranca del Panadés, near Barcelona, who, after their chapel had been closed, were caught by the police in a religious service in the home of the pastor. The pastor was imprisoned for a month, and each person present was fined fifty pesetas. The official document imposing the fine stated that the offence was 'celebrating without government authorization a meeting dedicated to the practice of the Evangelical religion'.[27]

One explanation of the prohibition of Protestant worship is that Protestants were identified with the enemies of the new State. It is true that most Protestants sympathized with the Republican cause during the civil war and feared the rise of a régime which emphasized Catholic unity; but few were the Protestants who were involved in politics, and purely imaginary was the danger which some people saw in the meetings for worship.

Foreign Protestants in Spain were more fortunate than their Spanish co-religionists. Freedom of worship was recognized for them in a police order which stated that 'through a generous tolerance of the religious opinions of foreigners who reside in our country' dissident chapels would be permitted to continue; but it warned that such chapels must not have any external signs or emblems which might cause them to be confused with Spanish Roman Catholic churches.[28] Here we find a continuation of the old belief that all good Spaniards are Catholics, whereas foreigners might well be Protestants. Members of the Anglican Church in Barcelona state that in the months following the civil war the police watched those who attended their services to make sure that no Spaniard was among them.

Catholic unity was affirmed in an agreement of 1941 between the Spanish government and the Vatican. It declared that until a new Concordat should be signed (which, as we shall see, meant until 1953) the first four articles of the Concordat of 1851 would be regarded as being in force, and it bound the Spanish government not to legislate on matters of interest to the Church without first consulting the Holy See.[29] It will be recalled that Article 1 of the Concordat states that the Roman Catholic religion is the only one of the Spanish nation and that it will be maintained with all the rights and privileges granted it by 'the law of God and the prescriptions of the sacred Canons'. The other articles which were recognized as still in force guaranteed that education in the schools should be in conformity with Catholic doctrine and under the watchcare of the Church; that the hierarchy and clergy should be protected and aided by the government in carrying out their functions, especially in combating efforts 'to pervert the souls of the faithful and to corrupt customs' and in preventing the publication and circulation of evil or harmful books; and that there should be freedom in the exercise of ecclesiastical authority. The Franco government felt much more keenly than did the monarchy the obligation to fulfil the terms of the Concordat.

It should not be supposed that the government was completely subservient to the Church. The nation was Catholic, but it was also avowedly Falangist or Fascist (especially during the first years of the régime); and the Falangists, though convinced that Catholicism should be cultivated as an integral part of Spanish life, were rather jealous of Church power. The government insisted on certain time-honoured rights with respect to the Church, and it did not hesitate to use those rights. By the terms of the agreement of 1941—continued by the Concordat of 1953 —when there is an episcopal vacancy, the Spanish government submits to Rome secretly a list of at least six candidates for the post. The Vatican returns three of the names, or in case it cannot approve three of the candidates it submits others, which in turn can be accepted or rejected by the government. From the names sent by the Pope, the head of the Spanish State makes his appointment.

Without the support of the Church, the Franco régime could probably not have come into existence, nor could it have maintained itself through the years. This does not mean, however, that the Spanish hierarchy approve of all of the policies of the government, nor that all Catholic leaders are faithful supporters of the régime. Some members of the hierarchy have especially resented the government censorship of their pastoral letters.[30] Some Catholics believe that the government uses the Church as a tool to fulfil its purpose and as a shield to protect itself.[31]

There can be no doubt, however, of the government's consistent intention to favour Catholicism. The new Penal Code promulgated in 1944 showed this intention. Religion was dealt with as in the Code of 1928. Catholics were thus given full protection of their religion, while Protestants were left with less defence than they had enjoyed during most of the monarchy.[32]

Foreign interest in the matter of religious freedom in Spain reached a high point towards the close of the Second World War. Religious freedom was one of the four freedoms which the Allies had announced their intention of establishing in the world. Protestants called upon the British Foreign Office and Parliament to use their influence with the Spanish government in favour of religious liberty in Spain. Newspapers took the matter up, and public opinion in Great Britain, the United States, and other countries was aroused.[33]

In July of 1945 the situation of Protestants in Spain improved markedly with the promulgation of the Charter of the Spanish People, a statement of the rights and duties of Spaniards. By Article 6, which was drawn up in consultation with the Holy See,[34] the Catholic religion was assured of official protection, but non-Catholics were guaranteed the right of private worship:

The profession and practice of the Catholic religion, which is that of the Spanish State, will enjoy official protection.

No one will be molested for his religious beliefs, nor for the private practice of his cult. No external ceremonies or manifestations other than those of the Catholic religion will be permitted.[35]

On the day the Charter of the Spanish People was unanimously adopted by the Cortes, Esteban Bilbao, President of the Cortes and chairman of the commission that had prepared the document, made a notable speech in which he said that Spain was continuing to give an example to the world in its recognition of human rights and liberties. The Charter, he said, guarantees the dignity of the human person and all his legitimate liberties, including liberty of conscience—not that which proclaims the absolute sovereignty of reason or which affirms unlimited freedom to choose truth and error, good and evil, but that which 'glorified in Calvary, maintained its rights before the absolutism of the Cæsars, was dyed with blood in the century of the martyrs, . . . practised true democracy, and fulminated and ever continues to fulminate, from Vatican Hill, its constant anathema against all the despots of the world and against all the tyrants of history'. He paid high tribute to the prelates who were members of the Cortes and had collaborated so well in the drawing up of the Charter, and he referred to them as 'indisputable rectors of our consciences'. The Charter, he said, 'is a commendable formula which, without violating in the least the supernatural essence of the Faith, . . . affirms without persecution and protects without violence that religious unity which is the soul of our history, the creed of a hundred generations, and the supreme ideal for which the heroes and martyrs of our glorious Crusade shed their blood and offered up their lives'.[36]

The real significance of Article 6 of the Charter of the Spanish People would depend upon the interpretation given to the right of private worship. Though the Constitution of the monarchy had not mentioned the word 'private' and had referred to 'public manifestations' rather than 'external manifestations', in reality it had been regarded as authorizing the private worship of non-Catholics, in the sense of worship within their chapels. The Republican Constitution guaranteed the right of all religions to 'practise their cults privately' —meaning within their places of worship—but required special authorization for public manifestations of religion; and Roman

Catholics complained that under the Republic they lost their right of public worship.[37]

It is evident that if the Charter of the Spanish People should be interpreted somewhat broadly and in harmony with the Spanish tradition of the preceding seventy years or so it would permit a return, so far as Protestant worship was concerned, at least to the pre-1910 situation. The leaders of the Roman Catholic Church, however, apparently regarded it as closer to the Concordat than was the Constitution of 1876, and therefore more restrictive of the liberties of non-Catholics. Quite obviously 'private worship' could be interpreted (and would be by some) as that of individuals or families within their own homes. The opposite extreme interpretation was that of the Protestant who suggested that 'private' meant 'not state, not national'.[38] One suspects that Article 6 was purposely made ambiguous so that it might be differently interpreted as expediency might demand.

Several months later the government gave an official interpretation of the article. It stated that certain non-Catholic chapels had been closed earlier because those in charge of them were hostile to the new régime and the chapels constituted a danger to 'the indispensable spiritual unity of the Spanish people', but that the reasons for the closing of the chapels had disappeared (presumably only the political reasons), and that the time had come for the re-establishment of normal conditions. Non-Catholic cults would therefore be permitted within dissident temples, provided there was no manifestation or evidence of these cults in the streets. Those who wished to open places of worship would have to request permission from the governor of the province concerned. The authorities would protect authorized worship, and would not interfere with it so long as there was no mixture of worship with propaganda, political activity, or other things not purely religious.[39] This order was similar to that drawn up by Cánovas del Castillo in 1876, but the mention of propaganda and the requirement that permission be obtained for the opening of chapels, instead of notification being given of their opening, indicated that Protestants might expect less freedom than they had enjoyed under the monarchy.

Shortly after the promulgation of the Charter of the Spanish People, its significance for Protestantism in Spain was summed up by an article entitled 'A Great Opportunity' in a Protestant periodical. 'We know that [the door of opportunity] is not fully open', stated the author, 'and we would desire a good many more things in order to be able to proclaim the Gospel with full freedom; but the fact that the door has begun to move is not only a reality which in itself should constitute a motive for the praise of our Lord but is, at the same time, a certain promise that we are to see greater things'.[40]

The years from 1945 to 1947 were good ones for Spanish Protestants. Religious freedom was not complete, for the earlier regulations concerning religion in the army, schools, burial, marriage, etc., continued in force; but Protestants easily obtained permits to open chapels (some even in places where there had never been Protestant churches), and they were largely unhindered in their work. Though they could not engage openly in evangelistic efforts outside their chapels and did not have use of ordinary means of propaganda, there were many conversions to the Evangelical faith, and the churches entered upon a period of new vitality. One missionary reported that during her thirty-five years of service in Spain she had not seen such a movement towards Evangelical Christianity as that which took place at this time.[41]

In August of 1947 General Franco was quoted in both the foreign and the Spanish press as saying:

In Spain non-Catholic confessions enjoy liberty and are protected by the article of the Charter of the Spanish People which respects liberty of conscience. Protestant churches now exist in the same places of Spain where they existed under other régimes, though they are necessarily few, since the religion of almost the totality of the Spanish people is Catholic and the majority of the few who do not profess it are atheists, thereby reducing Protestants to foreigners or persons of foreign origin or people who have lived for many years outside of Spain.[42]

Protestant churches did not then exist in all the places where there had been churches earlier, for there was a lack of leaders and also a lack of facilities, and some Protestant property which had been confiscated had not been returned; but it is true that Protestant churches (composed, incidentally, for the most part of Spaniards who had lived all of their lives in Spain), were about as numerous as they had ever been. It was not correct to say that 'non-Catholic confessions enjoy liberty', but there was a fairly generous religious toleration, and Protestants were making good use of it.

Roman Catholics were alarmed by Protestant progress, and they resolved to stop it. In the autumn of 1947 a determined anti-Protestant campaign got under way. Denunciations of Protestantism appeared in bishops' pastoral letters, in the pulpits of Catholic churches, in handbills distributed in the streets, in the daily press, and elsewhere. Some of the participants in the anti-Protestant drive wanted to close all non-Catholic churches, but others would be satisfied with the elimination of Protestant proselytism and the denial of permits to open new chapels. So striking were the pronouncements against dissident religions, and so strange in the middle of the twentieth century, that we shall take note of some of them.

Cardinal Segura of Seville, the great arch-enemy of Protestantism and of religious liberty, began the campaign with a protest against the opening of new Protestant chapels. He said that the hundreds of martyrs who gave their blood for the defence of the faith in the recent civil war cried out against it, and he quoted Balmes' statement that Protestantism if introduced into Spain would lead to factionalism, strife, vengeance, demoralization, and catastrophe.[43] A few weeks later Monseñor Vizcarra, the General Counsellor of Catholic Action in Spain, referred to the 'alarming growth' of Protestantism, which he called a new enemy; and he cast suspicions upon the motives of foreigners who gave aid to this enemy of Spain.[44]

A handbill distributed in the streets of Barcelona, apparently by Traditionalists (the bearers of the old Carlist zeal for religious unity), charged that Protestantism was attempting to establish itself on the blood of the martyrs of the civil war. It said further:

> For two years Protestantism has been struggling to take root in the soul of our dear country, thus threatening seriously to break our Catholic unity and even destroy our national unity, which has been forged on the anvil of Catholicism. . . .
> Upon those who exercise the function of authority rests the responsibility of vigorously extirpating to the roots this very serious evil.
> May there be constancy in fulfilling the duty which rests upon all Spanish Catholics, and to which we dedicate ourselves, not to permit Protestant activity in our national territory.[45]

A handbill distributed in Albacete contained the following statement:

> We will not be deceived by the empty words that float in the atmosphere of FARSE that characterizes our times. LIBERTY, TOLERANCE, UNDERSTANDING. Yes, But of these we cannot grant to the corrupters of souls more than the laws of all countries grant to the corrupters of minors or the editors of obscenities.[46]

The Archbishop of Zaragoza issued a pastoral letter warning against Protestantism:

> Educated Catholics are not led astray, but . . . [Protestants] seek chiefly ignorant, uneducated people. . . . The law in Spain does not permit either the public worship of other religions nor the diffusion of their doctrines, and they can engage in acts of proselytism only fraudulently and by flouting the vigilance of the authorities. Unfortunately, it is not a question just of increasing among us the number of adherents of the Reformation, so discredited and decadent, but of increasing the number of incredulous, of bad Spaniards, of internal enemies of the nation.[47]

An article in a Madrid newspaper repeated the old argument that Protestantism cannot have the same rights as Catholicism because error does not have the same rights as truth, and it continued:

> The government which declares that it does not know which religion is the true one cannot in good logic prohibit the propaganda of any (and that is the case, apparently, with the governments of Protestant countries like England); but a government, like that of

Spain, which affirms and believes that the Catholic is the true religion, cannot grant the same rights to others, which it knows positively to be false. That is why . . . in other nations liberty is granted to the Catholic minority and here it is not granted to the Protestant minority nor any other religious minority.[48]

One of the strongest and most frequently repeated arguments against Protestantism was that it is a foreign religion, whereas Catholicism is the religion of all true Spaniards. Protestant missionary work was regarded as definitely anti-Spanish, as can be seen in the following excerpt from a Barcelona newspaper:

We know that the plans and methods of this propaganda against our religious unity come to Spain from abroad. These foreigners who dedicate themselves to anti-Spanish activities in our country . . . are doubly guilty, for they take advantage of our hospitality and then attack the basis of our national unity. Once these people are discovered we have the obligation to return them to their respective countries. Our tolerance could go that far! And as for the Spaniards who help them—they are paid to do so, and many do not realize what it means for their own souls and for the unity of the nation—we must remind them of their duties as Spaniards and then, for the national good, of the existence of our legislation.[49]

The Bishop of Barcelona issued a pastoral letter on 'Catholic Unity and the Tolerance of Cults', which was published in the local press and widely commented on. He said that Protestants had taken advantage of a false interpretation of the Charter of the Spanish People, and were engaging extensively in propaganda and proselytism. Quoting Pope Leo XIII as denying the right of non-Catholics to toleration except when necessary in order to avoid some great evil or achieve some great good, he declared that such reasons did not exist in Spain, but, on the contrary, that great evils would come from the weakening or breaking of Catholic unity. He said that Spain, above all other countries, ought to hold Catholicism 'as the only religion of the State, to the exclusion of all other modes of worship', as taught by the *Syllabus of Errors*. He declared that the Charter of the Spanish People restricted toleration of dissident religions more than did the Constitution of the monarchy, and he called attention to the fact that the first four articles of the Concordat were in force. Toleration, he concluded, should be kept strictly within the limits of the law; and Catholics should do everything possible, but without violence, to maintain Catholic unity. Though no one must be forced to accept the Catholic faith against his will, care must be taken that no Catholic abandon the faith.[50]

The Spanish archbishops took up with General Franco the question of national policy on religion and wrote a joint pastoral letter warning the faithful against Protestant propaganda and proselytism. They called for Catholic unity and the limitation of Protestant freedom to the private worship permitted by the Charter of the Spanish People:

> The circumstances of Spain . . . are those of 'Catholic unity'. The Spaniards who do not profess the Catholic faith, and especially the adherents of confessions distinct from the Catholic, are so insignificant in number that they cannot be taken into account for a law looking to the social community. If in Article 6 of the Charter of the Spanish People there was introduced an element of tolerance of dissident cults it was for the foreigners who live in Spain. . . .
>
> This article . . . has a more restrictive sense than Article 11 of the Constitution of 1876. . . . [It] says clearly that what it authorizes or tolerates is the private practice of non-Catholic worship, but that other external ceremonies or manifestations than those of the Catholic religion will not be permitted. Therefore, Article 6 of the Charter of the Spanish People cannot be called, as has been done by some Protestants, a law of freedom of cults; and, what is worse, be used as a cover for engaging in public acts of worship and Protestant proselytism as if liberty of cults had been established in Spain—a procedure that has given rise to unpleasant acts commented on outside of Spain. What we Spanish bishops ask, in fulfilment of our duty, is the observance of what was established on this point in the fundamental law of the Charter of the Spanish People after this most delicate matter had been discussed with the Holy See.[51]

Some of the more hot-headed enemies of Protestantism in Spain did not limit themselves to talking or writing, but resorted to violence in an effort to frighten the Protestants and impress the government with the undesirability of giving freedom to non-Catholics. Several Protestant chapels were invaded by bands of young men who destroyed furniture, hymn books, and Bibles, and in a few instances did physical harm to those present.[52] The raid on a chapel in Granollers, near Barcelona, may be taken as typical. The following account appeared in a Carlist leaflet and will, therefore, permit us to look at what occurred through the eyes of persons in favour of the violence:

> On Sunday, September 21 [1947], in Granollers . . ., a group of Requetés assaulted the Protestant 'chapel' of the locality. Without wishing it or expressly planning it thus, they found themselves in the 'chapel' at the time an 'evangelical' (?) session was being held.
>
> The 'pastor' (who was reading a book which he declared to be the Bible) was told that we would not permit any offence against Catholic unity, especially after the Crusade of 1936, which was made expressly to sweep from Spain for ever all the evils and disasters of the Republic and the liberal monarchy; and that one of the evils which both intro- duced, to the detriment of our unity, was Protestant activity . . ., which the Requetés would not tolerate.
>
> The 'chapel' was left materially unserviceable after the action of our boys, and the heretical library which was there was also destroyed.[53]

One naturally wonders what was the responsibility of the Catholic Church for these acts of violence. A Catholic magazine of Madrid, in reply to a question, stated that it was permissible to enter Protestant chapels with the intention of creating disturbances and thus hindering the winning of proselytes when no other means was available for counteracting or stopping the harmful work of the Protestants. The writer added that if it were certain that good results would follow such acts of obstruction there would be an obligation to engage in them.[54] Another Catholic writer said that those who destroyed Protestant religious property were not obliged to make restitution, because they believed they were performing a good act in the service of the true religion. He went on to say that acts of violence were not to be recom- mended since the most they could achieve would be, first, a demonstration that in Spain Catholics and heretics cannot live together peacefully, and second, a reminder that the Charter of the Spanish People should strictly be enforced.[55]

6

The above statements should not be taken as expressions of a general attitude or policy of the Catholic Church in Spain, for the hierarchy made known its disapproval of the use of violence. We have already observed that the Bishop of Barcelona, while calling upon Spanish Catholics to protect Catholic unity, warned them not to resort to violence. The Spanish archbishops, in the joint pastoral letter from which we have already quoted, stated that Protestant efforts at proselytism should not be combated by violence but rather by denouncing violations of the law and calling for a strict fulfilment of the law. We must conclude, therefore, that in spite of the fact that encouragement was given by some Catholics in places of influence to violence against Protestant churches the Catholic Church as such did not plan or encourage it. Those who raided Protestant churches were irresponsible young men who felt that they were doing their religious duty by breaking up Protestant worship. The sense of duty had been heightened, to be sure, by pronouncements of the hierarchy and the clergy against Protestantism.

What was the attitude of the government towards the anti-Protestant violence? Since it received publicity abroad and had international repercussions, the government deplored it and sought to prevent it. Several Protestant churches were protected by police guards for months, and in some instances damage was recompensed by the State.

The government was, however, influenced by the anti-Protestant violence and propaganda. One of the chief purposes of both was evidently to impress the government with the inexpediency of freedom for Protestantism. After the anti-Protestant campaign got under way, religious liberty began to be reduced. Perhaps the change was due in part to the aggressiveness of Protestantism in Spain, and in part to developments in international affairs (Spain's gestures towards freedom had not brought acceptance by the United Nations),[56] but quite obviously a primary factor was the Catholic pressure upon the government. Protestants in Spain quite generally believe that they would have far greater freedom if it were not for this pressure.

It became extremely difficult, and generally impossible, to obtain permits to open Protestant chapels. Most applications for permits went unanswered. This meant a serious curtailment of Protestant efforts at expansion in new places, and it also meant in some cases a denial of freedom to open churches which had long been in existence, but which had for some reason not been opened in the months of comparative freedom following the promulgation of the Charter of the Spanish People. Numbers of chapels opened earlier were closed because of an irregularity in the matter of a permit or the lack of one. In 1949 British Foreign Secretary Ernest Bevan told the House of Commons that he had been trying unsuccessfully for more than a year to obtain the re-opening of seven Protestant chapels in Spain that were British property.[57]

Numerous petitions were sent by Spanish Protestants to the authorities for a correction of injustices and a fulfilment of the Charter of the Spanish People as it was originally interpreted. One of these stated that Protestants were grateful for the toleration introduced by the Charter of the Spanish People, but that they had noticed a reduction of the limits of that toleration since the Spanish archbishops and others had spoken out against Protestantism. Spanish Protestants, said the petitioners, at times found themselves in the unhappy situation of being forced to obey clandestinely the dictates of their consciences. They requested, therefore, the following things: (1) clear instructions concerning the conditions to be fulfilled for opening chapels, (2) guarantees of freedom of worship without impediments or disturbances, (3) the right to hold services in private homes in places where there was no chapel, (4) permission to print Bibles, hymn books, and other literature, (5) permission to reopen and establish schools for children of Evangelical families, (6) respect for the consciences of those attending State and private schools, (7) guarantees of freedom of civil marriage for members of Evangelical churches, (8) freedom to receive the benefits of public social welfare without religious conditions, (9) exemption from Catholic religious practices for Evangelicals in the armed services and penal institutions, and (10) guarantees of the right of Protestants to bury their dead with religious rites and in decorous cemeteries.[58]

The authors of the above petition received as a reply a copy of an order from the Minister of the Interior to the provincial governors. Referring to Protestant 'abuses and excesses' under the protection of the Charter of the Spanish People, and making the unsubstantiated charge that Protestant chapels had earlier been 'Masonic centres of conspirators against the public order', the Minister made clear that only private worship, meaning that which is strictly personal or that which is carried out in the interior of regular places of worship, was authorized to non-Catholics in Spain. He also stated that there could be no external or public manifestations of dissident religions, and that proselytism and propaganda by these religions were absolutely prohibited. Protestants were specifically forbidden to have schools, to make 'gifts with a beneficent appearance', and to have centres of recreation.[59] This order showed that restrictions on freedom were not just local occurrences, but followed a policy laid down by the government in Madrid.

There was a relaxation of the pressure upon Protestantism in 1951, when most nations resumed diplomatic relations with Spain, and the American Ambassador, apparently under instructions of the President, put the entire weight of his influence on the side of religious freedom. Though the authorities became less vigilant in controlling the activities of Protestants, there was, however, no clear-cut improvement in the legal situation, and the only concrete concession which the Ambassador was able to extract from the government was permission to open a new Baptist chapel in Alicante which had been kept closed for many months. A favourite joke among the Baptists of Alicante was that their chapel was the most expensive in the world, since its opening was made possible through millions of American dollars granted to the Spanish government.[60]

When the Ambassador's term of service ended, President Truman stated that he still did not like the Spanish régime, and

the Ambassador explained that the President's dislike was due
to the continued religious intolerance there. These statements
had wide repercussions in Spain, and America was accused of
attempting to intervene in Spain's internal affairs. The reaction
of the government was indicated in a note given to the press
by the Office of Diplomatic Information of the Ministry of
Foreign Affairs. Denouncing vigorously the words of the
President and all attempts at intervention by foreign powers in
the internal affairs of the country, it affirmed the policy of
Catholic unity and the toleration of private worship for dissident
religions. It stated that there were only about 20,000 Protestants
in Spain (only half of them Spaniards), representing less than
one-thousandth of the population, but that they had nearly 200
chapels and a number of pastors which in proportion to members
was far higher than that of the Catholic Church. The note ended
with the warning that if the rulers of some countries thought
that under the cover of friendly relations they could foment
religious dissidence in the nation they were greatly mistaken.[61]
The government had evidently decided that more was to be
gained through unqualified support of the Catholic Church than
through concessions which might please friends of religious
liberty in other countries. Representatives of the United States
became much more cautious about manifesting their interest in
religious freedom.

There were new denunciations of Protestantism by Catholic
leaders. Especially vociferous was Cardinal Segura, who not only
denounced Protestants and their activities, but accused the
government of forsaking Catholic unity. He said, 'Catholics are
apprehensive lest, under the pretext of politics, concessions
gravely prejudicial to religion may be made'. A Falangist newspaper took exception to his charge of official leniency towards
Protestantism and said, 'We doubt that anyone can point out
any nation in the world whose government has been more
diligent than the Spanish régime in the service of the Catholic
faith'.[62] Cardinal Segura's opposition to the Franco régime
eventually led to his retirement from active church leadership,

apparently by agreement between the Spanish government and the Vatican.[63]

Whatever doubts there had been as to the worthiness of the régime to receive Catholic support were to a great degree allayed by the signing of a new Concordat between Spain and the Holy See on 27th August 1953. The Spanish Foreign Minister pointed out that this Concordat is by no means a treaty of peace between hostile powers (as some Concordats have been), but is rather a systematization of the almost ideal relations that have existed between Church and State since the advent of General Franco.[64] This systematization involves the assertion by the State of some rights over the Church—the nomination of high ecclesiastics, for example—but more important are the guarantees of financial support and other rights and privileges of the Church and clergy. The Concordat reveals clearly the partnership of Church and State.

The new Concordat, like that of 1851, affirms Catholic unity, but without the alarming phrase, 'with the exclusion of all other cults', that is found in the earlier document. The first article reads as follows:

The Apostolic Roman Catholic religion continues to be the only one of the Spanish nation and will enjoy the rights and prerogatives which it should have in conformity with divine law and canonical law.[65]

A supplementary agreement reaffirms what was established by Article 6 of the Charter of the Spanish People. Thus is recognized the right of private worship without 'external ceremonies or manifestations' for non-Catholics. In a speech on the Concordat in the Cortes, General Franco said that the principle of religious unity had been combined perfectly with the right of private worship for members of dissident churches and the maintenance of the *status quo* in the African territories (where Mohammedanism not only enjoys full freedom but also receives support from the government). He made clear that the toleration of different beliefs and forms of worship does not mean freedom of propaganda or proselytism, for, said he, 'the totality of the nation wants to conserve, at whatever price, its Catholic unity'.[66]

Just after the signing of the Concordat, the Spanish Foreign Minister told the Press that the most striking parts of the agreement are those dealing with marriage and education. These, he said, could be taken as a model by any Catholic State.[67] For non-Catholics they mean, in two important areas of life, a continued denial of religious liberty.

On the subject of marriage the Concordat recognizes the absolute competency of the Roman Catholic Church so far as Catholics are concerned. In the case of mixed marriages it is agreed that the State will bring its legislation into harmony with canonical law. This means, among other things, that a Protestant and Catholic can be married only in the Catholic Church, after they have given the usual vows to bring up their children in the Catholic faith. The agreement provides also that in the case of unbaptized persons there will be no 'impediments opposed to natural law'. This is apparently a recognition of the right of unbaptized persons to marry according to their choice, except for reasons opposed to nature, such as impotence or insanity.

The Concordat does not solve the problem of those non-Catholics who were baptized as infants in the Catholic Church and now wish civil marriage. Their problem has grown in seriousness in recent years. After the Pope altered the Canonical Code in 1948, so as to make more binding the obligation of canonical marriage for all persons baptized as Catholics,[68] civil marriage became much more difficult in Spain. The authorities began to insist that only those who had not been baptized as Roman Catholics were not Catholics and, therefore, had the right to be married outside the Roman Catholic Church. Baptism, they said, imparts an indelible character which is not lost when one separates from the Roman Church, and civil marriage is authorized only for those who do not belong to the Roman Catholic religion.[69] An article (but not an official ruling) in the bulletin of the Ministry of Justice expressed a widespread opinion: 'From the examination of both Codes, canonical and secular, it is clear that civil marriage is not available to the subjects of the Catholic Church—whether they be Catholics by baptism or converted to the true faith—whether they remain submissive to the Church or separated from her, even by excommunication'.[70]

In a few places judges permitted the civil marriage of Protestants baptized as Catholics, but elsewhere such persons faced the alternatives of returning to the Catholic Church to be married, swearing that they had never been baptized as Catholics, or living together without legal marriage. Some pastors started blessing with a religious service the union of couples who could not be married legally without returning to the Catholic Church. Such couples, of course, were officially regarded as living in adultery, and their children were stigmatized as illegitimate.

A trend towards a broader interpretation of the right of civil marriage was indicated in a recent resolution of the General Directory of Registries and Notaries. Referring to the governmental order of 1941, which we have quoted, it stated that the intention had obviously been to hinder attempts of Catholics to avoid canonical marriage, but not to deny civil marriage to those of other religious confessions for whom canonical marriage was not 'adequate'. Confirmation was also given to an earlier interpretation that documental proof of non-Catholicity had to do with 'the notoriety of belonging to non-Catholic families'.[71] It is possible that letters from Protestant pastors will again be accepted as proof of the right to civil marriage.

With regard to education, the Concordat sanctions the Spanish policy of entrusting to the Church the general watchcare of all schools. The leaders of the Catholic Church are specifically charged with vigilance for the purity of faith and morality in the schools and are given the authority to withdraw any books or other materials which seem to them contrary to Catholic dogma and morality. The Spanish State guarantees that the Catholic religion shall be taught as a regular and obligatory course of study in all schools, whether State or private, from the lowest grade through the university. The one innovation in education presented by the Concordat is a provision that the children of non-Catholics may, on request, be excused from religious instruction. Spanish Protestants now have a legal basis for insisting that their children shall not be compelled to study the Catholic religion.

Shortly after the Concordat was signed, Spain and the United States completed their negotiations over military bases and economic aid.[72] The signing of the agreement ended Spain's political isolation and made her America's partner in the defence of western civilization. The Spanish government had acted on the assumption that it could get the foreign assistance it needed without any liberalization of policy with regard to minority religions, and the assumption proved correct.

Just after the signing of the pact between Spain and the United States, the official journal of Spanish Catholic Action made the following statement:

Looking at things from the point of view of Spanish Catholic Action, we want to emphasize the significance of the fact that at long last a Catholic power like our country is entering fully into the international political concert. . . . This is the occasion to recall that Spain is a Catholic nation, as—apart from other arguments—the expressive text of the recent Concordat with the Holy See declares. Wherever Spain goes, there goes her Catholicism.[73]

Spain's religious leaders certainly do not intend to permit the nation to forget its Catholic character. Shortly after the signing of the Concordat, the Archbishop of Toledo (who is the Primate of Spain), said that after the Holy See had very benevolently agreed to the toleration of private worship in order to prevent harm to the nation in the international realm it was obligatory upon the authorities to keep dissident worship strictly private. He especially called for the prohibition of all public meetings of Protestants, concentrations in the streets, and signs which could serve as external manifestations of non-Catholic religions. He said that the private worship of non-Catholics could be tolerated, but not 'propaganda of their errors', or attempts to convert the Catholic faithful.[74]

Early in 1954 the Bishop of Barcelona wrote a pastoral letter entitled 'In Defence of Our Faith and of Our Catholic Unity'. He declared that the present Spanish legislation guards Catholic unity better than did the Constitution of 1876, and he called upon Catholics to resist Protestant expansion with legal and religious arms. 'We prudently tolerate the tares', he said, '. . . but we cannot tolerate the sowing of tares'. He gave specific directions for the organization of Catholic forces in his diocese against the advance of Protestantism.[75]

This chapter could be prolonged for many pages by accounts of specific cases involving a denial of religious liberty in recent years. Only a few cases will be briefly cited as typical—all of them taken from the experience of one Evangelical denomination since 1952. During this period four Baptist churches have been closed by the authorities. The pretext for closing three of them was that they did not have permits to conduct services (though the permits had been properly requested). The other church had a written permit, and it was closed on the charge that the pastor and members had engaged in proselytism.[76] The pastor and a member of this church had been fined some months earlier for 'making proselytes'.[77] Another Baptist pastor was imprisoned for his religious activities.[78] Two men were fined for accompanying and permitting others to accompany to the cemetery the body of the eleven-year-old daughter of one of the men,[79] and in at least one case the expressed wish of an adult Baptist for burial according to the rites of his religion has been denied.[80] Missionary organizations have lost the right to purchase property in Spain,[81] and there has been interference with the holding of a convention.[82] Heavy fines were imposed upon several people who were planning to take part in a baptismal service in a river, and five were imprisoned.[83] A man who persisted in talking to his neighbours about his Evangelical faith was fined,[84] and another man was fined for holding services in his home.[85] Religious liberty is truly at low ebb in Spain.

Those in authority say that Spanish Protestants are too few to have the right to claim consideration in legislation. As we have already seen, some official estimates refer to 20,000 Protestants in Spain, of whom half are said to be foreigners. An article in the official organ of Catholic Action estimated the number of Spanish Protestants as 2,000, or .007 per cent of the population, and observed, probably quite correctly, 'Millions of Spaniards have never known a Protestant and have no idea of what it means to be one'. So few people, argued the writer, cannot expect that laws on marriage, education, military service, etc., should be adjusted to them. 'In Spain', he concluded, 'there is no religious persecution because, among other things, there is almost no one to persecute'.[86]

The Protestant minority in Spain is small, though not so small as some of its enemies believe or pretend to believe. Spanish Protestantism has more than recuperated the losses of the civil war and the years immediately following, and is stronger now than ever before. In 1952 there were 234 chapels, homes where services were held, or places where there were groups of Protestants,[87] many of them, of course, without permission to hold services. Baptists increased 85 per cent between 1933 and 1954 in spite of a minor schism involving the loss of about 400 members.[88] If this same percentage held good for all denominations (on the basis of the figures given by Araujo and Grubb in 1933), there would now be more than 11,600 communicant members of Protestant churches in Spain and about 40,000 members of the Protestant community, including children of Protestants and persons who attend church but are not members. Growth in some quarters has been slower, and we may conclude that the number of communicant church members is about 10,000.

The Protestant petition for religious freedom to which we have referred stated that in the region of Barcelona alone there were more than 2,000 communicant members of Evangelical churches, and it added: 'Furthermore, our Christian concept of liberty of conscience and worship does not admit at all that the concession of those liberties should be made to depend upon the number of believers benefited by them'.[89] Many people both in

Spain and abroad would agree with Spanish Protestants that the concession of religious liberty should not be made to depend upon the size of religious minorities. Whether there are ten or ten thousand or ten million non-Catholics in Spain, they have the right to religious liberty.

X

CONCLUSION

We have followed the ebb and flow of religious liberty in Spain. Both persecution and toleration existed in ancient and medieval times, and since then the range has been from extreme intolerance and persecution of dissident religions to toleration and even to full religious freedom. The tide has gone out again, however, and in perhaps no other country of the western world are Protestants so clearly and openly discriminated against today as in Spain. One lesson Spain teaches us is that religious liberty is never achieved once for all; it is ever in peril, and can be maintained only at the cost of eternal vigilance.

There can be no doubt that Catholicism has been the great obstacle to religious freedom in Spain. Catholic unity is incompatible with liberty. To be sure, the ideal of Catholic unity as developed in Spain is political as well as religious and has been defended by politicians who were really not devout Catholics; but Catholic unity is, after all, Catholic, and its driving power comes from the Catholic Church.

Not all Spanish Catholics, of course, are intolerant. Some of the ablest advocates of religious freedom have been Roman Catholics. They have not believed it expedient to maintain the principle of Catholic unity, or have not considered it right to do so. Their position calls for the gratitude and praise of friends of religious liberty everywhere, but it does not change the fact that the Catholic Church has been the enemy of religious freedom in Spain.

One constantly wonders when considering the attitude of Spanish Catholic leaders towards religious minorities whether this is the true Catholic attitude. There are noble statements concerning tolerance and freedom by Roman Catholics,[1] and even official Catholic publications have denounced Spanish intolerance. *The Indiana Catholic and Record*, for example, wrote in 1952:

We feel it is past time for American Catholics to be relieved from the oppressive burden of our Spanish brethren. We have spent weary hours cleaning up the blood the Spaniards overzealously spilled in the Inquisition. If they wish to call the cops on Protestantism four centuries late they can take the blame themselves. Let them fend for themselves against the slings and arrows of world opinion.

In time, we trust, even the Spaniards will recognize that although religious error has really no rights, the heretics who hold the error do have certain fundamental rights which the State must respect and protect—rights that the Popes as head of the Papal States preserved for the Jews and Waldensians in the Eternal City itself—to follow one's conscience, to build one's churches and to worship as one chooses, so long as this does not infringe upon the rights of others.[2]

The Spaniards who deny the right of freedom to dissident religions insist that theirs is the true Catholic position, at least for a country like Spain, in which the overwhelming majority of the people are Roman Catholics. The main weight of Roman Catholic authority rests on their side. Cardinal Segura and others who have contested such statements as the one we cited above have been able to quote papal encyclicals and other authoritative documents to prove their point.[3]

Throughout Spanish history those who have opposed freedom for all except 'the true religion' have had the support of the Vatican. We have seen how the Holy See insisted upon compliance with the Concordat of 1851, which recognized exclusive rights of the Roman Catholic Church in Spain, and has recently signed a new Concordat which is based upon the principle of Catholic unity. More than once the Vatican has made known its opposition to the introduction or extension of religious freedom. The Roman Catholic Church has insisted on privileges in Spain which it does not ask for everywhere because Spain has been regarded as a Catholic State—or at least as having possibilities of becoming one.

In a Catholic State it is thoroughly normal to limit freedom of worship. We have quoted the *Syllabus of Errors* and papal encyclicals to show Catholic opposition to such freedom. An American Catholic who speaks with authority on political science says that circumstances in a Catholic State may demand the toleration of dissident worship 'carried on within the family, or in such an inconspicuous manner as to be an occasion neither of scandal nor of perversion to the faithful'.[4] It is not strange that leaders of the Catholic Church in Spain have opposed the recognition of freedom of worship in Spanish law and have sought to prevent the opening of dissident chapels and the putting of signs on them.

Spanish Catholic opposition to propaganda and proselytism by dissident religions is in harmony with what is taught concerning the Catholic State. The American Catholic whom we have just quoted says,

Quite distinct from the performance of false religious worship and preaching to the members of the erring sect is the propaganda of the false doctrine among Catholics. This could become a source of injury, a positive menace, to the religious welfare of true believers. Against such an evil they have a right of protection by the Catholic State.[5]

It is probable that if Spanish Protestants would give up all attempts at evangelism and proselytism the opposition to them would disappear. It is certainly true that when Protestant evangelism gives signs of being successful Roman Catholic opposition increases. The governor of a Spanish province told the author in 1950 that the Jews in Spain were no cause of concern, since they were not engaging in proselytism, but that the case was quite different with Protestants. Lovers of religious liberty will never compromise for a freedom so limited that it does not include the right to win other people to a religious faith.

Another area in which Catholicism has limited religious freedom in Spain has been that of education. We have quoted the *Syllabus of Errors* and other documents to show the position of the Roman Church on this issue. It is common knowledge that the Catholic Church opposes secular education, and that it desires government aid for its own schools. The ideal arrangement, so far as the Catholic Church is concerned, is a system of public education which guarantees Catholic instruction for all. It is probably true, as the Spanish Government states, that Spain, more than any other country in the world, follows the norms of Catholic education.[6]

The Spanish Catholic position, and to a great extent the official Spanish position, on marriage has been in harmony with Roman Catholic teaching. The Catholic Church has always claimed the right to control the marriage of its own members. The effect of Roman Catholic teaching on Spanish practice regarding marriage needs no further commentary after a papal ruling in 1948 made marriage outside the Catholic Church almost impossible for persons baptized in that Church. No relief was provided by the new Concordat. Spanish law on marriage is what one should expect in a State which incorporates canon law in its own legal system.

Spanish Catholics have also been within the provisions of canon law when they have insisted on the burial of baptized persons in Catholic cemeteries. Canon law, however, does not place as great emphasis upon burial in Catholic cemeteries as has been placed upon the matter by the Spanish clergy. It permits the consecration of a section of public cemeteries for Catholics or even the consecration of individual graves in such cemeteries, although it is clear that wherever possible there are to be cemeteries for the use of Catholics only.[7] It is altogether possible that some persons whom the Catholic Church has insisted upon burying in Spain would in other countries be denied Catholic burial.

We must conclude that though the Spanish Catholic stand on religious liberty is not the only one possible for Catholics, it is, on most points, thoroughly orthodox and is likely to be the Catholic stand in a country where expediency does not rule otherwise. In 1948 the official organ of the Society of Jesus in Rome published an article in defence of the policy of the present Spanish Government on religion. It contained the following statements which show that it is the duty of the Catholic Church to insist on exclusive rights in a Catholic State:

The Catholic Church, convinced by her divine prerogative of being the only true Church, must claim for herself alone the right to liberty, because such a right can belong only to truth and never to error. As to other religions, she will not draw the sword, but she will exact, by means which are legitimate and worthy of the human person, that such religions shall not be allowed to propagate false doctrines. Consequently, in a State in which the majority are Catholic, the Church will ask that error not be given legal existence and that if religious minorities actually exist they have only *de facto* existence, without opportunity to spread their beliefs. But when concrete circumstances, either because of the hostility of a government or the numerical strength of the dissident group, are not such as to permit the full application of this principle, the Church will ask for herself the greatest possible concessions, resigning herself to accept as a lesser evil the legal toleration of other cults; and in some countries Catholics will be obliged to ask full religious liberty for all. . . . In this case the Church does not renounce her thesis, which remains as the most imperative of her laws, but rather adapts herself . . . to *de facto* conditions which she cannot ignore.[8]

A similar declaration was made in 1953 by Cardinal Ottaviani, of Italy, Pro-Secretary of the Congregation of the Holy Office. After recognizing the necessity of toleration under some circumstances, he denied the right for freedom to alter 'the secure and unanimous possession of truth and of religious practices' in countries such as Italy and Spain. Word came from the Vatican that his speech was 'unexceptionable', though not official. That there is some latitude allowed Roman Catholics on this subject was indicated by an American Catholic theologian, John Courtney Murray, who stated: 'It is still entirely possible and legitimate for Catholics to doubt or dispute whether Cardinal Ottaviani's discourse represents the full, adequate and balanced doctrine of the Church'.[9]

There will probably be no change of attitude on the part of

the Spanish hierarchy unless that change should be encouraged by the highest authority of the Roman Catholic Church. Criticisms of Spanish intolerance from non-Catholics, Catholic laymen, and even members of the Catholic hierarchy in other lands will be disregarded or considered as troublesome annoyances so long as the supreme voice of the Church remains silent. The Pope, if he wished, could change Spanish policy on religion. There has so far been no evidence of such a wish.

Is there, then, no hope that Catholicism may become a force for religious freedom in Spain? Some Spanish Catholics in the past have been friends of religious liberty. It is altogether possible that Catholic leaders will decide that intolerance is not expedient in Spain, just as they have decided that it is not expedient in other parts of the world. It hurts the nation, and it hurts the Roman Catholic Church. It breeds anti-clericalism, which is so deep-rooted in Spain and has so often resulted in the murder of priests and the burning of churches. The Catholic Church shows greatest spiritual strength where religious freedom is practised.

The *Syllabus of Errors* stated that it was an error to say that 'in the present day, it is no longer expedient that the Catholic religion shall be held as the only religion of the State, to the exclusion of all other modes of worship'. Some Catholics declare that 'in the present day' religious freedom or toleration has become a necessity everywhere, even in Spain.[10] Since no man and no nation can live in isolation, denials of freedom to non-Catholics in Spain may hurt the Catholic Church in other countries. This might be the avoidance of a 'great evil' which to Catholics would justify toleration of dissident religions.

By no means is the cause of religious liberty in Spain lost. The Liberals upon whom the cause has chiefly rested through the years have fallen into silence or have disappeared from the scene, but, fortunately, friends of religious toleration and even of freedom are found also among those who are not known as political Liberals. They are Catholics, Protestants, and free-thinkers. It is probably idle to hope for full religious liberty under the present régime, but it is not unreasonable to hope for broader toleration; and sooner or later the tide of full religious freedom will again come in. The good of the nation and the spirit of the times demand it.

NOTES

I

THE ORIGIN OF CATHOLIC UNITY

[1] *El correo catalan*, Barcelona, May 29, 1949.

[2] The author possesses a photostatic copy of a letter from a colonel of the 'Milicia Universitaria' written on July 12, 1946, to a young Protestant denying him his commission in the army because he practised 'the Evangelistic religion' and was 'a person of firm convictions in this religion'.
Further details, with documentation, concerning the present lack of religious liberty in Spain will be found in Chapter IX.

[3] Domingo de Arrese, *La España de Franco* (Madrid: Publicaciones Españolas, 1946), p. 18.

[4] Joseph Pohle, 'Toleration, Religious', *The Catholic Encyclopedia*, XIV, 771.

[5] John A. Ryan and Moorhouse F. X. Millar, *The State and the Church* (New York: The Macmillan Company, 1924), p. 37.

[6] Pope Leo XIII, 'The Christian Constitution of States. Encyclical Letter, *Immortale Dei*, November 1, 1885', in Ryan and Millar, *op. cit.*, p. 19.

[7] Vicente de la Fuente, *La pluralidad de cultos y sus inconvenientes* (Puebla: Imprenta de Narciso Bassols, Editor, 1868), pp. 200 ff.

[8] Marcelino Menéndez Pelayo, *Historia de los heterodoxos españoles* (Madrid: Librería Católica de San José, 1880–81), III, 834. This sentence is frequently quoted in Spain. On January 1, 1953, it appeared on the front page of *La vanguardia española* in connection with several pictures of General Franco participating in Roman Catholic ceremonies.

[9] Henry Charles Lea, *A History of the Inquisition in Spain* (New York: The Macmillan Company, 1906–07), I, 52–71.

[10] Fernando de los Ríos, *Religion y Estado en la España del siglo XVI* (New York: Instituto de las Españas en los Estados Unidos, 1927).

[11] G. G. Coulton, *Inquisition and Liberty* (London: William Heinemann, Ltd., 1938), p. 283.

[12] Lea, *op. cit.*, I, 156–73.

[13] *Ibid.*, p. 289.

[14] *Ibid.*, pp. 89–130.

[15] *Ibid.*, pp. 130–43.

[16] *Ibid.*, III, 318–406.

[17] Frederick Meyrick, *The Church in Spain*, Vol. 2 of *The National Churches*, ed. P. H. Ditchfield (New York: James Pott and Company, 1892), p. 423.

[18] Lea, *op. cit.*, III, 437–447.

[19] Jaime Balmes, *El protestantismo comparado con el catolicismo en sus relaciones con la civilización europea* (5th ed.; Paris: Librería de Rosa y Bouret, 1854), I, 466.

[20] Menéndez, *op. cit.*, II, 96–128; and C. Araujo Garcia and Kenneth G. Grubb, *Religion in the Republic of Spain* (London: World Dominion Press, 1933), pp. 24 f.

[21] Juan de Valdés, *Diálogo de doctrina cristiana* (Madrid: Librería Nacional y Extranjera, 1929), p. 128.

[22] Benjamin B. Wiffen, *Life and Writings of Juan de Valdés*, Vol. II, *The Hundred and Ten Considerations of Juan de Valdés*, trans. John T. Betts (London: Bernard Quaritch, 1865), pp. 324 f.

[23] *Ibid.*, p. 294.

[24] Menéndez, *op. cit.*, II, 164.

[25] Eward Boehmer, *Biblioteca Wiffeniana, Spanish Reformers of Two Centuries from 1520* (Strasburg: Karl Trubner, 1874), I, 65–84; and Wiffen, *op. cit.*

[26] Boehmer, *op. cit.*, I, 133–155.

[27] Roland H. Bainton, *The Travail of Religious Liberty* (Philadelphia: The Westminster Press, 1951), pp. 72–94.

[28] Thomas McCrie, *History of the Progress and Suppression of the Reformation in Spain in the Sixteenth Century* (Philadelphia: Presbyterian Board of Publication, 1842), pp. 114–34; and Boehmer, *op. cit.*, II, 5–9.

[29] Lea, *op. cit.*, III, 432–5.

[30] Menéndez, *op. cit.*, II, 314–56; and Lea, *op. cit.*, III, 429–41.

[31] Menéndez, *op. cit.*, II, 427.

[32] Lea, *op. cit.*, III, 427 ff., 443–8; and Boehmer, *op. cit.*, II, 1–18.

[33] Menéndez, *op. cit.*, II, 359–415; and Araujo and Grubb, *op. cit.*, pp. 32 f.

[34] Boehmer, *op. cit.*, II, 58–70, 165–88; and Menéndez, *op. cit.*, II, 455–520.

[35] Meyrick, *op. cit.*, p. 423.

[36] As late as October 31, 1947, a handbill calling for the elimination of Protestantism from Spain was distributed in the streets of Madrid. It said, among other things, 'We will not limit ourselves to talking. . . . For neither did the Holy Inquisition, guardian by divine commission of the unity of Spain in the true faith, limit itself to talking.

'We, Spanish university students of 1947, are full inheritors of the inquisitorial spirit.'

[37] *Diario de Barcelona*, June 8, 1950, pp. 5 f.

II

THE RISE OF LIBERALISM

[1] Rafael Altamira, *A History of Spain from the Beginnings to the Present Day*, trans. Muna Lee (New York: D. Van Nostrand Company, Inc., 1949), pp. 507 ff.

[2] A. Boulenger, *Historia de la iglesia*, trans. and completed with *Historia eclesiástica de España y America*, by Arturo García de la Fuente (Barcelona: Editorial Lutúrgica Española, 1947), pp. 631 ff., 639, 648.

[3] Altamira, *op. cit.*, pp. 511 ff., 540, 561, 569, 587.

[4] John T. Reid, *Modern Spain and Liberalism. A Study in Literary Contrasts* (Stanford University: Stanford University Press, 1937), p. 18.

[5] Altamira, *op. cit.*, pp. 532-8.

[6] Arnold R. Verduin, *Manual of Spanish Constitutions* (1808-1931). *Translation and Introductions* (Ypsilanti, Michigan: University Lithoprinters, 1941), p. 12.

[7] Menéndez, *op. cit.*, III, 439-85.

[8] *Ibid.*, pp. 459-75.

[9] *Ibid.*, pp. 492-536.

[10] *Ibid.*, pp. 524 f.

[11] Antonio Ballesteros y Beretta, *Historia de España y su influencia en la historia universal* (Barcelona: Salvat Editores, 1919-41), VII, 230 ff., 521-7, 536-41.

[12] Menéndez, *op. cit.*, III, 590-5.

[13] *Ibid.*, pp. 594-611; and James MacCaffrey, *History of the Catholic Church in the Nineteenth Century* (1789-1908) (Dublin: M. H. Gill and Son, 1910), I, 167 f.

[14] Verduin, *op. cit.*, p. 41.

[15] Menéndez, *op. cit.*, III, 614-18.

[16] *Ibid.*, 625-32; and MacCaffrey, *op. cit.*, I, 168 f.

[17] Ballesteros, *op. cit.*, VIII, 2-10.

[18] Verduin, *op. cit.*, p. 45.

[19] Joaquín Francisco Pacheco, *El código penal concordado y comentado* (Madrid: Imprenta de D. Santiago Saunaque, 1848), I, 336 f.; II, 11 f., 17 f., 35.

[20] Agreement of June 7, 1941, between Spain and the Vatican, Arrese, *op. cit.*, p. 47.

[21] *Diccionario de la administración española*, edited by Marcelino Martinez Alcubilla, 6th ed., IV, 132. Hereafter referred to as Alcubilla.

[22] Menéndez, *op. cit.*, III, 641-4.

[23] Royal Order of April 29, 1855, *Gaceta de Madrid*, May 3, 1855, pp. 1 f.

[24] Menéndez, *op. cit.*, III, 644-9; and 'Un discurso de hace medio siglo en las Cortes españolas sobre la tolerancia religiosa,' *El cristiano*, XL (October 21, 1909), 337.

[25] Verduin, *op. cit.*, p. 52.

[26] Ballesteros, *op. cit.*, VIII, 53-98.

[27] Law of June 22, 1864, *Gaceta de Madrid*, June 23, 1864, p. 1.

[28] Menéndez, *op. cit.*, III, 650-4.

[29] Pope Pius IX, *Syllabus Errorum*, Latin and English text, by Philip Schaff, in W. E. Gladstone, *The Vatican Decrees in Their Bearing on Civil Allegiance* (New York: Harper and Brothers, 1875), pp. 113-29.

[30] Menéndez, *op. cit.*, III, 654-7. Nocedal was the speaker.

[31] *Ibid.*, 658 f.

[32] *Ibid.*, 664-8; and C. Gutierrez Marin, *Historia de la Reforma en España* (Mexico: Casa Unida de Publicaciones, 1942), pp. 177-81.

[33] George Borrow, *The Bible in Spain*, ed. Ulick Ralph Burke (New York: G. P. Putnam's Sons, 1896), 2 vols.

[34] William I. Knapp, *Life, Writings and Correspondence of George Borrow* (1803-1881) (New York: G. P. Putnam's Sons, 1899), I, 256-78.

[35] *Ibid.*, p. 278.

[36] *The Sixty-sixth Report of the British and Foreign Bible Society*, 1870, p. 112.

[37] Juan B. Cabrera, 'Bienaventurados los muertos que de aquí en adelante mueren en el Señor,' [Obituary of Francisco de Paula Ruet], *La luz*, X (November 30, 1878), 169-72; and Manuel Carrasco, *Antonio Carrasco* [Published in serial form], *Revista cristiana*, XXXIX (September 1918), 133 ff.

[38] Mrs. Robert Peddie, *Los albores de la segunda reforma en España* [Published in English in 1871 and translated by Fernando Cabrera, to be published in serial form], *España evangélica*, V (September 18, 1924), p. 315.

[39] *The Sixty-fifth Report of the British and Foreign Bible Society*, 1869, pp. 139f.

[40] Menéndez, *op. cit.*, III, 675-81; and Araujo and Grubb, *op. cit.*, pp. 56 f.

[41] Guillermo Greene, *Vida y Muerte de Don Manuel Matamoros* [Also printed in English] (2nd ed.; Madrid: Librería Nacional y Extranjera, 1897); and various articles in *Evangelical Christendom* for 1860-3.

[42] Manuel Trigo, quoted in *The Christian Herald*, XIX (May, 1868), 149.

[43] Antonio Carrasco, 'Report of the State of Religion in Spain,' *Evangelical Alliance Conference*, 1873, ed. Philip Schaff and S. Irenaeus Prime (New York: Harper and Brothers, 1874), p. 117.

[44] *The Missionary Herald of the Presbyterian Church in Ireland*, February 1, 1870, p. 27.

III

THE ESTABLISHMENT OF RELIGIOUS FREEDOM

[1] Ballesteros, *op. cit.*, VIII, 93–150.

[2] Proclamation of Generals Topete, Prim, Serrano, and others, September 19, 1868, quoted in Nicolás María Serrano and Melchor Pardo, *Anales de la guerra civil (España desde 1868 a 1876)* (Madrid: Astort Hermanos, Editores, 1875–76), I, 497 ff.

[3] *Evangelical Christendom*, IX (November 2, 1868), 412 f.

[4] Edward Henry Strobel, *The Spanish Revolution, 1868–75* (Boston: Small, Maynard and Company, 1898), pp. 9–21.

[5] Menéndez, *op. cit.*, III, 762 f.

[6] Petition of Seville Women, October 15, 1868, in Serrano and Pardo, *op. cit.*, I, 585–8.

[7] Manifesto of the Revolutionary Committee of Seville, September 22, 1868, *Revista cristiana*, XXXIV (September 15, 1913), 207.

[8] Manifesto of the Revolutionary Committee of Madrid, October 8, 1868, in Serrano and Pardo, *op. cit.*, I, 555.

[9] *The New York Times*, October 14, 1868, pp. 3 and 5; and *Gaceta de Madrid*, October 15, 1868, pp. 4 f.

[10] Manifesto of Provisional Government, October 25, 1868, in Serrano and Pardo, *op. cit.*, I, 601–6.

[11] Letter of General Serrano to the Local Committee of the Universal Israelite Alliance in Bordeaux, December 1, 1868, in Serrano and Pardo, *op. cit.*, I, 724.

[12] *The Sixty-fifth Report of the British and Foreign Bible Society*, 1869, pp. 140–3; and *Fifty-fifth Annual Report of the American Bible Society*, 1871, pp. 98 f.

[13] Serrano and Pardo, *op. cit.*, I, 649–800.

[14] Manifesto of the Association of Catholics, December 24, 1868, in *ibid.*, p. 728.

[15] Decree of January 1, 1869, *Gaceta de Madrid*, January 26, 1869, p. 1.

[16] Jerónimo Becker, *Relaciones diplomáticas entre España y la Santa Sede durante el siglo XIX* (Madrid: Imprenta de Jaime Ratés Martín, 1908), p. 241.

[17] Manifesto of the Provisional Government, January 28, 1869, *Gaceta de Madrid*, January 28, 1869, p. 1.

[18] Becker, *op. cit.*, pp. 238–45.

[19] Letter from Madrid, February 15, 1869, in *Evangelical Christendom*, X (March 1, 1869), 101.

[20] Ballesteros, *op. cit.*, VIII, 149 f.

[21] Becker, *op. cit.*, pp. 244 f.

[22] *Diario de sesiones de las Cortes Constituyentes*, Appendix to March 30, 1869, p. 2. Hereafter referred to as *Diario Constituyentes*.

[23] *Ibid.*, p. 4.

[24] *Ibid.*, April 6, 1869, p. 850.

[25] *Ibid.*, February 24, 1869, p. 179.

[26] *Ibid.*, April 1, 1869, p. 782.

[27] Becker, *op. cit.*, pp. 245–51.

[28] *Diario Constituyentes*, April 12, 1869, pp. 977–86.

[29] *Ibid.*, April 26, 1869, pp. 1379–83, and April 27, 1869, pp. 1394–8.

[30] *Ibid.*, April 27, 1869, pp. 1409–15.

[31] Bishop Monescillo, of Jaen, *ibid.*, April 14, 1869, p. 1029.

[32] Ortiz de Zárate, *ibid.*, April 28, 1869, p. 1437.

[33] Cruz Ochoa, *ibid.*, April 29, 1869, pp. 1451, 1453.

[34] *Ibid.*, April 26, 1869, pp. 1359–62.

[35] *Ibid.*, May 4, 1869, pp. 1596–99, 1611.

[36] *Ibid.*, May 3, 1869, pp. 1565–71.

[37] *Ibid.*, April 7, 1869, pp. 899–902.

[38] *Ibid.*, April 12, 1869, pp. 986–91 (Quotation, p. 991).

[39] *Ibid.*, May 5, 1869, p. 1640.

[40] Eugenio García Ruiz, *ibid.*, April 26, 1869, pp. 1364 ff.

[41] Juan Garrido, *ibid.*, April 30, 1869, p. 1509.

[42] Estanislao Figueras, *ibid.*, April 6, 1869, p. 874.

[43] *Ibid.*, April 9, 1869, pp. 953 f.

[44] *Ibid.*, April 26, 1869, p. 1378.

[45] *Ibid.*, May 4, 1869, pp. 1611–15.

[46] *Ibid.*, April 14, 1869, pp. 1044–51.

[47] *Ibid.*, May 5, 1869, pp. 1652 ff.

[48] *Ibid.*, May 5, 1869, pp. 1633–9 (Quotation, p. 1637).

[49] Antonio Romero Ortiz, *ibid.*, April 27, 1869, pp. 1415 f., and May 4, 1869, p. 1608.

[50] Antonio de los Ríos y Rosas, *ibid.*, April 9, 1869, pp. 957 f.

[51] Aguirre, *ibid.*, April 28, 1869, p. 1421.

[52] Rojo Arías, *ibid.*, May 4, 1869, p. 1601.

[53] *Ibid.*, April 8, 1869, p. 935.

[54] *Ibid.*, May 5, 1869, p. 1655.

[55] *Gaceta de Madrid*, June 7, 1869, p. 1.

[56] Fernando Cabrera, 'La primera capilla evangélica, o así se escribe la historia,' [Published in serial form], *España evangélica*, II (June 21, 1921), 232;

and Enrique Calamita, 'Rectificaciones. La Primera capilla evangélica, o así se escribe la historia,' *España evangélica*, II (September 8, 1921), 288 f.

[57] *Evangelical Christendom*, X (April 1, 1869), p. 141.

[58] Fernando Cabrera, 'La primera capilla evangélica, o así se escribe la historia,' *España evangélica*, II (July 28, 1921), 240; and Manuel Carrasco, *op. cit.*, XL (January, 1919), 10 f.

[59] Fernando Cabrera, 'La primera capilla evangélica, o así se escribe la historia,' *España evangélica*, II (August 4 and 11, 1921), 247 f., 257 f.; and Antonio Vallespinosa, *Memorias de un protestante* [Written in 1881. Published in serial form], *España evangélica*, XII (January 15, 1931), 23.

[60] Letter from Madrid, January 15, 1869, in *Evangelical Christendom*, X (February 1, 1869), 56.

[61] *The Pictorial Missionary News*, June 1, 1869, p. 69.

[62] *The Missionary Herald of the Presbyterian Church in Ireland*, January 1 and February 1, 1870, pp. 10 and 27.

IV

THE PRACTICE OF RELIGIOUS FREEDOM

[1] Strobel, *op. cit.*, pp. 68–107.

[2] Circular Letter of July 26, 1869, *Gaceta de Madrid*, September 28, 1869, p. 1.

[3] *Diario Constituyentes*, January 15, 1870, p. 4928.

[4] Circular Letter of Minister of War, January 28, 1870, Alcubilla, *op. cit.*, IV, 295.

[5] Alcubilla, *op. cit.*, III, 732, 738, 750, 775.

Forcing a person to practise a religion not his own, or keeping a person from practising his own religion; hindering or disturbing by acts, words, gestures, or threats a minister of any religion while performing his functions, or disturbing in the same way any religious acts in the place regularly set apart for them; making mock of the dogmas or ceremonies of any religion having adherents in Spain, or publicly profaning images, vessels, or objects of worship would be punished by imprisonment for a term of two years, four months, and one day up to six years, and a fine of 250 up to 2500 pesetas. Disturbing in a tumultuous manner the acts of any cult in the place set apart for such acts would be punished with imprisonment for a term of six years and one day up to ten years. Scandalous performance of other acts offensive to the religious sentiments of those present in a place of religion would be penalized by imprisonment for a term of one month and one day up to four months. Otherwise disturbing the acts of a cult or offending the religious sentiments of those present at such acts would be punished by arrest for one to ten days and a fine of five to fifty pesetas.

[6] Law of the Civil Register, June 17, 1870, *Gaceta de Madrid*, June 20, 1870, pp. 1 f.; and Law of Civil Marriage, June 18, 1870, *Gaceta de Madrid*, June 21, 1870, pp. 1 f.

[7] Ballesteros, *op. cit.*, VIII, 157.

[8] *Diario Constituyentes*, April 2, 1870, pp. 7049–82.

[9] Circular Letter of Minister of Public Works, October 4, 1870, *Gaceta de Madrid*, October 5, 1870. p. 5.

[10] Decree of Minister of Grace and Justice, August 5, 1869, *Gaceta de Madrid*, August 7, 1869, p. 1.

[11] Becker, *op. cit.*, pp. 254–8.

[12] *Diario Constituyentes*, October 23, 1869, p. 4026.

[13] *The Sixty-sixth Report of the British and Foreign Bible Society*, 1870, pp. 111 f., 116.

[14] Strobel, *op. cit.*, pp. 109–76.

[15] Becker, *op. cit.*, pp. 259 f.

[16] Royal Order of July 16, 1871, Alcubilla, *op. cit.*, III, 178.

[17] Circular Letter of Minister of Interior, February 28, 1872, *Gaceta de Madrid*, March 1, 1872, pp. 643 ff.

[18] 'Un atentado contra el derecho', *La luz*, III (June 15, 1871), 5.

[19] Antonio Carrasco and Felix Moreno Astray, for the Assembly of the Spanish Christian Church, 'Al pueblo español', *La luz*, IV (June 1, 1872), 2 f.

[20] Strobel, *op. cit.*, pp. 177–237.

[21] *Diario de sesiones de las Cortes Constituyentes de la República Española de 1873*, June 13, 1873, p. 139.

[22] *Ibid.*, Appendix No. 1 to July 26, 1873.

[23] *Ibid.*, Appendix No. 2 to July 17, 1873.

[24] Becker, *op. cit.*, pp. 261–4.

[25] Menéndez, *op. cit.*, III, 776–82.

[26] Letter of José Alhama, November 7, 1873, in *La luz*, V (November 15, 1873), 7; and Letter from Juan B. Cabrera, quoting letter from José Alhama to the Governor and one from the Governor to Alhama, in *La luz*, V (December 1, 1873), 7 f.

[27] Strobel, *op. cit.*, 235–88.

[28] Ballesteros, *op. cit.*, VIII, 244–51.

[29] Serrano and Pardo, *op. cit.*, II, 779.

[30] *La luz*, VI (June 1, 1874), 4.

[31] American Baptist Missionary Union, *Sixty-first Annual Report*, 1875, p. 70.

[32] A. B. O., 'The State of Spain', *Evangelical Christendom*, XV (June 1, 1874), 192.

[33] Letter of A. Benoliel, July 10, 1874, in *Evangelical Christendom*, XV (September 1, 1874), 288.

[34] Letters from A. Benoliel, June 25, 1874, July 10, 1874, and February, 1875, in *Evangelical Christendom*, XV (August 1, 1874), 255, XVI (March 1, 1875), 80–83.

[35] Antonio Carrasco, *op. cit.*, p. 117.

[36] *The Sixty-seventh Report of the British and Foreign Bible Society*, 1871, pp. 142 f.

[37] *The Sixty-eighth Report of the British and Foreign Bible Society*, 1872, p. 137.

[38] *The Seventieth Report of the British and Foreign Bible Society*, 1874, pp. 92 f.

[39] *The Missionary Herald of the Presbyterian Church in Ireland*, December 1, 1870, pp. 233 f.

[40] *The Home and Foreign Missionary Record of the Free Church of Scotland*, June 1, 1871, p. 111.

[41] *The Missionary Herald of the Presbyterian Church in Ireland*, September 1, 1871, pp. 445 ff.

[42] *El cristiano*, III (April 20, 1872), 7.
Vicente de la Fuente states that at this time the number of Protestants in Madrid was 3623 and that they attended nine chapels, seven of which had schools connected with them. Vicente de la Fuente, *Respuesta al manifiesto de la Asamblea*, quoted in Menéndez, *op. cit.*, III, 794.

[43] *The Home and Foreign Missionary Record of the Free Church of Scotland*, September 1, 1873, pp. 186 f.

[44] *La luz*, II (March 12, 1870), 2 f.

[45] John S. Black, 'Spanish Evangelization. Opening of the New Church in Seville', *The Church of Scotland Home and Foreign Missionary Record*, VIII (June 1, 1872), 61 f.

[46] *La luz*, V (February 15, 1873), 7.

[47] *The Missionary Herald of the Presbyterian Church in Ireland*, September 1, 1871, p. 445.

[48] *La luz*, VI (April 15, 1874), 2 ff.

[49] *Ibid.*, V (September 15, 1873), 1.

[50] *Ibid.*, VI (February 1, 1874), 1.

[51] *Protestantism in Spain* [A pamphlet appealing for support of the work of Herr Fliedner. New York: Committee for Co-operation with Latin America, 1924].

[52] Antonio Carrasco, *op. cit.*, p. 117.

[53] *Forty-fifth Annual Report of the American Tract Society*, 1870, p. 118.

[54] Letter from Henry C. Hall, in *Fifty-sixth Annual Report of the American Bible Society*, 1872, p. 100.

[55] Letter from William Moore, in *The Missionary Herald of the Presbyterian Church in Ireland*, March 1, 1870, p. 43; and Letter from William Knapp, April 5, 1870, letter from William Knapp, William Moore, and John Jameson,

and letter from John Jameson, April 4, 1870, in *Missionary Record of the United Presbyterian Church* [Scotland], III (May 2, 1870), 139 f.

[56] American Baptist Missionary Union, *Fifty-seventh Annual Report*, 1871, p. 93; Letter from William Knapp, September 1, 1870, in *The Missionary Magazine*, L (December, 1870), 449; and Letter from William Knapp, May 11, 1871, in *The Missionary Magazine*, LI (October, 1871), 383 ff.

[57] American Baptist Missionary Union, *Sixtieth Annual Report*, 1874, pp. 73 ff.

[58] American Baptist Missionary Union, *Fifty-ninth Annual Report*, 1873, p. 7.

[59] *The Report of the Wesleyan Methodist Missionary Society for the Year Ending April, 1871*, pp. 20 f.

[60] *The Report of the Wesleyan Methodist Missionary Society for the Year Ending April, 1874*, p. 29.

[61] *Sixty-third Annual Report of the American Board of Commissioners for Foreign Missions*, 1873, p. 93.

[62] *Sixty-fourth Annual Report of the American Board of Commissioners for Foreign Missions*, 1874, pp. 76–9.

[63] Statistical Tables compiled by William H. Gulick, August 12, 1874, *The Missionary Herald, Containing the Proceedings of the American Board of Commissioners for Foreign Missions*, LXX (November, 1874), 366 ff. There was Protestant work in the following places: Madrid, Barcelona, Santander, Seville, Cadiz, San Fernando, Rio Tinto, Jerez, Balearic Islands (Mahon), Valencia, Alicante, Cartagena, Granada, Huelva, Cordova, Linares, Camuñas, Valladolid, and Zaragoza.

[64] *The Sixty-eighth Report of the British and Foreign Bible Society*, 1872, p. 137.

[65] Antonio Carrasco, *op. cit.*, p. 114.

[66] A. B. O., 'The State of Religion in Spain', *Evangelical Christendom*, XVI (June 1, 1874), 192.

[67] Balmes, *op. cit.*, I, 430.

V

THE ESTABLISHMENT OF RELIGIOUS TOLERATION

[1] Ballesteros, *op. cit.*, VIII, 253–7.

[2] *Ibid.*, pp. 284 ff.

[3] Carlos Navarro y Rodrigo, *Un período de oposición* (Madrid: Imprenta de los hijos de J. A. García, 1886), pp. 13–29.

[4] Ballesteros, *op. cit.*, VIII, 288–98.

[5] Manifesto of Sandhurst, December 1, 1874, in Strobel, *op. cit.*, pp. 269–72.

[6] Circular Letter of Minister of Grace and Justice, January 2, 1875, *Gaceta de Madrid*, January 7, 1875, pp. 52 f.

[7] Decree of January 29, 1875, *Gaceta de Madrid*, January 30, 1875, p. 248.

[8] *La luz*, VII (February 6, 1875), 37.

[9] Circular Letter of Minister of Interior, February 7, 1875, *Gaceta de Madrid*, February 8, 1875, p. 340.

[10] Decree of February 9, 1875, *Gaceta de Madrid*, February 10, 1875, pp. 363 f.

[11] Letter from Señor Giménez, February 16, 1875, in *The Missionary Herald of the Presbyterian Church in Ireland*, May 1, 1875, p. 582.

[12] Circular Letter of Minister of Public Works, February 26, 1875, *Gaceta de Madrid*, February 27, 1875, pp. 531 f.

[13] Becker, *op. cit.*, pp. 269 f.

[14] *Ibid.*, pp. 267–72.

[15] *La luz*, VII (May 15, 1875), 135 f.

[16] American Baptist Missionary Union, *Sixty-first Annual Report*, 1875, p. 71; American Baptist Missionary Union, *Sixty-second Annual Report*, 1876, p. 70; and Letter from Henry Duncan, in *The Thirty-ninth Annual Report of the Board of Foreign Missions of the Presbyterian Church of the United States of America*, 1876, p. 86.

[17] *The Seventy-first Report of the British and Foreign Bible Society*, 1875, pp. 74 ff.

[18] Letters of the Bishop of Cadiz and the Governor of Cadiz, in Serrano and Pardo, *op. cit.*, II, 1012.

[19] Becker, *op. cit.*, pp. 273–78.

[20] *Diario de las sesiones de Cortes. Senado*. Appendix No. 1 to May 30, 1876, p. 4. Hereafter referred to as *Diario. Senado*.

[21] Becker, *op. cit.*, p. 279.

[22] Speech of Cánovas del Castillo, *Diario. Senado*, June 16, 1876, p. 791.

[23] Becker, *op. cit.*, pp. 280 ff.

[24] 'Se generaliza la lucha', *La luz*, VIII (January 22, 1876), 25.

[25] Ballesteros, *op. cit.*, VIII, 313 ff.

[26] 'A las Cortes', *La luz*, VIII (April 22, 1876), 130.

[27] Becker, *op. cit.*, pp. 284–301.

[28] *Diario de las sesiones de Cortes. Congreso de los Diputados*. May 11, 1876, pp. 1328–42. Hereafter referred to as *Diario. Congreso*.

[29] *Diario, Senado*, June 14, 1876, pp. 735–55.

[30] *Ibid.*, June 13, 1876, pp. 709–20.

[31] *Ibid.*, June 16, 1876, pp. 777 f.

[32] *Diario, Congreso*. April 24, 1876, p. 907.

[33] *Diario. Senado*, June 2, 1876, pp. 482–5.

[34] *Diario Congreso*, March 15, 1876, p. 431.

[35] *Ibid.*, May 12, 1876, p. 1392.

[36] *Ibid.*, May 3, 1876, pp. 1081–7, 1091 f.

[37] *Diario, Senado,* June 14, 1876, pp. 755–60.

[38] *Diario. Congreso,* April 20, 1876, pp. 829–33, 838.

[39] *Diario. Senado,* June 13, and 14, 1876, pp. 720–3 and 727–33.

[40] Becker, *op. cit.,* pp. 291 f., 301.

[41] Verduin, *op. cit.,* pp. 77 ff.

VI

THE PRACTICE OF RELIGIOUS TOLERATION

[1] Pope Leo XIII, 'The Christian Constitution of States. Encyclical Letter *Immortale Dei,* November 1, 1885', in Ryan and Millar, *op. cit.,* pp. 18 f. (Quoted by permission of The Macmillan Company, New York.)

[2] Pope Leo XIII, Encyclical Letter *Libertas Humana,* June 20, 1886, in Joseph Husslein, *Social Wellsprings,* Vol. I. *Fourteen Epochal Documents by Pope Leo XIII* (Milwaukee: The Bruce Publishing Company, 1943), pp. 115–39.

[3] J. B. Trend, *The Origins of Modern Spain* (New York: The Macmillan Company, 1934), pp. 50–132.
The school was opened in 1876.

[4] Ballesteros, *op. cit.,* VIII, 316–24.

[5] Note of Papal Secretary of State, August 16, 1876, in Becker, *op. cit.,* p. 304.

[6] 'El artículo 11 de la Constitución', *La luz,* VIII (September 16, 1876), 298 ff. The church building referred to was in San Fernando.

[7] Letter of Augusto Binion, September 21, 1876, about church in Port Mahon, Minorca, in 'Prosigue el artículo 11', *La luz,* VIII (September 30, 1876), 314.

[8] Royal Order of October 23, 1876, *Gaceta de Madrid,* October 25, 1876, pp. 225 f.

[9] *The Seventy-third Report of the British and Foreign Bible Society,* 1877, p. 79.

[10] Royal Order of October 23, 1876, *Gaceta de Madrid,* October 24, 1876, pp. 217 f.

[11] Royal Order of October 21, 1877, *Gaceta de Madrid,* October 22, 1877, pp. 233 f. The Protestant father lived in the village of Iznatoraf.

[12] *Evangelical Christendom,* May 1, 1877, p. 135.

[13] *El cristiano,* VIII (1877), *passim.*

[14] Royal Order of November 21, 1877, in *La luz,* IX (December 30, 1877), 191.

[15] *The Seventy-fifth Report of the British and Foreign Bible Society,* 1879, p. 67.

[16] 'La cuestion de Alcoy', *La luz,* X (January 30, 1878), 10 f.; and 'Causa célebre', *La luz,* X (August 30 and September 30, 1878), 127 f. and 142 ff.

[17] Decision of Second Chamber of Supreme Court, December 27, 1879, Alcubilla, *op. cit.,* V, 520.

[18] Decision of Supreme Court, October 20, 1886, *ibid.*, V, 521.

[19] Antonio García Illana, 'Crónica de la obra evangélica en España', *La luz*, XII (February 15, 1880), 24.

[20] Royal Order of November 8, 1890, *Gaceta de Madrid*, December 7, 1890, pp. 778 ff.

[21] Law of June 15, 1880, *Gaceta de Madrid*, June 16, 1880, p. 671.

[22] Ballesteros, *op. cit.*, VIII, 323–33.

[23] Circular Letter of Minister of Public Works, March 3, 1881, *Gaceta de Madrid*, March 4, 1881, p. 615; and MacCaffrey, *op. cit.*, I, 387.

[24] Circular Letter of Chief Attorney of Supreme Court, March 5, 1881, in B. Castrell, 'Pro libertad de cultos', España evangélica, XI (October 16, 1930), 333.

[25] *The Missionary Herald of the Presbyterian Church of Ireland*, October 1, 1881, p. 667.

[26] Ballesteros, *op. cit.*, VIII, 336–52.

[27] Pastor Fliedner, 'The Religious Condition of Spain', *The Religious Condition of Christendom, Described in a Series of Papers Presented to the Eighth General Conference of the Evangelical Alliance Held in Copenhagen, 1884*, ed. Lewis Barrett White (London: Office of the Evangelical Alliance, 1885), p. 129.

[28] Royal Decree of July 4, 1884, Alcubilla, *op. cit.*, X, 16 f.

[29] Royal Decree of August 18, 1885, *Gaceta de Madrid*, August 25, 1885, pp. 598–602.

[30] Decision of Second Chamber of Supreme Court, April 30, 1885, Alcubilla, *op. cit.*, V, 518.

[31] Ballesteros, *op. cit.*, VIII, 341, 348–418, 445.

[32] 'Ponapé', *Revista cristiana*, VIII (October 15–December 31, 1887), 295–8, 311 ff., 325–9, 346–50, 364–7, 374 ff.

[33] *Seventy-eighth Annual Report of the American Board of Commissioners for Foreign Missions*, 1888, pp. 111 f.

[34] Becker, *op. cit.*, pp. 374–8.

[35] Alcubilla, *op. cit.*, III, 420, 424.

[36] 'Criptana', *Revista cristiana*, XI (May 31, 1890), 153.

[37] *El cristiano*, XXIII (December 8 and 22, 1892), 388 ff., 406 f.; XXIV (March 16 and 23, 1893), 85, 93 f. This church is the principal unit—the 'cathedral'—of the Spanish Reformed Church.

[38] 'La libertad religiosa en España', *Revista cristiana*, XXVI (May 31, 1905), 154–8. The chapel was inaugurated on March 17, 1893, and permission to open the front door was given in 1905.

[39] Count de Canga Argüelles, *Diario. Senado*, April 19, 1893, pp. 76–81.

[40] Montero Ríos, *ibid.*, pp. 79–81.

[41] Royal Decree of February 5, 1886, Alcubilla, *op. cit.*, IX, 599.

[42] Royal Order of December 19, 1885, *ibid.*, X, 18 f.

7

[43] Royal Decree of January 25, 1895, *Gaceta de Madrid*, January 27, 1895, p. 306.

[44] Marqués de Pidal, *Diario. Senado*, February 11, 1895, pp. 1087–94.

[45] Lopez Puigcerver, *ibid.*, 1094–9.

[46] *Ibid.*, February 14, 1895, pp. 1142–6.

[47] George Fliedner, *Missionary College, Madrid* [Pamphlet], Madrid, 1926.

[48] *Revista cristiana*, XVIII (August 15, 1897), 238 f.

[49] Ballesteros, *op. cit.*, VIII, 418–45.

[50] Order from Office of the Civil Register, December 28, 1900, Alcubilla, *op. cit.*, XI, 224 f.

[51] Reid, *op. cit.*, p. 40.

[52] *The Report of the Wesleyan Methodist Missionary Society for the Year Ending April, 1902*, p. 26.

[53] Señor Marín, quoted in American Baptist Missionary Union, *Eighty-eighth Annual Report*, 1902, p. 228.

[54] American Baptist Missionary Union, *Sixty-third Annual Report*, 1877, p. 70.

[55] J. N. Murdock, 'Signs of Promise in Our Missions', American Baptist Missionary Union, *Sixty-sixth Annual Report*, 1880, p. IX.

[56] Vicente Mateu, *Memoria sobre el orígen y desarrollo de la Iglesia Evangélica Bautista en Valencia de 1888 a 1898* (Valencia: Imprenta de Francisco Vives Mora, 1898).

[57] American Baptist Missionary Union, *Eighty-seventh Annual Report*, 1901, p. 220.

[58] *Ninety-second Annual Report of the American Board of Commissioners for Foreign Missions*, 1902, pp. 155 f.; and Elizabeth Putnam Gordon, *Alice Gordon Gulick, Her Life and Work in Spain* (New York: Fleming H. Revell Company), [1917].

[59] 'La Iglesia Española', *La Luz*, XII (April 15, 1880), 60.

[60] Juan B. Cabrera, quoted in John E. Mayor, *Spain, Portugal, and the Bible* (Cambridge: Macmillan and Bowes, 1892), p. 44.

[61] José Viliesid, Rafael Blanco, and Manrique A. Lallave, 'Instituto Evangélico de Teología. A las iglesias evangélicas de España', *El cristiano*, XIV (October 6, 1883), 320.

[62] 'La Iglesia Evangélica Española', *Revista cristiana*, VII (May 31, 1886), 154 f.

[63] *Eighty-ninth Annual Report of the American Board of Commissioners for Foreign Missions*, 1899, p. 165.

[64] Letter from John Jameson, in *The Missionary Herald of the Presbyterian Church in Ireland*, June 1, 1886, p. 119.

[65] Report from Mr. Jameson, *The Eighty-eighth Report of the British and Foreign Bible Society*, 1892, pp. 76–9.

⁶⁶ W. H. Gulick, quoted in H. A. Schauffler, 'Continental Mission. Missions in Spain', *The Missionary Herald of the Presbyterian Church in Ireland*, October 1, 1894, p. 243.

⁶⁷ Schauffler, *op. cit.*, p. 243.

VII

THE PRACTICE OF RELIGIOUS TOLERATION—*continued*

¹ For general information on this period see Ballesteros, *op. cit.*, VIII, 471–603.

² *The Hundred and Seventh Report of the British and Foreign Bible Society*, 1911, p. 84.

A strong appeal for religious freedom had been sent to the Congress of Deputies in 1908 by the Spanish Evangelical Church. The petition stated that there were about a hundred Protestant churches in Spain, an equal number of groups not organized as churches, and about a hundred schools. Cipriano Tornos and Miguel Barroso, 'Mensaje de la Asamblea de la Iglesia Evangélica Española al Congreso de Señores Diputados', [July 13, 1908], *El cristiano*, XXXIX (July 23, 1908), 233 ff.

³ Juan B. Cabrera and Others, Message to the Cortes, October 30, 1910, quoted in 'La campaña de la juventud evangélica en pro de la libertad de cultos: Presentación del mensaje en el Congreso', *El cristiano*, XL (December 8, 1910), 391.

The letter stated that there were more than 100,000 signatures. There were probably additional signatures obtained after the letter was written, though it is possible that estimates of 150,000 signatures were too high.

⁴ "La campaña de la juventud evangélica en pro de la libertad de cultos: Presentación del mensaje en el Congreso', *El cristiano*, XL (December 8, 1910), 391–5.

⁵ Fernando Cabrera Latorre and Julián Saco, Letter of April 7, 1923, quoted in 'Por la libertad de cultos—Mensaje de la Alianza Evangélica Española al Presidente del Consejo de Ministros', *España evangélica*, IV (April 12, 1923), 117.

⁶ Melchor Fernández Almagro, *Historia del reinado de Don Alfonso XIII* (2nd ed.; Barcelona: Montaner y Simón, S. A., 1934), pp. 94 f.; and Fernando Cabrera, 'Tocando a rebato', *España evangélica*, IV (April 5, 1923), 112.

⁷ Pope Pius X, Letter to Cardinal Aguirre y García, Archbishop of Toledo, April 20, 1911, quoted in Pastoral Letter of Cardinal Segura, June 20, 1952, Pedro, Cardenal Segura y Saenz, *Por la unidad católica de España* (Seville: Editorial Edelce, 1952), p. 64.

⁸ Cipriano Tornos and Miguel Barroso, *op. cit.*, p. 235.

⁹ Juan B. Cabrera and Others, *op. cit.*, p. 392.

¹⁰ Royal Order of September 29, 1904, *Gaceta de Madrid*, October 1, 1904, p. 3.

[11] Royal Order of August 27, 1906, *Gaceta de Madrid*, August 28, 1906, pp. 830 f.

[12] Count de Romanones, quoted in 'El matrimonio civil', *Revista cristiana*, XXVII (August 31, 1906), 249.

[13] Royal Order of February 28, 1907, *Gaceta de Madrid*, March 1, 1907.

[14] Royal Order of June 28, 1913, *Gaceta de Madrid*, July 4, 1913, p. 35.

[15] Royal Decree of April 25, 1913, *Gaceta de Madrid*, April 26, 1913, pp. 286 f.

[16] *Diario. Congreso*, March 2, 1906, pp. 2952–6. Nocedal was the Carlist speaker, and Romanones and Moret spoke for the government.

[17] Royal Order of July 3, 1906, quoted in Royal Order of January 25, 1913, *Gaceta de Madrid*, January 29, 1913, pp. 237 f.

[18] 'El soldado evangélico y la prensa española', *Revista cristiana*, XXXIII (Supplement to August 15, 1912); and 'La libertad de conciencia en España', *Revista cristiana*, XXXIII (December 31, 1912), 260 f.

[19] *Diario. Congreso*, December 14, 1912, pp. 5890–3.   Luis Zulueta was the deputy, and Count de Romanones was President of the Council of Ministers.

[20] Royal Order of January 25, 1913, *Gaceta de Madrid*, January 29, 1913, p. 237.

[21] 'Enseñanzas de un proceso', *Revista cristiana*, XXXIV (January 15, 1913), 1–4; and 'Una carta del marinero Pablo Fernández', *Revista cristiana*, XXXIV (February 28, 1913), 40.

[22] Royal Order of March 17, 1919, cited in Juan Labrador, 'Para los evangélicos militares', *España evangélica*, VI (January 1, 1925), 4 f.

[23] *The Hundred and Tenth Report of the British and Foreign Bible Society*, 1914, p. 75; and 'El coronel Labrador', *Revista cristiana*, XXXV (January 20, 1914), 1–5.

[24] Juan Labrador, 'Para los evangélicos marinos', *España evangélica*, VI (June 25, 1925), 223 f.

[25] Royal Order of June 10, 1910, *Gaceta de Madrid*, June 11, 1910, p. 553.

[26] C. Tornos, 'La Real Orden sobre las manifestaciones exteriores de los cultos disidentes', *El cristiano*, XLI (June 16, 1910), 193 f.

[27] Juan B. Cabrera and Cipriano Tornos, 'Mensaje al Excmo. Sr. Presidente del Consejo de Ministros, presentado el dia 29 de Junio, a nombre de los cristianos evangélicos de España, enfrente de la protesta de los obispos y damas católico-romanas', *El cristiano*, XLI (June 30, 1910), 205 f.

[28] *Diario. Congreso*, July 18 and 19, 1910, pp. 707, 732–40.   Diaz Aguado y Salaberry was the one who presented the Catholic point of view, and Melquíades Álvarez was the Republican speaker.

[29] Agustín Arenales, 'La libertad de conciencia y la Constitución', *España evangélica*, III (June 8, 1922), 187; Fernando Cabrera, 'Tocando a rebato', *España evangélica*, IV (April 5, 1923), 112; and Fernando Cabrera, 'La cuestión del artículo 11', *España evangélica*, IV (April 12, 1923), 118.

[30] Decision of December 5, 1914, Alcubilla, *op. cit.*, Appendix for 1915, p. 703.

[31] Decision of June 2, 1915, *ibid.*, Appendix for 1915, p. 704.

[32] Decision of February 23, 1916, *ibid.*, Appendix for 1917, p. 524.

[33] Decision of April 19, 1918, *ibid.*, Appendix for 1918, p. 429. (A typical case.)

[34] Decision of April 2, 1918, *ibid.*, Appendix for 1918, p. 453. (A typical case.)

[35] Ballesteros, *op. cit.*, VIII, 604–30.

[36] Domingo de Ramos, 'Bajo el gobierno militar', *España evangélica*, IV (November 8, 1923), 373.

[37] Fernando Cabrera and Julián Saco, 'La Alianza Evangélica Española al Presidente del Directorio Militar', *España evangélica*, IV (November 8, 1923), 369.

[38] Domingo de Ramos, 'Bajo el gobierno militar', *España evangélica*, IV (December 20, 1923), 426.

[39] *One Hundred and Sixteenth Annual Report of the American Board of Commissioners for Foreign Missions*, 1926, p. 179.

[40] Fernando Cabrera and Julián Saco, Letter of the Spanish Evangelical Alliance, February 14, 1927, in 'Alianza Evangélica Española, *Españá evangélica*, VIII (February 24, 1927), 59.

[41] 'Carmen Padín Álvarez en Madrid—Lo que la Alianza Evangélica ha hecho por ella', *España evangélica*, IX (July 26, 1928), 237 f.; and Royal Order of July 17, 1928, *Gaceta de Madrid*, July 19, 1928, p. 335.

[42] 'Código penal de 8 de Septiembre de 1928', Alcubilla, *op. cit.*, Appendix for 1928, pp. 325 f., 433 f.

[43] C. A. G., 'Crónica', *España evangélica*, X (September 19, 1929), 304.

[44] 'El segundo congreso evangélico español—Nuestra información', *España evangélica*, X (August 29, 1929), 269.

[45] Fernando Cabrera and Julián Saco, Letter of the Spanish Evangelical Alliance, November 11, 1929, 'Petición reiterada—La Alianza Evangélica Española, a nombre del II Congreso Evangélico Español, solicita de los poderes públicos la libertad de cultos', *España evangélica*, X (November 21, 1929), 381.

[46] Teodoro Fliedner ¡'¡A luchar, a luchar, a luchar!' *España evangélica*, XI (February 13, 1930), 52.

[47] Ballesteros, *op. cit.*, VIII, 630–44.

[48] Fernando Cabrera, 'Crónica. Monárquicos o evangélicos?' *España evangélica*, XII (February 19, 1931), 44.

[49] 'La Alianza Evangélica Española y su obra', *España evangélica*, IX (February 23, 1928), p. 61; and 'El segundo congreso evangélico español—Nuestra información', *España evangélica*, X (August 29, 1929), 269–83. The Spanish Evangelical Alliance was organized in 1914.

[50] Araujo and Grubb, *op. cit.*, pp. 79–82. *España evangélica* began publication in 1920.

[51] 'XIV Asamblea de la Iglesia Evangélica Española celebrada en los dias 24, 25, y 26 en la ciudad de Málaga', *España evangélica*, IX (May 3, 1928), 141 f.

[52] J. H. Horstmann, 'The Progress of the Gospel in Spain', *The Missionary Review of the World*, LI (September, 1928), 725. The committee was formed in 1924.

[53] Gutierrez, *op. cit.*, pp. 343 ff., 365–8.

[54] *Ninety-third Annual Report of the American Board of Commissioners for Foreign Missions*, 1903, p. 138; and *One Hundred and Twenty-first Annual Report of the American Board of Commissioners for Foreign Missions*, 1931, p. 112.

[55] Araujo and Grubb, *op. cit.*, pp. 76 f.

[56] *One Hundred and Twenty-first Annual Report of the American Board of Commissioners for Foreign Missions*, 1931, p. 112.

[57] Everett Gill, 'First Annual Report on New European Missions', *Annual of the Southern Baptist Convention*, 1922, p. 305; and *Annual of the Southern Baptist Convention*, 1931, p. 271.

[58] Araujo and Grubb, *op. cit.*, p. 74.

[59] Everett Gill, 'Annual Report', *Annual of the Southern Baptist Convention*, 1923, p. 114.

VIII

SEPARATION OF CHURCH AND STATE

[1] Salvador de Madariaga, *Spain* (London: Jonathan Cape, 1946), pp. 292–8.

[2] Decree of April 14, 1931, *Gaceta de Madrid*, April 15, 1931, p. 195.

[3] 'La República Española—La soberanía del pueblo implanta la república en España', *España evangélica*, April 16, 1931, p. 109.

[4] James Hastings Nichols, *Democracy and the Churches* (Philadelphia: The Westminster Press, 1951), p. 203; and Luis Villaoz, 'Crónica. ¡A rebato!' *España evangélica*, May 14, 1931, p. 146.

[5] Luis Villaoz, 'Crónica. ¿Quién quemó los conventos?' *España evangélica*, May 21, 1931, p. 152. It is suggested that the burning of religious buildings might have been the work of monarchists who wished to discredit the Republic.

[6] Circular Letter of April 18, 1931, for Army, Alcubilla, *op. cit.*, Appendix for 1931, p. 267; and Order of May 6, 1931, for Navy, *Gaceta de Madrid*, May 9, 1931, p. 624.

[7] Decree of August 4, 1931, *Gaceta de Madrid*, August 5, 1931, p. 978. Even earlier, compulsory attendance at religious services in prisons had

been abolished. Decree of April 22, 1931, *Gaceta de Madrid*, April 23, 1931, p. 283.

[8] 'Un decreto importante. Hacia la libertad de cultos', *España evangélica*, May 14, 1931, p. 145.

[9] Decree of May 6, 1931, *Gaceta de Madrid*, May 9, 1931, pp. 619 f.

[10] Circular Letter of May 13, 1931, *Gaceta de Madrid*, May 22, 1931, pp. 874 f.

[11] Decree of May 22, 1931, *Gaceta de Madrid*, May 23, 1931, pp. 878 f.

[12] Decree of July 9, 1931, *Gaceta de Madrid*, July 10, 1031, p. 275.

[13] *Diario de sesiones de las Cortes Constituyentes de la República Española*, October 8, 1931, pp. 1521–8.

[14] Rodriguez Piñero, *ibid.*, October 9, 1931, pp. 1554 f.

[15] De Tapía, *ibid.*, pp. 1555–8.

[16] *Ibid.*, October 8, 1931, pp. 1528–32.

[17] Molina Nieto, *ibid.*, October 9, 1931, pp. 1548–54.

[18] Beunza, *ibid.*, October 10, 1931, pp. 1632–9.

[19] *Ibid.*, pp. 1602–11.

[20] *Ibid.*, October 13, 1931, pp. 1666–72.

[21] *Ibid.*, October 14, 1931, pp. 1725 ff.

[22] *Gaceta de Madrid*, December 10, 1931, pp. 1578–88. Articles 70 and 87 state that ecclesiastics, ministers of the different religions, and certain other persons are ineligible for the Presidency of the Republic and of the Council of Ministers.

[23] Fernando Cabrera, 'Crónica. La constitución española', *España evangélica*, December 10, 1931, p. 384.

[24] 'Revista del año 1931,' *España evangélica*, December 31, 1931, p. 411.

[25] Agustín Arenales, 'Crónica. Hay que insistir en la verdad de la situación presente del Romanismo en España bajo la República', *España evangélica*, December 31, 1931, p. 413.

[26] Adolfo Araujo, 'El primer presidente de la República', *España evangélica*, December 17, 1931, pp. 389 f.

[27] Madariaga, *op. cit.*, pp. 302 f., 308 ff.

[28] Decree of March 12, 1932, *Gaceta de Madrid*, March 17, 1932, p. 1923.

[29] Madariaga, *op. cit.*, p. 310.

[30] Law of January 30, 1932, *Gaceta de Madrid*, February 6, 1932, p. 946.

[31] Order of March 14, 1932, *Gaceta de Madrid*, March 15, 1932, p. 1860.

[32] Circular Letter of June 14, 1932, Alcubilla, *op. cit.*, Appendix for 1932, p. 75.

[33] Order of February 10, 1932, *Gaceta de Madrid*, February 17, 1932, pp. 1182 f.

[34] Law of June 28, 1932, *Gaceta de Madrid*, July 3, 1932, p. 60.

[35] Penal Code of 1932, *Gaceta de Madrid*, November 5, 1932, pp. 818–856. See especially articles 218, 228, and 236.

[36] This information was obtained through Mr. Percy Buffard from a member of the delegation who does not wish his name revealed.

[37] Law of June 2, 1933, Alcubilla, *op. cit.*, Appendix for 1933, pp. 78–84.

[38] Pope Pius XI, Encyclical Letter *Dilectissima Nobis*, June 3, 1933, in Joseph Husslein, *Social Wellsprings*, Vol. II, *Eighteen Encyclicals of Social Reconstruction* (Milwaukee: The Bruce Publishing Company, 1943), pp. 293–302.

[39] Madariaga, *op. cit.*, pp. 311, 321.

[40] *Ibid.*, pp. 322–39.

[41] *Ibid.*, pp. 339–43.

[42] Agustín Arenales, 'Crónica, Las elecciones que vienen', *España evangélica*, January 30, 1936, p. 9; and *La situación del protestantismo en España* (Seis estudios sobre una campaña de difamación contra España) (Madrid: O. I. D., 1949), p. 17.

[43] Madariaga, *op. cit.*, pp. 339–49.

[44] *Ibid.*, pp. 349–52.

[45] *Ibid.*, pp. 367–420.

[46] *Ibid.*, pp. 376 ff.

[47] Fernando Cabrera, 'Crónica. ¡Salud, Vasconia!' *España evangélica*, October 15, 1936, p. 125.

[48] *The Hundred and Thirty-third Report of the British and Foreign Bible Society*, 1937, p. 35.

[49] *The Hundred and Thirty-fourth Report of the British and Foreign Bible Society*, 1938, p. 29.

[50] Ambrosio Celma, quoted by Everett Gill, 'Spain', *Annual of the Southern Baptist Convention*, 1938, p. 244.

[51] Fernando Cabrera, 'Crónica. Una iglesia disidente', *España evangélica*, June 11, 1931, pp. 176 f.

[52] Araujo and Grubb, *op. cit.*, pp. 68–102.

[53] Ambrosio Celma, quoted by Everett Gill, 'The Word of the Lord That Came to Spain', *Annual of the Southern Baptist Convention*, 1934, p. 224.

[54] Everett Gill, 'God Hath Given Europe the Spirit of Power', *Annual of the Southern Baptist Convention*, 1935, p. 218.

[55] One mention of new church buildings is by Everett Gill, 'The Word of the Lord That Came to Spain', *Annual of the Southern Baptist Convention*, 1934, p. 224.

[56] One typical meeting was described by Juan Cabrera and Germán Araujo, 'Una fecha histórica. El mítin de afirmación evangélica en Madrid', *España evangélica*, June 25, 1931, pp. 189–94.

[57] *Annual of the Southern Baptist Convention*, 1931, p. 271.

[58] *Annual of the Southern Baptist Convention*, 1936, p. 216.

IX

RETURN TO CATHOLIC UNITY

[1] Arrese, *op. cit.*, p. 18.

[2] Pastoral Letter of July 10, 1937, quoted in lecture by Fernando Valls Taberner, 'La revalorización de la vida religiosa en España', in Universidad de Barcelona, *Aspectos y problemas de la nueva organización de España* (Barcelona, 1939), pp. 128 f.

[3] For general information on this period see Gerald Brennan, *The Spanish Labyrinth* (Cambridge: University Press, 1950); and Madariaga, *op. cit.*

[4] General Franco, quoted in lecture by Valls Taberner, *op. cit.*, p. 134.

[5] Letter from Lord Phillimore, quoting letter from the Duke of Alba, *The Times* (London), November 19, 1937, p. 12.

[6] *The Times*, November 22, 1937, p. 8.

[7] Letter from Lord Phillimore, *The Times*, November 27, 1937, p. 8.

[8] Order of October 5, 1938, Estanislao de Aranzadi (ed.), *Repertorio cronológico de legislación* (Pamplona), 1938, pp. 839 f.

[9] Order of June 14, 1938, *ibid.*, 1938, p. 553.

[10] Decree of May 3, 1938, *ibid.*, 1938, pp. 399 f.

[11] Law of February 3, 1939, Arrese, *op. cit.*, p. 71.

[12] Law of November 9, 1939, *ibid.*, p. 72.

[13] Order of November 12, 1937, Aranzadi, *op. cit.*, 1937, p. 820.

[14] Confirmation of Royal Order of 1913, Postal telegram to army units from the Secretariat of War, November 4, 1938, in Pedro Cantero, 'La libertad religiosa en España', *Ya* (Madrid), February 12, 1950, p. 6.

[15] One such case is referred to in the government publication, *La situación del protestantismo en España* (Seis estudios sobre una campaña de difamación contra España) (Madrid: O.I.D., 1949), p. 24.

[16] *The Hundred and Thirty-sixth Report of the British and Foreign Bible Society*, 1940, p. 25.

[17] Religion in primary schools, Order of September 21, 1936, Aranzadi, *op. cit.*, 1936, p. 791; Religion in 'bachillerato', Order of October 7, 1937, *ibid.*, 1937, p. 773; Religion included in law of secondary education, Law of September 20, 1938, *ibid.*, 1938, p. 807; Religion required in universities, Decree of January 26, 1944, Alcubilla, *op. cit.*, Appendix for 1944, pp. 102 f.

In 1945, the right of foreigners to have non-Catholic schools for their children was written into a law, but the Catholic character of education was recognized as follows: 'The law does not hesitate to gather, perhaps as no other (law) in the world, and at times with manifest literalness, the postulates set forth by Pius XI as norms of Christian educational law in his immortal

Encyclical *Divini illius Magistri'*. Law of July 17, 1945, Aranzadi, *op. cit.*, 1945, p. 1150.

When a new law on education was proposed in 1952, it did not meet with the unqualified approval of the hierarchy and the Vatican, but was accepted. It continued earlier guarantees of the Catholic character of education. Enrique, Cardinal Pla y Deniel; and Balbino Santos y Olivera, 'El apostolado de la educación y los derechos en ella de la iglesia (Instrucción de Conferencia de Metropolitanos)', *Ecclesia*, October 4, 1952, pp. 375 ff.

[18] Order of July 27, 1939, Aranzadi, *op. cit.*, 1939, pp. 560 f.

[19] Law of December 10, 1938, *ibid.*, 1938, pp. 1085 f.

[20] *La situación del protestantismo en España* admits that in villages or small towns and cities a civil cemetery is sometimes lacking (p. 23).

The British and Foreign Bible Society, in its report for 1941 (p. 18), stated that generally funerals according to the will of the deceased were permitted, but that sometimes it was insisted that those baptized as Catholics be buried by the Catholic Church.

[21] Decree of March 2, 1938, Aranzadi, *op. cit.*, 1938, p. 173.

[22] Law of March 12, 1938, *ibid.*, 1938, p. 209.

[23] Order of March 10, 1941, *Boletín oficial del estado* (Madrid), March 12, 1941, p. 1775.

[24] *The Hundred and Thirty-sixth Report of the British and Foreign Bible Society*, 1940, p. 25; and Letter from Paul Culbertson, of the United States Department of State, November 9, 1942, in *Tidings from Spain*, January–March, 1944, pp. 12 f.

In 1947 the Bible Society sold 16,129 copies of the Bible or Bible portions, in comparison with 305,000 copies in 1935. Sociedad Bíblica, *Notas de la obra bíblica*, Número 5 (Madrid, 1948), p. 6.

[25] Interview with José Flores, Spanish Secretary of the British and Foreign Bible Society, November 28, 1952.

[26] *The Hundred and Thirty-sixth Report of the British and Foreign Bible Society*, 1940, pp. 24 f.

[27] The service was on January 10, 1943. Benjamín Santacana, *Memoria de la obra evangélica en Vilafranca del Panadés* (a brief unpublished manuscript).

[28] Letter from Paul Culbertson, citing police order of September, 1940, *Tidings from Spain*, January–March, 1944, pp. 10 f.

[29] Agreement of June 7, 1941, Aranzadi, *op. cit.*, 1941, pp. 811 f.

[30] Pedro, Cardinal Segura y Saenz, Archbishop of Seville, Pastoral Letter of April 17, 1952, included in *Por la unidad católica de España* (Seville: Editorial Edelce, 1952), pp. 25 ff.

[31] 'El vaticano y el régimen', *La víspera* (Barcelona), August, 1951, pp. 1, 3. This was a clandestine monarchist magazine.

[22] Decree of December 23, 1944, Alcubilla, *op. cit.*, Appendix for 1945, pp. 709–801. See especially pages 710, 737 f.

[33] 'Religious Liberty in Spain', *Tidings from Spain*, July–September, 1945, pp. 4 ff.

[34] Enrique, Cardinal Pla y Deniel, Archbishop of Toledo, and Balbino, Archbishop of Granada, 'Instrucción de la conferencia de metropolitanos españoles sobre la propaganda protestante en España', *Ecclesia*, VIII (July 19, 1948), p. 675.

[35] 'El Fuero de los Españoles', Law of July 17, 1945, Aranzadi, *op. cit.*, 1945, p. 1133.

[36] *La vanguardia española* (Barcelona), July 14, 1945, p. 4.

[37] *La situación del protestantismo en España*, p. 16.

[38] A.A.G., 'El Fuero de los Españoles', *Carta circular a los evangélicos españoles* (Madrid), August–September, 1945, pp. 16–20.

[39] Letter of the Minister of the Interior, November 12, 1945, quoted in *La situación del protestantismo en España*, Appendix No. 6, pp. 21 f.

[40] T.F., 'Una gran oportunidad', *Carta circular a los evangélicos españoles*, August–September, 1945, pp. 1–7.

[41] Elin Bengtson, 'Treading the Way of Peace in Spain', *Annual of the Southern Baptist Convention*, 1946, p. 250.

[42] General Franco, to the American reporter, Merwin K. Hart, in *La vanguardia española*, August 19, 1947. Also published in Hearst papers and International News Service.

[43] Pastoral Letter of Cardinal Segura, September 10, 1947, in *Religious Liberty in Peril. Documents Illustrating the Condition of Protestants in Spain* (Paris: 'Pro Hispania', 1948), pp. 2 ff.

[44] Speech of Manseñor Vizcarra, copied from *Signo* of October 18, 1947, in *Religious Liberty in Peril*, p. 8.

[45] November, 1947. The author has in his possession a copy of this handbill and the following one.

[46] December, 1947.

[47] Pastoral Letter of Rigoberto, Archbishop of Zaragoza, December 22, 1947, *El correo catalán* (Barcelona), January 11, 1948.

[48] P. Vemancio Marcos, 'Libertad de los protestantes en España,' *Pueblo* (Madrid), February 7, 1948.

[49] 'La unidad religiosa nacional,' *La prensa* (Barcelona), June 21, 1948.

[50] Gregorio, Bishop of Barcelona, 'Unidad católica y tolerancia de cultos,' *El correo catalán*, March 10–17, 1948.

[51] Enrique, Cardinal Pla y Deniel, and Balbino, Archbishop of Granada, 'Instrucción de la conferencia de metropolitanos sobre la propaganda protestante en España,' *Ecclesia*, VIII (July 19, 1948), pp. 673 ff.

[52] The following are some of the chapels that were raided: the Baptist chapel of Granollers, on September 21, 1947; the Methodist Church of Ripoll Street, in Barcelona, on October 11, 1947; the Church of the Brethren, on Trafalgar Street, Madrid, in November of 1947; the Baptist Church of Valencia,

on December 9, 1947, and again on April 12, 1949; the Baptist Church of Albacete, on January 4, 1948; the Church of the Brethren, in Linares, on June 24, 1948; and the Reformed Church, in Seville, on March 3, 1952.

[53] '¿ Protestantes extranjeros?' *Requetés*, September, 1947.

[54] Antonio Peinador, 'Cuestiones morales', *El iris de paz o El immaculado corazón de María* (Madrid), January 1, 1948.

[55] *Mensajero del corazón de Jesús*, quoted in José Julio Martinez, *Protestantes* (Bilbao: El Mensajero del Corazón de Jesús, 1948), p. 53.

[56] Dean Acheson, Letter to Chairman of Committee on Foreign Relations of the United States Senate concerning American Policy towards Spain, January 18, 1950, *Documents on American Foreign Relations*, Vol. XII, January 1–December 31, 1950, ed. Raymond Dennett and Robert K. Turner (World Peace Foundation, Princeton University Press, 1951), pp. 617–22.

[57] *New York Herald Tribune*, April 29, 1949.

[58] Fernando Cabrera and Carlos Araujo, 'Mensaje de los evangélicos españoles a S.E. el Jefe del Estado Español,' February 15, 1950, *Carta circular a los evangélicos españoles*, May, 1950, pp. 3–6.

[59] Order of February 23, 1948, in *Carta circular a los evangélicos españoles*, June, 1950, pp. 3, 11.

[60] Permission to build a chapel in Alicante was requested on November 7, 1947, but no reply was ever received. In the summer of 1949 a building was bought with the intention of renovating it for a chapel. The city authorities gave permission to do the necessary work before they realized that the building was to be used as a Protestant church, and later they withdrew it. Appeals to city, provincial, and national authorities proved fruitless; but eventually enough work was done on the building secretly to make it usable as a place of worship. The governor, however, refused to permit the Baptists to use their chapel, and it was only in September of 1951, after Ambassador Griffis had presented the matter to the highest officials of the nation, that permission was finally given for the chapel to be used.

[61] *La vanguardia española*, February 12, 1952.

[62] *Arriba* (Madrid), March 12, 1952.

[63] *Tages-Anzeiger* (Zürich), March 17, 1955.

[64] *La vanguardia española*, August 29, 1953, p. 3.

[65] *Ibid.*, p. 5.

[66] *Diario de Barcelona*, October 27, 1953, p. 9.

[67] *La vanguardia española*, August 29, 1953, p. 3.

[68] The *Motu Proprio* of Pope Pius XII on August 1, 1948, eliminated from Canon 1099 the paragraph exempting from canonical marriage the children of non-Catholics who were baptized in the Catholic Church but not educated in it. T. Lincoln Bouscaren and Adam C. Ellis, *Canon Law. A Text and Commentary* (Milwaukee: Bruce Publishing Company, 1948), p. 583.

[69] The municipal judge of Manresa, on August 26, 1949, rejected the request

of two members of the Manresa Baptist Church for civil marriage and emphasized that the order of 1941 gave the right of civil marriage to those who do not *belong to* the Roman Catholic Church, not to those who do not *profess* the Roman Catholic religion. His written judgment stated that after the *Motu Proprio* of the Pope in 1948 there was no exception to the rule that a person baptized as a Catholic was subject to the requirement of canonical marriage. A photostatic copy of the judgment is in the possession of the author of this book.

A resolution of the General Directory of Registries and Notaries on June 28, 1951, stated with regard to the case of a couple in Algeciras that a document certifying that they were baptized in 'the evangelical sect' was not proof of non-membership in the Roman Catholic Church, since they had earlier been baptized in the Catholic Church. *Diario de Barcelona*, March 23, 1952.

On February 6, 1952, a municipal judge in Alicante rejected the petition of two members of the Baptist Church there for civil marriage, on the grounds that they had been baptized in the Roman Catholic Church, and he stated that, according to Canon Law, baptism imparts an indelible character which is not lost when one separates from the Roman Church. The author has a copy of the judge's written decision.

[70] José Pere Raluy, 'Concepto de la acatolicidad a efectos de la celebración del matrimonio civil' (reprinted), *Ecclesia*, October 3, 1953, pp. 11 f.

[71] Authorization of civil marriage on December 27, 1954, to Francisco Manzanares Martín and Julia Calvo after appeal to a higher court, which in turn received an interpretation or resolution of the General Directory of Registries and Notaries dated December 17, 1954. The author has a copy of this decision.

[72] *La vanguardia española*, September 29, 1953.

[73] *Ecclesia*, October 3, 1953, p. 3.

[74] Cardinal Pla y Deniel, quoted by Gregorio, Bishop of Barcelona, 'En Defensa de nuestra fé y de nuestra unidad católica', *La vanguardia española*, March 19, 1954.

[75] Gregorio, Bishop of Barcelona, 'En Defensa de nuestra fé y de nuestra unidad católica', *La vanguardia española*, March 19, 20, 21, 1954.

[76] The Baptist Church of Elda was closed on September 5, 1952, then permitted to reopen for a while and finally closed again. The Baptist Church of Lerida was closed on April 9, 1953; the Second Baptist Church of Madrid (which had a written permit) on July 17, 1954; and the Second Baptist Church of Valencia on November 8, 1954.

The first case, and also some of the matters which follow, are referred to in my article, 'From Bad to Worse in Spain', *The Christian Century*, December 10, 1952, pp. 1438 f. I am indebted to friends in Spain for keeping me informed of recent occurrences there.

[77] In April of 1953 the pastor and a member of the Second Baptist Church of Madrid were fined 500 pesetas (about $12.50) each. They were not told the

specific charges against them, nor were they given a chance to defend themselves; but they supposed that the reason for the fine was that the church member had permitted some Catholic children to accompany him and his children to Sunday school.

[78] Aurelio del Campo, pastor of the Baptist church in Navarrés, was fined 3000 pesetas for blaspheming, causing a public scandal, and distributing unauthorized literature. When he did not pay the fine he was sentenced to forty-five days in prison. After fifteen days he was released on the condition that he give up his residence in Navarrés.

[79] The fine was imposed upon two men of the province of Valencia on April 2, 1952. It amounted to ten thousand pesetas (about $250).

[80] On February 7, 1954, a member of the Baptist Church of Badalona was denied the right of burial according to the religion she professed. It was claimed that she was Catholic, since she had been baptized in the Catholic Church and married in it, and since her husband had been buried as a Catholic.

[81] On May 6, 1952, the author requested from the Institute of Foreign Money a permit to buy a piece of property in Barcelona for the Foreign Mission Board of the Southern Baptist Convention. Several other such requests had been previously granted. This application was repeated four times, and the American Embassy inquired about the matter, but the most that could ever be learned was that the request had been referred to the Council of Ministers. No permits have been granted since then.

[82] A Baptist convention was planned for September, 1952. The pastor of the church in Alicante, where the convention was to be held, was advised by the police that a special authorization was necessary. The authorization was requested, and the pastor even went to Madrid to try to obtain it. He was told that a reply would be given after the Council of Ministers had discussed the matter. No reply was ever received.

[83] Members and friends of the Baptist Church of Játiva who had met in the country for a baptismal service were dispersed by the police before the service could be held. Twenty-three people were fined from 250 to 2,000 pesetas, and five who would not or could not pay their fines were imprisoned, some for eight days and the others for fifteen days. Two of those fined were later pardoned.

[84] A fine of 2,000 pesetas was paid by a man from a village near Játiva.

[85] A man of Madrid was forced to pay a 500 peseta fine in spite of his protest that the meetings for which he was fined were family devotional services.

[86] Jesús Iríbarren, 'El protestantismo español, problema artificial. III. Política y fantasía', *Ecclesia*, May 21, 1949, pp. 573 ff.

[87] *Vademecum evangélico* (Madrid), 1952.

[88] Araujo and Grubb listed 1037 members in 1933, *op. cit.*, p. 100. The *Annual of the Southern Baptist Convention* for 1954 reported thirty-three Baptist churches in Spain, with a membership of 1920 (p. 184).

[89] Cabrera and Araujo, *op. cit.*, p. 4.

X

CONCLUSION

¹ During the war a group of prominent European Catholics living in America made a clear and forceful statement in favour of religious freedom which included the following: 'It is not the function of the State either to dominate or to control consciences. The creeds which, in the present state of religious disunity, share souls' allegiance should be free to establish their rites, to preach their teachings, to shape souls, to exercise their apostolate, without the civil authority's mixing into their proper province. We are aware, moreover, that by its teachings on the act of faith, God's free gift, freely accepted, and which no constraint can produce in souls, it is Christianity itself which lays the basis for civil tolerance in religious matters'. José Antonio de Aguirre et al, 'In the Face of the World's Crisis', *Commonweal*, XXXVI (August 21, 1942), 418 f.

² 'The Cardinal Is Calling the Cops Four Centuries Late', *The Indiana Catholic and Record*, Indianapolis, March 14, 1952.

³ Pedro, Cardinal Segura y Saenz, *Par la unidad católica de España*.

⁴ John A. Ryan, 'Comments on "The Christian Constitution of States",' in Ryan and Millar, *op. cit.*, p. 35. (Used by permission of The Macmillan Company, New York.)

⁵ *Ibid.*, pp. 35 f. (Used by permission of The Macmillan Company, New York.)

⁶ Law on Education, July 17, 1945, Aranzadi, *op. cit.*, 1945, p. 1150.

⁷ See especially canons 1012, 1016, 1058, 1070, 1072, 1099, 1206, 1212, 1239, 1240. They are quoted or summarized in T. Lincoln Bouscaren and Adam C. Ellis, *Canon Law. A Text and Commentary* (Milwaukee: The Bruce Publishing Company, 1948).

⁸ F. Cavalli, 'La condición de los protestantes en España', [translation of article in *La civilta cattolica*, April 3, 1948], *Ecclesia*, VIII (May 1, 1948), p. 5 (481).

⁹ *Time*, August 3, 1953, pp. 32 f.

¹⁰ This is the position of Joseph Pohle, Toleration, Religious', *The Catholic Encyclopedia*, XIV, 769.

BIBLIOGRAPHY

The various items in the bibliography are books, pamphlets, magazines, newspapers, and reports. In order to avoid lengthening the list unduly, magazine and newspaper articles, with their authors, are not listed here.

Altamira, Rafael. *A History of Spain from the Beginnings to the Present Day.* Translated by Muna Lee from 2nd ed. New York: D. Van Nostrand Company, Inc., 1949.

America. National Catholic Weekly Review, New York, 1952.

American Baptist Missionary Union. Annual Reports, 1871–1902. Boston.

American Board of Commissioners for Foreign Missions. Annual Reports, 1872–1931. Boston.

American Tract Society. *Forty-fifth Annual Report,* 1870. New York.

Aranzadi, Estanislao de (ed.), *Repertorio cronológico de legislación.* One volume for each year since 1931. Pamplona.

Araujo Garcia, C., and Grubb, Kenneth G., *Religion in the Republic of Spain.* London and New York: World Dominion Press, 1933.

Arrese, Domingo de, *La España de Franco.* Madrid: Publicaciones Españolas, 1946.

Arriba. Daily Newspaper of Madrid, 1952.

Bainton, Roland H., *The Travail of Religious Liberty.* Philadelphia: The Westminster Press, 1951.

Ballesteros y Beretta, Antonio. *Historia de España y su influencia en la historia universal.* 9 vols. Barcelona: Salvat Editores, 1919–41.

Balmes, Jaime. *El protestantismo comparado con el catolicismo en sus relaciones con la civilización europea.* 2 vols. 5th ed. Paris: Librería de Rosa y Bouret, 1854. A new edition of this book was printed by Editorial Araluce of Barcelona in 1951.

Bates, M. Searle. *Religious Liberty: An Inquiry.* New York: International Missionary Council, 1945.

Becker, Jerónimo. *Relaciones diplomáticas entre España y la Santa Sede durante el siglo XIX.* Madrid: Imprenta de Jaime Ratés Martín, 1908.

Boehmer, Edward. *Biblioteca Wiffeniana, Spanish Reformers of the Two Centuries from 1520, Their Lives and Writings according to the Late Benjamin B. Wiffen's*

Plan and with the Use of His Materials. 2 vols. Strasburg: Karl Trubner, 1874.

Boletín oficial del estado. Official periodical for publication of laws, decrees, etc. Madrid, 1941.

Borrow, George. *The Bible in Spain; or, The Journeys, Adventures, and Imprisonments of an Englishman in an Attempt to Circulate the Scriptures in the Peninsula.* New Edition, with notes and a glossary by Ulick Ralph Burke. 2 vols. New York: G. P. Putnam's Sons, 1896.

Boulenger, A., *Historia de la iglesia.* Translated and enlarged with *Historia eclesiástica de España y America,* by Arturo García de la Fuente. Third edition. Barcelona: Editorial Litúrgica Española, 1947.

Bouscaren, T. Lincoln, and Ellis, Adam C. *Canon Law. A Text and Commentary.* Milwaukee: Bruce Publishing Company, 1948.

Brennan, Gerald. *The Spanish Labyrinth.* Cambridge: University Press. 1950.

British and Foreign Bible Society. Annual Reports, 1869–1941. London.

Carta circular a los evangélicos españoles. Periodical of the Spanish Evangelical Church, published in Madrid. 1945–52.

The Christian Century. Chicago. 1952.

The Catholic Encyclopedia. Encyclopedia Press. 1913,

The Christian Index. Georgia Baptist periodical, Atlanta. 1951.

The Christian World. Organ of the American and Foreign Christian Union, New York. 1868–75.

The Church of Scotland Home and Foreign Missionary Record. Edinburgh. 1872.

Clarke, H. Butler. *Modern Spain. 1815–1898.* In *Cambridge Historical Series.* edited by G. W. Prothers. Cambridge: University Press, 1906.

The Commission. Journal of Southern Baptist Foreign Board. Richmond. 1954.

Commonweal. Catholic periodical, New York, 1942.

El correo catalán. Daily newspaper of Barcelona. 1948.

Coulton, G. G. *Inquisition and Liberty.* London: William Heinemann, Ltd., 1938.

El cristiano. A Protestant periodical published in Madrid. 1872–1910.

Dennett, Raymond, and Turner, Robert K. (ed). *Documents on American Foreign Relations.* Vol. XII, January 1–December 31, 1950. World Peace Foundation, Princeton University Press, 1951.

Diario de Barcelona. Daily newspaper of Barcelona. 1950–3.

Diario de las sesiones de Cortes. Congreso de los Diputados. Government publication, Madrid. 1872, 1876, 1906, 1910, 1912, 1916.

Diario de las sesiones de Cortes. Senado. Government publication, Madrid. 1876, 1893, 1895.

Diario de sesiones de las Cortes Constituyentes. Government publication, Madrid. 1869–70.

Diario de sesiones de las Cortes Constituyentes de la República española de 1873. Government publication, Madrid.

Diario de sesiones de las Cortes Constituyentes de la República española. Government publication. 1931.

Ecclesia. Official organ of Spanish Catholic Action, Madrid. 1948–53.

El eco de la verdad. Baptist periodical published in Barcelona. 1928.

España evangélica. A Protestant periodical published in Madrid. 1920–36.

Evangelical Alliance. *Evangelical Alliance Conference, 1873. Hixtory, Essays, Orations, and Other Documents of the Sixth General Conference of the Evangelical Alliance, Held in New York, October 2–12, 1873.* Edited by Philip Schaff and S. Irenaeus Prime. New York. Harper and Brothers, 1874.

Evangelical Alliance. *The Religious Condition of Christendom, Described in a Series of Papers Presented to the Eighth General Conference of the Evangelical Alliance Held in Copenhagen, 1884.* Edited by Lewis Barrett White. London: Office of the Evangelical Alliance, 1885.

Evangelical Christendom. Periodical published by the Evangelical Alliance, London. 1860–77.

Fernández, Almagro, Melchor. *Historia del reinado de Don Alfonso XIII.* Second edition. Barcelona: Montaner y Simón, 1934.

Fliedner, George. *Missionary College, Madrid.* Pamphlet. Madrid, 1926.

Fuente, Vicente de la. *Historia eclesiástica de España.* Second edition. 6 vols. Madrid: Compañía de Impresores y Libreros del Reino, 1873–5.

Fuente, Vicente de la. *La pluralidad de cultos y sus inconvenientes.* Puebla: Imprenta de Narciso Bassols, 1868.

Gaceta de Madrid. Government publication of decrees, laws, etc., Madrid. 1855–1936.

Gladstone, W. E. *The Vatican Decrees in Their Bearing on Civil Allegiance; a Political Expostulation, to Which Are Added: A History of the Vatican Council; together with the Latin and English Text of the Papal Syllabus and the Vatican Decrees,* by Philip Schaff. New York: Harper and Brothers, 1875.

Gordon, Elizabeth Putnam. *Alice Gordon Gulick, Her Life and Work in Spain.* New York: Fleming H. Revell [1917].

Greene, Guillermo. *Vida y muerte de Don Manuel Matamoros. Relación de la última persecución de cristianos en España, extractada de cartas originales y otros documentos.* Second edition. Madrid: Librería Nacional y Extranjera, 1897.

Gutierrez Marín, Claudio. *Historia de la reforma en España.* Mexico: Casa Unida de Publicaciones, 1942.

The Home and Foreign Missionary Record of the Free Church of Scotland. Edinburgh. 1871–3.

Husslein, Joseph. *Social Wellsprings.* [Vol. I] *Fourteen Epochal Documents by Pope Leo XIII.* Milwaukee: The Bruce Publishing Company, 1943.

Husslein, Joseph. *Social Wellsprings.* Vol. II. *Eighteen Encyclicals of Social Reconstruction by Pope Pius XI.* Milwaukee: The Bruce Publishing Company, 1943.

The Indiana Catholic and Record. Indianapolis. 1952.

El iris de paz o el inmaculado corazón de María. Catholic periodical, Madrid. 1948.

Knapp, William I. *Life, Writings and Correspondence of George Borrow (1803–1881).* 2 vols. New York: G. P. Putnam's Sons, 1899.

Lea, Henry Charles. *A History of the Inquisition in Spain.* 4 vols. New York: The Macmillan Company, 1906–7.

Levante. Daily newspaper of Valencia. 1952.

Llorente, Juan Antonio. *Historia crítica de la inquisición de España.* 10 vols. Madrid: Imprenta del Censor, 1822.

La luz. A Protestant periodical published in Madrid, 1870–80.

MacCaffrey, James. *History of the Catholic Church in the Nineteenth Century (1789–1908).* 2 vols. Second edition. Dublin: M. H. Gill and Son, 1910.

McCrie, Thomas. *History of the Progress and Suppression of the Reformation in Spain in the Sixteenth Century.* Philadelphia: Presbyterian Board of Publications, 1842.

Madariaga, Salvador de. *Spain.* London: Jonathan Cape, 1946.

Martinez, José Julio. *Protestantes.* Booklet. Bilbao: El Mensajero del Corazón de Jesús, 1948.

Martinez Alcubilla, Marcelo (ed.). *Diccionario de la administración española.* Sixth edition. 13 vols. containing legislation through 1913. An appendix for each year since then. Madrid. Referred to as Alcubilla.

Mateu, Vicente. *Memoria sobre el origen y desarrollo de la Iglesia Evangélica Bautista en Valencia de 1888 a 1898.* Booklet. Valencia: Imprenta de Francisco Vives Mora, 1898.

Mayor, John E. B. *Spain, Portugal and the Bible.* Cambridge: Macmillan and Bowes, 1892.

Menéndez Pelayo, Marcelino, *Historia de los heterodoxos españoles.* 3 vols. Madrid: Librería Católica de San José, 1880-1. A new edition of eight volumes was published in 1946-8 by the Consejo Superior de Investigaciones Científicas as a part of the complete works of Menéndez Pelayo.

Meyrick, Frederick. *The Church in Spain.* Vol. II of *The National Churches.* edited by P. H. Ditchfield. New York: James Pott and Company, 1892.

The Missionary Herald, Containing the Proceedings of the American Board of Commissioners for Foreign Missions. Cambridge, Massachusetts. 1874.

The Missionary Herald of the Presbyterian Church in Ireland. Belfast. 1870-94.

The Missionary Magazine. Published by the American Baptist Missionary Union, Boston. 1870-1.

Missionary Record of the United Presbyterian Church, Edinburgh. 1870.

The Missionary Review of the World. 1928.

Navarro y Rodrigo, Carlos. *Un período de oposición.* Madrid: Imprenta de los. Hijos de J. A. García, 1886.

New York Herald Tribune, Paris. 1949-52.

The New York Times. 1868, 1946.

Nichols, James Hastings. *Democracy and the Churches.* Philadelphia: The Westminster Press, 1951.

Pacheco, Joaquín Francisco. *El código penal concordado y comentado.* 3 vols. Madrid: Imprenta de D. Santiago Saunaque, 1848.

The Pictorial Missionary News. London. 1869.

La prensa. Daily newspaper of Barcelona. 1948.

Presbyterian Church of the United States of America. *The Thirty-ninth Annual Report of the Board of Foreign Missions,* 1876. New York.

Protestantism in Spain. Pamphlet. [New York: Committee on Co-operation with Latin America, 1924.]

Pueblo. Daily newspaper of Madrid. 1948.

Reid, John T. *Modern Spain and Liberalism. A Study in Literary Contrasts.* Stanford University Press, 1937.

Religious Liberty in Peril. Documents Illustrating the Condition of Protestants in Spain. Booklet. Paris: 'Pro Hispania', 1948.

Religious Tract Society. *The Seventy-eighth Annual Report,* 1877. London.

Requetés. A clandestine Carlist leaflet. September, 1947.

Revista cristiana. A Protestant periodical published by the Fliedner family of Madrid. 1886–1919.

Ríos, Fernando de los. *Religión y estado en la España del Siglo XVI.* New York: Instituto de las Españas en los Estados Unidos, 1927.

Ryan, John A., and Millar, Moorhouse F. X. *The State and the Church.* Vol. III of *Social Action Series.* New York: The Macmillan Company, 1924. A revised edition of this book, by Ryan and Boland (Francis J.), was published by Macmillan in 1940.

Santacana, Benjamín. *Memoria de la obra evangélica en Vilafranca del Panadés.* A brief unpublished manuscript.

Segura y Sáenz, Pedro, Cardenal. *Por la unidad católica de España.* A collection of pastoral letters. Seville: Editorial Edelce, 1952.

Serrano, Nicolás María, and Pardo, Melchor. *Anales de la guerra civil (España desde 1868 a 1876).* 2 vols. Madrid: Astort Hermanos, 1875–6.

La situación del protestantismo en España (Seis estudios sobre una campaña de difamación contra España). Published under auspices of the Spanish government. Madrid: O. I. D., 1949. Most of this material was published in English in the *Spanish Cultural Index,* of Madrid, in 1951.

Shannon, Albert Clement. *The Popes and Heresy in the Thirteenth Century.* Villanova, Pennsylvania: Augustinian Press, 1949.

Sociedad Bíblica. *Notas de la obra bíblica, Número 5,* 1948. Report of Madrid office of the British and Foreign Bible Society.

Southern Baptist Convention. Annual Reports, 1922–54, Nashville.

Strobel, Edward Henry. *The Spanish Revolution, 1868–1875.* Boston: Small, Maynard and Company, 1898.

Tidings from Spain. Periodical of the Spanish Gospel Mission, published in England. 1944–8.

Time. Chicago. 1953.

The Times. London. 1937.

Torres de Castilla, Anfonso. *Historia de las persecuciones políticas y religiosas ocurridas en Europa desde la edad media hasta nuestros días.* Vol. VI. Barcelona: Imprenta y Librería de Salvador Manero, 1866.

Trend, John Brande. *The Origins of Modern Spain.* New York: The Macmillan Company, 1934.

Universidad de Barcelona. *Aspectos y problemas de la nueva organización de España*. Ciclo de conferencias organizado por la Universidad de Barcelona. Barcelona, 1939.

La vanguardia española. Daily newspaper of Barcelona. 1945–54.

Valdés, Juan de. *Diálogo de doctrina cristiana*. Madrid: Librería Nacional y Extranjera, 1929.

Verduin, Arnold R. *Manual of Spanish Constitutions, 1808–1931. Translation and Introductions*. Ypsilanti, Michigan: University Lithoprinters, 1941.

La víspera. Clandestine Monarchist magazine published in Barcelona for eight months. 1951.

Wesleyan Methodist Missionary Society. Reports for 1871–6, 1901–2. London.

Wiffen, Benjamin B. *Life and Writings of Juan de Valdés, Otherwise Valdesso, Spanish Reformer in the Sixteenth Century, with a Translation from the Italian of His Hundred and Ten Considerations by John T. Betts*. 2 vols. London: Bernard Quaritch, 1865.

Ya. Daily newspaper of Madrid. 1950.

INDEX